THE
HUNDREDTH
ARCHBISHOP
OF CANTERBURY

Michael Cantuar:

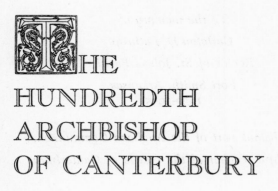

THE HUNDREDTH ARCHBISHOP OF CANTERBURY

BY JAMES B. SIMPSON

HARPER & ROW, PUBLISHERS
NEW YORK AND EVANSTON

To the memory of

Carleton D. Lathrop

Rector of St. John's Parish

Fort Smith, Arkansas

1930-1955

In a distant part of the Anglican Communion,

a faithful teacher of the creeds of Canterbury

Library of Congress catalog card number: 62-14581

CONTENTS

Not unto us, O Lord, not unto us,
but unto Thy Name give Thee praise.

INSCRIPTION ON FIFTEENTH-CENTURY CENTRAL TOWER ARCH
IN CANTERBURY CATHEDRAL

PREFACE

At breakfast on January 20, 1961, the snowy day John F. Kennedy was inaugurated president of the United States, I noted on the front page of *The New York Times* a dispatch from London announcing the appointment of a new Archbishop of Canterbury —one Arthur Michael Ramsey.

The majestic aura surrounding this ancient title stirred in my mind some dim associations: Thomas Becket's martyrdom in the Cathedral, Cosmo Lang's grave eagle face during the abdication crisis, Geoffrey Fisher lifting high the jeweled crown in the most solemn moment of Elizabeth II's coronation. I recalled a visit to Canterbury and a stroll in the courtyard of Lambeth Palace in London.

During the next few months the new Archbishop's public statements evidenced remarkable insight and imagination. I studied his impressive countenance looming out from newspapers and magazines. I learned that he was a great preacher, a brilliant author, a profound philosopher. Clergy and laity spoke of him with deep respect. Presently, there evolved the idea of a book which would tell Episcopalians, and others who follow with interest the Anglican Communion's widespread life, something of the background and thought of the hundredth Archbishop of Canterbury. In the course of my research there also evolved a portrait of a warm, uniquely gifted figure who is without doubt one of the outstanding personalities of our time.

My first interviews with Dr. Ramsey were in New Delhi late in 1961 at the Third Assembly of the World Council of Churches. These conversations were continued at Lambeth Palace and the Old Palace, Canterbury, after I had completed a fascinating round of visits to the places where he has lived and worked: London and Liverpool, the old cathedral towns of Lincoln, Durham, York, and Canterbury, as well as Cambridge, Oxford, Boston, Repton, Cuddesdon, Kelham and Mirfield.

Rarely did a day pass that I was not told that biographies of living archbishops *simply aren't done*. Yet scores of people asked me in for a cup of tea and talked with affection and admiration of Michael Ramsey.

The Archbishop may have regarded this proposed biography as the last unwarranted invasion of the small amount of privacy that remained for him and his family. Nonetheless, he kindly responded by relating incidents and details which greatly helped my study.

Never at any time did we speak of this book as an official biography. Dr. Ramsey is much too humble and astute to authorize such a volume. An assessment of his private correspondence and some current relationships must await a biographer of future years just as a thorough analysis of his theology must remain the province of the professional theologian.

A biography, perhaps more than any other book, leaves its author indebted to many. I thank those in this country and abroad who have generously given me hours of their time in interviews and correspondence. To the former American Ambassador to Ireland, the Honorable Grant Stockdale, and Mrs. Stockdale, go my special thanks for the Christmas and New Year holidays spent with them in Dublin, a delightful respite from my archiepiscopal adventures.

Valuable and encouraging help was rendered by Dr. Clifford P. Morehouse, President, House of Deputies of the Episcopal Church, and the public relations staffs of the National Council of the Episcopal Church, World Council of Churches, and British Information Service. I am grateful to Edward M. Story for exacting research and indexing and to Eleanor Jordan for her careful attention to the technical preparation of the manuscript. I appreciate the use of the Frederick Lewis Allen Memorial Room of the New York Public Library, where most of this book has been written, and the access granted me to libraries of St. Bede's, General Theological Seminary, Lambeth Palace, the British Museum, and St. Augustine's College, Canterbury.

The Church of the Resurrection, of which I am a communicant, has had a strong influence in the interests that shaped this book. My thanks and good wishes go to its rector, Dr. Albert Chambers, now Bishop-elect of Springfield, Illinois, an unfailing witness to the Catholic faith and the sacramental life and work of the whole Church.

JAMES B. SIMPSON

New York
July 3, 1962

THE
HUNDREDTH
ARCHBISHOP
OF CANTERBURY

A NOTE ON THE COATS-OF-ARMS

Dean and Chapter of the Cathedral Church of Christ, Canterbury (p. 1): Silver cross on blue field has Greek text letters for Jesus Christ.

St. Augustine's Chair (p. 8): Occupied by Archbishop of Canterbury at enthronement and at ceremony opening Lambeth Conference.

Cambridge (p. 32): Municipal arms feature castlement [or bridge], ships, fleur-de-lis and Tudor roses.

Repton (p. 40): Arms of founder, Sir John Port. Motto added in 1870's.

Magdalene (p. 46): Eagles and "martlets" characterize arms granted Lord Audley who re-established college after dissolution of monasteries.

Cuddesdon (p. 59): Uses arms of its founder, Samuel Wilberforce, Bishop of Oxford, 1845-1870.

Liverpool (p. 69): Mythical Liver (rhymes with diver) is on city arms.

Lincoln (p. 74): Cathedral's symbols balance arms of Bishop Christopher Wordsworth in whose tenure, 1869-1885, college was founded.

Boston (p. 81): Three crowns of graduated size distinguish coat-of-arms of town of Boston in Lincolnshire.

St. Benet's, Cambridge (p. 103): Symbol of the Atonement, pelican tearing breast for young, adapted from arms of patron, Corpus Christi College.

Durham University (p. 106): Cross of St. Cuthbert, forerunner of Bishops of Durham, dominates shield with diocesan heraldry in upper corner.

Cambridge University (p. 116): Four golden leopards surround book at center of arms granted in 1573.

See of Durham (p. 122): Gold cross divides silver lions on blue field. Coronet at base of mitre denotes bishop's status as a Prince Prelate.

See of York (p. 144): Recalls Christ's gifts of "the keys of the kingdom" to St. Peter, to whom York Minster is dedicated. Granted in 1515.

See of Canterbury (p. 200): Y-shaped length of white wool of a young lamb, bestowed by Popes on early Archbishops of Canterbury, became treasured symbol of office. It was attached to primate's vestments by iron pins representing the nails of the Passion. Primatial Cross is at center.

Anglican Communion (229): Designed by the Rev. Edward West, Canon Sacrist of the Cathedral of St. John the Divine, New York, for the 1954 Anglican Congress at Minneapolis, this compass and shield surmounted by a mitre was subsequently adapted for use by the Lambeth Conference of 1958.

I ENTHRONEMENT AT CANTERBURY

Lifting its spires where the praises of God have been sung for more than a thousand years, Canterbury Cathedral that day was filled with one of the greatest congregations in its long history. Nearly four thousand persons had assembled for the solemn ceremony of an enthronement, a timeless spectacle, a medieval tapestry woven of gold and sky blue and scarlet and purest white. The long gray nave became a blaze of color bathed not only by the summer sun streaming through the windows but by the brilliant light of television floodlamps.

Arthur Michael Ramsey, Lord Archbishop of Canterbury, Primate of All England, Metropolitan, one hundredth in direct succession to the Chair of St. Augustine, at his throne in the choir chose as the text for his enthronement sermon a strong and simple sentence from the Old Testament First Book of Samuel: "There went with him a band of men, whose hearts God had touched."

The mystery and promise of the Biblical verse hung for a moment in the hushed silence of the gloriously beautiful afternoon of June 27, 1961. The new Archbishop, a powerfully built man with a face of craggy splendor, spoke in a slow, compelling voice:

1

"These words describe how many centuries ago there was the first choice of a man to be King in Israel: it was a task beyond all human strength, and many in the land were sure to be hostile and estranged. But he was not alone, there went with him a band of men who had felt the touch of God. It made all the difference. Do not these words come true today, as words can do across the lapse of centuries? Today a man enters his task as the chief shepherd of a great portion of the Christian Church: it is a task beyond all human strength, and many in the country are not so much hostile as indifferent and aloof. But he sets out not alone: there goes with him the great band of those hearts God has touched with the faith of Christ. We call today's ceremony an enthronement. What does that mean? It is the putting of a man into the seat of a ruler, for in Christ's name he will rule in the Church of God, not indeed as lording over it, but as serving it; for, under Christ, authority and humility must always go together. It is also the putting of a man into the chair of a teacher —let that not be forgotten—for a bishop is the shepherd of the people as being also the teacher of God's truth. . . . : to this there is called one more man, the hundredth in this place, with all the frailties of human flesh and blood."

The initial processions had converged upon the Cathedral a half hour before. First came the Coronation Barons of the Cinque Ports and with them the mayors of York and Lambeth and Canterbury and towns within the Diocese of Canterbury, wearing their chains of office and accompanied by bewigged town clerks.

The high-ranking officials of Her Majesty's government and members of Parliament walked together, their presence a reminder that it was a State occasion as well as a religious ceremony.

After them came the deans and chapters of York Minster and Durham Cathedral, among whom the new Archbishop had lived and served, and then the somberly dressed representatives of the Church of Scotland and the non-conformist groups of the United Kingdom—Methodists, Congregationalists, Presbyterians, Baptists, Free Churchmen—walking in measured pace with the clergy of foreign churches: the Lutheran bishops of the Scandinavian countries, notable in their white ruff collars; ministers of the German Evangelical and the French Reformed and the Netherlands Reformed churches; the Old Catholic bishops in cope and mitre; and lastly, dignified and impressive as always, nineteen black-garbed prelates of the Orthodox Church of Greece, Russia, Cyprus, Rumania, Bulgaria, Serbia, Poland, and Armenia.

Boy choristers in purple cassocks and white surplices sang in the lay clerks and minor canons, the cathedral preachers and honorary canons, and fifty King's Scholars escorting the priceless Canterbury Gospels traditionally believed to have been given St. Augustine by Pope Gregory the Great.

The bishops of the world-wide Anglican Communion were a moving stream of crimson robes and billowing white sleeves— the Primus of the Episcopal Church in Scotland; the Archbishop-elect of York, the immediate successor in Michael Ramsey's former see in the north of England; the Archbishops of Dublin, Wales, and Jerusalem; all of the English bishops of the provinces of York and Canterbury; the Bishops of Glasgow and Galloway, Gibraltar, Borneo, Amritsar, Jordan, and the Sudan. There were two Americans—the Bishop of New York, Horace Donegan (who also represented the Presiding Bishop of the Protestant Episcopal Church in the United States), and the Anglican Communion's executive officer, the Rt. Rev. Stephen Bayne.

The Anglican prelates vested in the Old Palace, the Archbishop's residence within the Cathedral precincts. The new Archbishop, walking behind them in the procession, bowed his head in a final prayer before entering the Cathedral.

The road which had brought Michael Ramsey to this hallowed hour had begun ninety-five miles away at Cambridge in the year 1904. Ramsey had followed it as a student, curate, tutor, lecturer, vicar, canon theologian, and professor, to the bishopric of Durham, the archiepiscopal throne of York, and finally to Canterbury. Now he had come to a spiritual office in the Western Churches second in prominence only to the Pope of Rome.

There waited to greet him at the Cathedral doors the eighty-seven-year-old Dean of Canterbury, Dr. Hewlett Johnson, whose avowed Communist viewpoint has made him famous as the "Red Dean." He has been confused in the public mind with every Archbishop of Canterbury since 1932.

Fifteen uniformed men of the Royal Military School of Music raised their silver trumpets to announce the Archbishop's presence. When the Dean had read aloud Elizabeth II's mandate of enthronement, the grandest procession in the whole ceremonial of processions began traversing the full length of the nave and choir with all the pomp and beauty that only a great cathedral can offer. Officials of the Diocese of Canterbury and bishops suffragan led the procession followed by a dozen men chosen as the new primate's honorary chaplains. In the Archbishop's path was borne the Primatial Cross of Canterbury, flashing with diamonds and precious stones.

Ramsey, wearing cloth-of-gold cope and mitre, surged majestically down the center aisle, pastoral staff in hand, looking far more a patriarch of old than a man of fifty-six, the first Archbishop of Canterbury born in the twentieth century. In the distance was the high altar. Its large cross and candles, a study in exquisite simplicity, were flanked by immense bowls of fragrant white lilies. The Archbishop ascended the stairs before the richly carved stone choir screen, passed through the choir, and dropped to his knees in prayer—a solitary, humble figure almost engulfed by the heavy cope.

Arising, he took his solemn oath on the Canterbury Gospels and was seated in the archiepiscopal throne. From there he returned to the steps in front of the choir screen, in full view of the crowded nave, for the time-honored ritual's supreme moment at the Chair of St. Augustine. The massive chair, made in 1205, had been brought from its usual place in the corona, the bay called "Becket's Crown," at the extreme east end of the Cathedral. The bishops, law officers, and members of the Cathedral Foundation grouped around the ancient seat beneath the gently curving arch of the central tower. Here enthroned, the new Archbishop received "the real, actual and corporal possession of the Archbishopric of Canterbury, with all its metropolitical rights, dignities, honors, privileges, and appurtenances whatsoever. . . ."

The afternoon sun, filtering through the stained glass, burnished the tall mitre and seemed to set aflame the golden cope touched with deep rose-pink. In this moment the choir burst into *Te Deum Laudamus*, the Church's devout act of praise to Almighty God. The wondrous music swelled and carried to every corner as the Dean and bishops moved slowly up the chair stairs, bowing in acknowledgment to the seated Archbishop.

When the last had passed, the Archbishop was accompanied to his throne in the choir by two chaplains of his household, and there he prepared to address the clergy and the people. This very human prelate, who had not wished to be seen walking up the nave wearing glasses, fumbled beneath his robes for his spectacles case and pocket handkerchief. He wiped each lens, donned his glasses, then, almost as an afterthought, blotted a little moisture from the palm of one hand. It was the only outward sign of inner emotion, and it was over in a second. He laid aside his mitre and began to tell of the band of men "whose hearts God had touched" in Israel long ago and what they might have in common with the congregation assembled in Canterbury Cathedral.

"We must be sure what we have and where we stand in our own Church of England. We are a Church reformed and scriptural: let there be no doubt about that. We rejoice too in our catholic continuity, and of this the enthronement today is a valid symbol. No less must we cherish that quest of intellectual freedom, that passion for truth which has marked our great thinkers and teachers, a passion never more needed than today when we have to present the Christian faith amid the scientific culture of our time. Scriptural, Catholic, Liberal, we shall go out from today pledged to every part of what, as Anglicans, we have received and need still to stir ourselves to use. But, as we go, we look more widely. Our Church must reach out in the quest of unity, for Christ is longing that there will go with him not separated bands of followers, but, as one band, all those whose heart God has touched."

He spoke as the son of a Free Churchman father and an Anglican mother, the grandson of a country vicar and a Congregationalist preacher. He spoke out of his long, sometimes frustrating experiences in the World Council of Churches, keenly aware of the patience and understanding and compromise needed in the search for unity. This was a significant subject to broach in a gathering of men of so many persuasions. Now he moved to another sensitive issue:

"Here in England the Church and the State are linked together, and we use that link in serving the community. But, in that service and in rendering to God the things that are God's we ask for a greater freedom in the ordering and in the urgent revising of our forms of worship. If the link of Church and State were broken, it would not be we who ask for this freedom who broke it, but those—if there be such—who denied that freedom to us."

Some thought the Archbishop half turned, as he spoke, to the government bench in the choir. Although such an obvious gesture would not be characteristic, there is no doubt that the bold statement indicated another side of his thinking. Gone was the parish priest entreating a congregation; here was the voice of a primate of a Church that urgently desired to loosen at least a few of its bonds with the State. To some extent what he asked was already in the making. But Ramsey was determined to point the way. For many people the reference to Church and State recalled Parliament's rejection of the revised Book of Common Prayer in the 1920's. It rankled still.

The Archbishop moved on to problems beyond the boundaries of England:

" . . . there is . . . the supreme task to bring home to the people God himself. . . . We cannot fulfil the task for this country unless we are striving to fulfil it towards the whole of the world. It therefore demands the service of men and women who will go anywhere in the world in Christ's obedience, who will witness to Christ's love in the insistence that races, black and white, are brothers together of equal worth."

In embracing all races, Archbishop Ramsey came to an issue more delicate than the relationship of Church and State. The statement would not be welcomed in many quarters where apartheid and segregation are upheld. But there Ramsey stood and the only judgment he made was that all men, regardless of color, "are brothers together of equal worth." Several rows of monks and nuns, representatives of religious communities in the Church of England, knew from personal experience in the mission fields the full meaning of the Archbishop's words.

". . . at home our mission means for the Church a constant involvement in the community: we shall strive to penetrate the world of industry, of science, of art and literature, of sight and sound, and in this penetration we must approach as learners as well as teachers. We need to be learning not only many new techniques, but also what God is saying to us through the new and exciting circumstances of our time."

The Archbishop's expression bespoke his sincere determination to see a Church totally absorbed in the life of the parish, not aloof or remote or detached. He envisioned such a Church at work in factories and laboratories and in the world of the artist and the intellectual. He would use all the techniques of modern communication to spread the word of God. He counseled that his people should sift carefully the tumultuous news of the day, remembering at the same time to wait upon God in prayer. He came to his closing plea:

". . . We must help one another, and serve one another, both in our family of the Church of England and in Christendom near and far. Help one another, serve one another, for the times are urgent and the days are evil. Help one another, serve one another, as from this hundredth ceremony at St. Augustine's throne there goes a band of those whose hearts God has touched."

The magnificent enthronement ceremony ended with the Archbishop's three blessings—the first from the high altar, the second at St. Augustine's Chair in the nave, and the third outside the Cathedral. Michael Ramsey raised his hand to make in broad and reverent strokes the sign of the cross in blessing for the city, the diocese, and the province.

Wildly, joyously, the bells rang out, joined by the peal of others across the countryside, as the hundredth Archbishop of Canterbury entered on his primacy, upheld by the prayers of the faithful in Jesus Christ, to lead and serve the Church throughout the world.

II ACROSS THE CENTURIES

What does it take to be an Archbishop of Canterbury?

"The strength of a horse," declared the ninety-ninth Archbishop, Dr. Geoffrey Fisher, a few months after his retirement, "and the ability to be a cart horse one day and a race horse the next."

Intellect, perseverance, and vigor in generous measure are outstanding traits, indeed, of most of the Canterbury archbishops parading across the centuries in steady succession from the first, St. Augustine, to the hundredth, Arthur Michael Ramsey.* Those are the qualities that with prayerful service and devotion have made Canterbury the rallying point and fortress of faith for forty-two million Anglicans in dioceses and parishes around the world.

Once a precious jewel in the Roman pontiff's triple crown, Canterbury was destined to break free during the rebellious years of the sixteenth century that split the allegiances of Europe. In the next three centuries the missionary zeal that reached abroad from Canterbury was parallel to England's success in establishing a global commonwealth of nations.

The monks of Canterbury elected the first archbishops, although history reveals that the monarchs and popes often imposed their own choices. With the Reformation the Crown

* A complete list of the Archbishops of Canterbury appears on page 252.

8

acquired the sole right to select the Archbishop, with the Cathedral dean and chapter, who had replaced the monks, giving their token approval. The formation of more democratic government, in which the monarch reigned but did not rule, brought the choice of archbishops and bishops into the hands of the Prime Minister. He acts on the recommendations of his ecclesiastical appointments secretary, sometimes called "the Bishop-spotter," whose discreet business it is personally to know opinion and sentiment among the clergy and laity.

The Prime Minister submits his choice to the sovereign, who in turn places the name in nomination—a step tantamount to appointment. Canterbury's dean and chapter then go through the formality of election.

The last fifty years have seen a total of ten Prime Ministers, but only three of them have participated in the choice of an Archbishop of Canterbury. Prime Minister Stanley Baldwin suggested Cosmo Gordon Lang for nomination by George V. Winston Churchill advanced two nominees to George VI—William Temple in 1942 and Fisher in 1944. Harold Macmillan proposed Ramsey to Elizabeth II. (George III in 1805 personally offered the primacy to the aristocratic Charles Manners-Sutton, overstepping the Prime Minister's prerogative in the matter.)

The system of selection is criticized by many who say that Church leaders should not be chosen by a Prime Minister who, according to law, need not be a member of the Church nor for that matter a Christian. Others point out that it has worked well for several centuries. (Victoria and George VI are among the monarchs who are known to have been extremely conscientious in securing a personal knowledge of their appointees.) Whether fair or unfair, wise or unwise, it is a part of the integral working of Church and State.

What Augustine of Canterbury stirred up in a corner of England has spread to every continent: the great Anglican Communion, with the Archbishop of Canterbury its titular head, traditionally and realistically one of Christendom's most revered leaders. He is often called *alterius orbis papa*, the other pope of the world. Officially he is *primus inter pares*, first among equals, standing at the head of more than three hundred bishops of the Anglican Communion. He receives them once each decade at the

Chair of St. Augustine in Canterbury Cathedral. And in his London residence, Lambeth Palace, he presides over their deliberations, the Lambeth Conference.

As Primate of All England the Archbishop crowns the sovereign in Westminster Abbey. In the House of Lords he speaks on Church affairs and spiritual issues. He is the first subject of the realm, coming directly after the Royal Family with precedence even over the Prime Minister. Another traditional role of wide influence appears to be shaping itself in the World Council of Churches, in which both Geoffrey Fisher and Michael Ramsey have served as presidents.

Neither Fisher nor Ramsey is an expert on the archbishops of the past. Both name William Temple as the modern Archbishop they most admire. Fisher ventures an opinion that "Cranmer stands out. Yes, Cranmer—and Matthew Parker. They are side by side in serving the Church and keeping it on an even keel."

The courageous chronicle of Canterbury began in a monastery in Italy. It was the house of a young order, the Benedictines; the founder, St. Benedict, was not long dead. On that day in the year 590 the monks were celebrating the election of one of their brothers as Pope Gregory I. But not even the wisest of these tonsured heads could predict that this monk would be an extraordinary pope, a man of enormous energy and vision, whom history would know as Gregory the Great. Under him the Roman patriarchate rose to supremacy over all others and was transformed into the papal system that has endured to the present.

One of Gregory's foremost objectives was the evangelizing of England. Christianity as established by the early Romans existed in England but did not flourish. Seeking an able man who could be entrusted with the reviving of the faith, the Pope's discerning eyes fell upon the assistant abbot of a Benedictine monastery in Rome. His name was Augustine.

Like many great movements of history, Augustine's mission to Canterbury almost died aborning. As his band of forty monks traveled through France, they heard frightening talk of torture and death at the hands of the barbarians of England. Augustine was sent as envoy to plead with the Pope to let them return to the cloister.

Instead, Gregory ordered them to proceed. He sent a letter of encouragement: "Forasmuch as it were better not to begin a good work, than to think of desisting from that which has begun, it behooves you, my beloved sons, to accomplish the good work which, by the help of the Lord, you have undertaken."

Pope Gregory was as considerate, however, as he was firm. He sent letters to kings and important persons in France asking, among other favors, for interpreters to join the band of monks. And he appointed Augustine to be abbot of the group.

Today a Celtic cross marks the spot where Augustine and his monks first came ashore in 597. They proceeded cautiously, but it was soon evident that the King of Kent, Ethelbert, was kindly disposed toward them. His wife, Bertha, was a Christian, the daughter of the King of Paris, and together they received Augustine and his missionaries in a ceremony under a spreading oak tree.

Not only did the King welcome the missionaries, but he also became a Christian. He was baptized on Whitsunday. On Christmas Day, ten thousand of his subjects followed the royal example.

At the end of the first year of startling growth Augustine was made an archbishop—the first Archbishop of Canterbury. He went to France for his consecration by Vergilius, Archbishop of Arles.

In Canterbury, King Ethelbert presented to Augustine the holdings that befitted an archbishop—the king's own palace and, next to it, a church built by the early Romans. Augustine dedicated the church "to Christ our Saviour," a dedication still in use 1,364 years later, when the hundredth Archbishop of Canterbury took the traditional oath to "protect the rights and liberties of this Cathedral and Metropolitical Church of Christ, Canterbury."

Both Augustine and Gregory died in 604 without seeing their evangelization of England successfully carried beyond Canterbury. Their efforts elsewhere failed because Augustine did not recognize the consideration due to the Church which had existed in Britain for three centuries. Moreover, he was not sufficiently tolerant of the diversity of British and Roman usage. Ill feeling continued until the decisive Council of Whitby in 661. In that conference Church leaders chose between the Celtic form of worship that prevailed isolated and loosely organized, in the north, and the Roman form in southern England, well ordered and valuing its association with Rome and the Continent.

The choice of a single system, the Roman, brought the churches and clergy of Britain together in the *Ecclesia Anglicana*. Thus the seventh Archbishop of Canterbury, Theodorus of Tarsus, became the first primate whose authority was recognized by the whole English Church. The ecclesiastical organization he ruled was a reality some three hundred and fifty years before Britain was unified as a nation.

The archbishops of the eighth, ninth, and tenth centuries creep past in the shadows of history—good, able men, perhaps, but totally undistinguished except for Dunstan, adviser to kings and advocate of education for the clergy. Especially revered is the twenty-ninth Archbishop, Aelfheah, sometimes called Alphege. This selfless soul went without food and sleep to stay constantly with the people of Canterbury during the terrible month of September, 1011, when the city was besieged by the Danes. On the twentieth day a traitor set a fire inside the walls. When the garrison rushed to fight the flames, the enemy burst in from the other side, unopposed, and began dreadful pillage, rape, and murder. Archbishop Aelfheah was dragged to witness the burning of his cathedral. In the flickering light of the consuming fire, the monks of Canterbury were slain, one after the other, in front of the primate. During the next seven months, Aelfheah was led in chains wherever the army went while the Danes demanded a ransom from the cathedral treasury. "Money, Bishop, money," they cried, knowing full well that several of the archbishops had minted their own coins. As they taunted the old man they tore off mouthfuls of roast oxen and drank many cups of the good English wine. "What is mine to give I freely offer, the knowledge of the one true God," Aelfheah declared. In reply a soldier threw a heavy ox bone that knocked Aelfheah to the ground. More of the heavy bones struck the prostrate, weeping form until finally a grief-stricken Dane, a young soldier whom the primate had baptized, lifted an ax and brought it crashing down on the head of his beloved Archbishop. He had rendered what he considered a stroke of mercy. With it Aelfheah became the first Archbishop of Canterbury to walk in the Church's "noble army of martyrs."

The next hundred and fifty years saw ten Archbishops of Canterbury, of whom Lanfranc and his pupil, Anselm, are the most notable. They were stalwart, patient men who served in an age of impetuous kings—William the Conqueror, William Rufus, and Henry I. An archbishop who followed soon after Anselm was Theobald, and it is in his history that one of Canterbury's most celebrated names is written for the first time—Thomas Becket. Archbishop Theobald had young Becket as a confidential secretary, or archdeacon, and it was in that role that Becket became an intimate of Henry II. The first part of their saga celebrates one of the great friendships of history. The King appointed Becket to the office of Chancellor of England. And when Theobald died in 1161 the King had no other thought than to appoint Becket as the fortieth Archbishop of Canterbury.

Then one comes to a fascinating instance of how human nature can literally change overnight. The new Archbishop was far different from the lighthearted companion King Henry had known. At Canterbury, Becket fasted and drank only water in which hay had been boiled. He prayed for long hours in his secret cell and daily kept the memory of Christ by washing the feet of thirteen beggars. He disputed continually Henry's supposed power over the Church. Finally, in the darkness of a November morning in 1164, Becket sat in a tiny open boat manned by two monks who took him to voluntary exile in France. For six years the quarrel smoldered between the King and the Archbishop. It flared again when Becket decided to return, only to find that Henry had allowed Roger, Archbishop of York, to have the role of crowning Henry's son as "the boy King." On Becket's appeal to the Pope, Roger of York was excommunicated. King Henry was enraged and asked the fateful words, "Will none avenge me on this low clerk?"

Henry's cry set in motion the deed that was recorded in blood in the history of Canterbury. Four knights of Henry's household plotted the Archbishop's murder to avenge their King. First there was a loud quarrel in the Archbishop's palace, and when the knights momentarily withdrew the monks persuaded Becket to come into the cathedral for Evensong. They thought he would be safe in that hallowed sanctuary. But as they sang the vesper prayers the knights broke in, crying out for Becket "the traitor." In the twilight came Becket's answer, "Here! No traitor, but a Priest of God and Archbishop!" Moments later he lay slain in his cathedral.

Henry was plunged into sobbing grief. He had not really desired the death of his old friend. He mourned him for months, and four years later walked barefoot through the streets of Canterbury to keep an all-night vigil of fasting and prayer at Becket's tomb.

Canterbury was a place of pilgrimage for many besides the guilt-ridden King. After the cathedral burned on a September day in 1174, the monks and the new Archbishop, Robert of Dover, built a magnificent edifice which included the ornate Altar of the Sword's Point, honoring Becket. Dedicated in 1180, Canterbury Cathedral as it is known today became one of the great churches of Christendom centuries before Michelangelo glorified Rome with St. Peter's.

John Cardinal Morton was occupying St. Augustine's Chair the year Columbus discovered America. Two other cardinals, John Kemp and Thomas Bourchier, had immediately preceded him at Canterbury in a period when Rome was obviously choosing its most skilled and trusted men for the primatial see. For nearly half a century the scarlet robes of three successive cardinal archbishops swept the aisles of Canterbury, but their august reigns did little to close the widening breach between Rome and difficult, rebellious England.

Henry VIII, whose barrel coat, ruff collar, and broad-brimmed hat have been seen in countless history books, became King of England in 1509. By the early 1530's his longing for a male heir had made miserable his marriage to his brother's widow, Catherine of Aragon, and William Warham, the Archbishop who crowned him, could do nothing to soothe the unhappy monarch.

Fretting for an annulment on some grounds acceptable to Rome, Henry believed he had discovered the solution in the plans outlined by a Cambridge tutor, Thomas Cranmer. A man who had not come to ordination in the Church until his early thirties, Cran-

The King's Library

mer had diligently studied ecclesiastical law and felt the English Church courts could circumvent Rome in granting the annulment. "This man has got the right sow by the ear," Henry cried, and promptly installed Cranmer as one of the royal chaplains. It was the first step toward the day when Cranmer would become Archbishop of Canterbury. There was not long to wait, for Archbishop Warham died the next year. Cranmer granted Henry's annulment but Pope Clement VII, strongly influenced by Catherine's royal ties in Europe, refused to concur. The enraged Henry broke openly with Rome.

The monasteries were dissolved, their treasures swept away with righteous, misdirected enthusiasm. Almost everything that could be called Roman or popish, including Becket's shrine at Canterbury, was destroyed. Soldiers and townspeople stripped the cross from altars, chipped and hacked at statues, and defaced beautiful brasses and paintings. (During this same era, much of Europe—influenced by Martin Luther, John Calvin, and John Knox—shared these anti-Roman feelings.)

Cranmer ordered services conducted in English and the English-language Bible displayed for the public to read in every parish. In a tower room at Lambeth he phrased beautiful prayers and liturgies for The Book of Common Prayer, one of the major adornments of Anglican worship.

Certainly Cranmer's appointment was made in the hope and trust he would approve Henry's annulment and sanction his next marriage. It is, however, a grievous error to regard annulment as the only factor in the break with Rome. Quarrels, misunderstandings, disagreements had festered for centuries between the independently-minded English and the Roman pontiffs. The terrible sore was lanced by the issue of Royal progeny. There continued in England, without allegiance to a pope, the same "one Lord, one Faith, one Church" proclaimed by Augustine of Canterbury.

After Henry VIII died, in 1547, Cranmer crowned Henry's ten-year-old son King Edward VI. The death of the young sovereign six years later led Archbishop Cranmer to stand in support of Lady Jane Grey, Henry VIII's non-Roman grandniece. But it was Mary Tudor, the Roman Catholic daughter of Henry's first marriage, who successively established her right to the Crown. She ordered Cranmer confined first to Lambeth and then, in September, 1553, to the Tower of London. Hearings dragged on until early 1556, when the Pope pronounced Cranmer "contumacious" and ordered a degrading ceremony officially relieving him of the office of Archbishop. By royal order Cranmer was burned at the stake.

Mary Tudor's cousin, Reginald Cardinal Pole, was her choice for the primacy. He had almost married her years before. In 1530, strongly disapproving of Henry VIII, Pole had rejected an opportunity to be Archbishop of York and later had barely missed being elected pope. His was a long history in which prominence and power had been elusive. But he was to have only two years at Canterbury. His death in 1558, within a few hours of Mary Tudor's, ended the reign of the last Archbishop of Canterbury in communion with Rome.

The throne fell to Mary Tudor's half-sister, Elizabeth I, the only daughter of Henry VIII and Anne Boleyn. The first archbishop in the long Elizabethan era was the able Matthew Parker. Heavy-set and somewhat resembling Martin Luther, Parker filled long-vacant bishoprics, upheld canonical observances, and tempered the Puritanical reforms that threatened the Church's heritage.

The Puritan movement continued for more than fifty years, reaching a tragic climax during the primacy of William Laud. He was determined to maintain the historic continuity of the English Church, to permit no breach of her constitution and no departure from her teaching. The Puritan party, among others, regarded him with suspicion. When tried for popery in 1644, Laud confided to his diary the fear that he would be deported to New England. Instead, he was beheaded, a fate which King Charles I also met within the next few years as the Commonwealth government swept into power. After Laud's execution in 1645 the See of Canterbury fell vacant for an unprecedented period of fifteen years.

Charles I had been ministered to on the scaffold by William Juxon, an Anglican bishop, who told him, "You are exchanged from a temporal to an eternal crown, a good exchange." When the monarchy was restored in 1660, Charles II chose Juxon as Archbishop of Canterbury.

It was not until 1689 that Church and State began an era of harmony and stability that has continued through the years. The

"Declaration of Rights" achieved under William and Mary was a revolution without bloodshed, and thenceforth the supreme ruler was to be a constitutional monarch, a servant and not the master of the legislature. It became impossible for anyone to be monarch of England who would not uphold the Church.

With the arrival of the eighteenth century the American colonies became a concern of the Archbishops of Canterbury. In 1715 Archbishop Thomas Tenison bequeathed one thousand pounds to provide bishops for the colonial clergy. No action was taken, however, and more than forty years later Archbishop Thomas Secker was overruled in his desire to consecrate "two or three" bishops for America.

Frederick Cornwallis reigned as the eighty-seventh Archbishop of Canterbury during the years of the American Revolution. After the fledgling States won their independence, the English prelates refused to overstep their allegiance to the Crown by consecrating bishops for a land so recently in revolt. That was the reasoning outlined to Dr. Samuel Seabury, who had been sent from Connecticut to seek the bestowal of the episcopacy. He subsequently was consecrated in 1784 in the Episcopal Church of Scotland.

Relaxing its stern policy, the British government decreed within three years after the Scottish ceremony that an oath of allegiance was not necessary for bishops consecrated for other countries. That cleared the way for the historic Lambeth Palace ceremony in 1787, when the eighty-eighth Archbishop, John Moore, consecrated the second and third members of the American episcopate, the Bishops of New York and Philadelphia. The eighteenth century also saw dioceses established in Canada, India, and Australia, a part of the spirited movement in which the Anglican faith was spread far beyond the shores of England.

Early on the morning of June 20, 1837, the Archbishop of Canterbury, William Howley, accompanied the Lord Chamberlain to Kensington Palace to tell the young Victoria that she had become Queen of England. During her reign of sixty-four years Victoria knew personally seven Archbishops of Canterbury—Howley, Sumner, Longley, Tait, Benson, Frederick Temple, and Davidson.

Most outstanding of these Victorian archbishops is Charles

Thomas Longley, a man of strong character, recalled as "handsome and winning." In his study at Lambeth Palace he reviewed a plan suggested by the Bishop of the small American Diocese of Vermont, and forwarded to London by the Canadian bishops. Longley approved this outline for a meeting of all the bishops of the Anglican Communion, first called the Pan Anglican Synod and later known as the Lambeth Conference. Convening in September, 1867, the seventy-six bishops described themselves as "Bishops of Christ's Holy Catholic Church in Communion with the United Church of England and Ireland, professing the Faith delivered to us in the Holy Scripture, maintained by the Primitive Church and by the Fathers of the English Reformation, now assembled, by the good providence of God, at the Archiepiscopal Palace of Lambeth, under the presidency of the Primate of All England."

One of them, the Bishop of London, Archibald Campbell Tait, succeeded Longley at Canterbury the following year. He was Archbishop when disestablishment, constitutional separation from the State, was discussed for the first time. The proposal was defeated in the House of Commons by a vote of 374 to 89.

The same year the Canadian Church asked for the scheduling of another Lambeth Conference. Its request was seconded by the West Indian bishops in 1873 and the American bishops in 1874. On June 29, 1878, Archbishop Tait took his place in the Chair of St. Augustine, on the steps of the high altar of Canterbury Cathedral, to welcome to the second Lambeth Conference one hundred bishops of the Anglican Communion.

As a young man, Tait had known shattering sorrow in the loss of five of his six daughters to scarlet fever in five weeks' time. The one who survived, the lovely Edith, gave the Archbishop a link with the twentieth century, for she met and married at Lambeth Palace her father's chaplain, Randall Thomas Davidson. They returned together to Lambeth in 1903 when Davidson became the ninety-sixth Archbishop of Canterbury.

Between Tait and Davidson there were two superb archbishops—Edward White Benson, a statesman of considerable stature, and Frederick Temple. It was Benson who presided over the third Lambeth Conference in 1888, attended by one hundred and forty-five bishops, almost twice the number who had converged on Lambeth two decades earlier.

Benson was succeeded in 1897 by Frederick Temple, who brought to Canterbury the experience of sixteen years as Bishop of Exeter and ten years as Bishop of London. His primacy saw the fourth Lambeth Conference. In thirty years its attendance had climbed to one hundred and ninety-four prelates, a hearty reflection of the growth of the whole Anglican Communion during the Victorian age. Colonial bishoprics had soared from seven to ninety-six. In the same period the American Church's sixteen bishoprics had increased to seventy-four. It was an impressive score to tally in this year of 1897—the thirteen hundredth anniversary of Augustine's arrival.

Three years past the turn of the century Randall Thomas Davidson came back to the Lambeth he had known as a young chaplain to Archbishop Tait. His primacy was to last twenty-five years. It was the longest reign since that of the sixty-eighth Archbishop, William Warham, who had occupied the Chair of St. Augustine exactly four hundred years before. Davidson was the first Archbishop born in the reign of Queen Victoria, and he was in thought and action a Victorian who had to adapt to the rapidly changing world of Church and State in the twentieth century. He presided at the Lambeth Conference of 1908 and again in 1920.

Davidson crowned George V, guided the Church through World War I, and helped found the Church Assembly of laity and clergy. The last great project of his life, the revision of the Prayer Book, was rejected by Parliament in 1927, and Archbishop Davidson saw the work of years undone in one evening.

In 1928 he became the first Archbishop to retire. A grateful nation of friends and clergy marked the long primacy and the Davidsons' fiftieth wedding anniversary with a tall stone cross that stands in the central courtyard of Lambeth Palace. George V created the retiring Archbishop a life baron, Lord Davidson of Lambeth.

The regal Cosmo Lang, Archbishop of York since 1909, was nominated to succeed Davidson. (The last Archbishop to have known Queen Victoria, Lang often recalled that he had mistaken Kaiser Wilhelm for a family servant at Victoria's funeral.) His was a troubled era—the 1930 Lambeth Conference in the midst of a crippling economic depression, the abdication of Edward VIII, the outbreak of World War II. Lang was seventy-eight when in 1942 he followed Davidson's precedent of retirement, believing he should make way for a younger man, the brilliant theologian and social thinker, William Temple. For the first time the Chair of St. Augustine received the son of a former primate.

William Temple's stout figure had become familiar in England and America during his years as Archbishop of York. He found Lambeth almost in ruins from the heavy bombings of London. In an improvised apartment, he and his wife endured further air raids, and at the Old Palace in Canterbury they crouched under the staircase during the Germans' most devastating attack on the cathedral city.

An archbishop's role in wartime was exhausting, but Temple looked forward to quieter days and even to retirement. "I must give up in time for Geoffrey to have his whack," he once said, referring to his old friend, Geoffrey Fisher, who had succeeded him as headmaster at Repton and in 1939 had become Bishop of London. Temple's primacy was to be even briefer than his father's five-year reign. His death in April, 1944, shocked the world—especially Cosmo Lang who lived on in retirement, the first Archbishop of Canterbury to see a successor die in office.

Geoffrey Francis Fisher came to his enthronement at Canterbury in the momentous month of April, 1945, when Franklin D. Roosevelt died, Adolf Hitler perished, and the war in Europe was ending. In the sixteen years ahead he conducted a comprehensive program of reconstruction and expansion in the Anglican Communion.

Fisher is in appearance the epitome of an English priest. He is old-fashioned enough to like high-topped shoes. But he is sufficiently modern to joke about the day's headlines, his eyes twinkling and the coins jingling in his pockets.

"I am glad to be remembered as an administrator, provided I may add that if anybody will read the epistle to the Corinthians he will see that administration is the heart of the Gospel," Fisher said in an interview a few months after retirement. He inaugurated four independent provinces of the Anglican Communion —West Africa, Central Africa, East Africa, and Uganda. He worked for the appointment of an Anglican "executive officer," a full-time bishop-administrator to serve as a link of continuity between the Lambeth Conferences. And he helped shape "an operative canon law that, more than a code of conduct, would pull the Church together."

Fisher recalls going to the United States in 1946 "to restart the idea of the Anglican Communion. That was the preparation for the 1948 Lambeth Conference which marked a rebirth of the feeling of the Anglican Communion. It was a far happier thing than 1930 when the American bishops felt they were treated like country cousins."

In his ex-officio role of parish priest to the Royal Family he solemnized the marriage of Princess Elizabeth, baptized her son, buried her father, and crowned her Queen.

In a speech to the Episcopal Church triennial convention at Philadelphia in 1946 Fisher declared that "the name Anglican is already a misnomer; it indicates remote origin, but does not at all describe the present condition." At the World Council of Churches at Evanston in 1954 he described the ecumenical trend as "a movement of churches toward their own center, a concentration of Christendom on Christ."

American journalists liked Archbishop Fisher for his terse and often witty statements, but he had a far less friendly press in England. His own clergy sometimes felt he treated them as if he were still a headmaster. He annoyed the bishops in Convocation and the Church Assembly by keeping up a constant stream of comment as he presided. Yet a great deal of it was amusing, even to the moment when he disclosed to the Convocation his plans to retire: "My vigor has not declined. I am convinced that day by day my wisdom increases. But I am also satisfied that my stock of patience diminishes, and that is why I think, really, that the time has come. My feelings are those of a schoolboy getting in sight of the holidays . . . or perhaps those of a matador who has decided not to enter the ring."

The ninety-nine men who march ahead of Ramsey on the roster of Canterbury are as different from one another as the ages of history in which they lived and reigned. Almost all have left their marks for good on the Church they loved. Some have made dur-

able contributions—selfless examples of martyrdom, great cathedrals, literary masterpieces, significant leadership toward the
freedom of man, and inspired development of religious thought.

The best known of the fourteen saints of Canterbury are Augustine and Becket. Others are Laurentius, Mellitus, Justus,
Honorius, Deusdedit, Theodorus, Tatwine, Breguwine, Oda,
Dunstan, Anselm, and Edmund Rich. Miracles were reported at
the grave of Robert Cardinal Winchelsey, but he was never
canonized. After the Reformation, the formal machinery of
canonization was discontinued in the Church of England, the only
reason the list is not longer.

Names of all the archbishops are engraved on a huge tablet of
red-veined marble in Canterbury Cathedral. Archbishop Lang,
pointing out this roll to visitors in 1930, referred to it as "the
place of my humiliation. . . . Lanfranc, Anselm, Becket, Laud,
Davidson—and then, at the end, my unworthy self, Cosmo Gordon." A glance at this list hints of the history of the office and of
England itself—a gradual change from Romans, Saxons, Vikings,
and Normans to the English family names that began to predomi-
nate by the end of the thirteen century.

Nothing is recorded of the birthplaces of Augustine, Laurentius, and Mellitus. The fourth and fifth archbishops, Justus and
Honorius, were born in Rome. The sixth, Deusdedit, was the first
native-born Saxon to become Archbishop of Canterbury. The
seventh, Theodorus, was born in Tarsus in Cilcia. Succeeding
archbishops frequently came from either Saxony or Mercia, an
ancient kingdom in central England. The twenty-second, Oda,
was a Dane. The thirty-third, Robert, was the first of several
from Normandy and France.

The line does not appear to have become exclusively British
until the forty-ninth, John Pecham, a native of Sussex, occupied
the Chair of St. Augustine in 1279. After Pecham, the birthplaces
of archbishops read like a road map of England—Windsor, London, Derby, Halifax, Wakefield, Norfolk, Norwich, Kenilworth,
Reading, Ashford, Guildford, Blandford, Chichester, Exeter, Winchester, Rochester, Nottingham, Cottenham, and Birmingham.
Four bore the names of their towns—Robert Winchelsey, John
Stratford, Simon Islip, and Simon Sudbury. The fifty-seventh, William Whittlesey, was born in Cambridge, as was Ramsey. Three

since 1868 have been Scotsmen—Tait, Davidson, and Lang.

The archbishops of recent centuries are British in the same tradition that the popes are Italian. The College of Cardinals need not, however, confine its choice. But the man who becomes primate and head of the established Church of England must be a British subject. It would be difficult to imagine a foreign-born Archbishop of Canterbury so widely regarded is he as the embodiment of everything British.

Since the Reformation most have come from upper-middle-class homes—sons of merchants, civil servants, professors, and parsons. (In early years a few were of royal blood.) Four of the five archbishops of this century have been the offspring of clergymen. Davidson and Lang were children in a Presbyterian manse. William Temple was born in the Bishop's Palace at Exeter when his father was head of that diocese. Fisher's father was a country priest. Ramsey comes near to continuing this pattern. Although he is the son of a Cambridge don, both his grandfathers were of the clergy—one a priest of the Church of England, the other a Congregationalist minister.

Whether the children of noblemen or commoners, the primates have usually received the best educations available in their times. When monasteries gave way to universities as the centers of learning, the University of Paris became a place of study for several destined to be archbishops. By the middle of the thirteenth century Oxford University had begun to attract future clerics. Since then, nearly every archbishop has studied at either Oxford or Cambridge.

In their Church careers most of the archbishops have served at one time or other as curates, vicars, prebendaries, or canons. Not a few have been university chancellors. Experience as a diocesan bishop has become an unwritten prerequisite for archiepiscopal office. Several of the archbishops, consequently, have passed along the same route to Canterbury. For example, Longley became Bishop of Durham in 1856, Archbishop of York in 1860, and Archbishop of Canterbury in 1862. Ramsey followed these same steps, almost as swiftly, in 1952, 1956, and 1961.

Nine Archbishops of York have been translated to Canterbury. (Once a man is consecrated the transfer to another bishopric is known as a translation.) The first five—Arundel, Kemp, Grindall,

Herring, and Hutton—found their way to Canterbury in the years from 1396 to 1862. But the last four—Longley, Lang, William Temple, and Ramsey—have been translated within the last hundred years. This suggests that a man who qualifies for the second-ranking see, York, is a likely nominee for Canterbury if he should be relatively young. (Ramsey's successor at York, Frederick Donald Coggan, was a strong contender for Canterbury in 1961 and would doubtlessly vie with the Bishop of London, Robert Stopford, for advancement to Canterbury should Ramsey die or resign during his early years in office.)

It is, however, the Diocese of London that over the centuries has had the largest number of its bishops translated to Canterbury. This is an ironic twist of history, since Pope Gregory's grand plan originally called for London, the seat of the ancient Roman Church, to be the principal see after Augustine's death. Eighteen bishops were translated from London between 619 and 1945. (In the years from 1604 to 1663 five successive Bishops of London advanced to the primacy.) The last hundred years have seen three more—Tait, Frederick Temple, and Fisher. Every Archbishop of Canterbury since 1862 has come from York or London except for Benson's translation from Truro and Davidson's from Winchester.

The ages of the men called to Canterbury have ranged from the early forties to the late seventies. (That some early-day archbishops may have been younger is indicated by Boerhtweald's thirty-eight-year reign in the eighth century and Ceolnoth's primacy of thirty-seven years in the ninth century.) Both Becket and Cranmer were enthroned at forty-four; Juxon at seventy-eight. Fisher at the age of fifty-eight and Ramsey at fifty-six were slightly younger than the average, while Lang was sixty-four and William Temple sixty-one. Frederick Temple was seventy-six and almost blind when he ascended to the primacy in 1897.

The primate's age has a direct bearing, of course, on the length of service. The average reign over the centuries is thirteen years. The shortest on record is that of Thomas Bradwardine who died of the plague in 1349, only forty days after his enthronement. The longest reigns of the nineteenth and twentieth centuries have been those of Moore, twenty-two years; Manners-Sutton, twenty-three years; and Davidson, twenty-five years.

The archbishops' relationships with royalty have always been close—frequently cordial, sometimes stormy. Often it has been an amiable association that has led to a cleric's nomination to Canterbury. Robert of Jumièges became Archbishop after he had befriended Edward the Confessor while the King was in exile. The camaraderie of Becket and Henry II is famous. Reynolds was the indulgent tutor of Edward II who later appointed him to Canterbury. Thomas Cranmer sympathized with Henry VIII's desire for an annulment. Davidson became as a young priest the favorite ecclesiastical adviser of Queen Victoria, an acquaintance that led to his rapid advancement.

In the Middle Ages the archbishops sometimes reigned hand in hand with the monarchs, holding simultaneously the primacy and the office of Lord Chancellor. Hubert Walter was the virtual ruler of England while Richard the Lion-Hearted was being held a prisoner in Germany. In the reign of the next monarch, King John, Walter continued as Lord Chancellor. When Walter died, John sighed, "Now for the first time am I truly King of England."

John spoke too soon. He opposed the papal selection of Stephen Langton as the next Archbishop, but eventually gave in. The delay only made Langton more determined to restrain the King's lawlessness. The result was the signing in 1205 of the historic document known as the Magna Carta. It declared that no man should be kept in prison without trial and judgment by his peers and that "the Church of England shall be free and have her rights entire and her liberties uninjured."

While Langton triumphed, others fell before royal power—deprived of office, exiled, sometimes executed. "Exile was almost an occupational risk," writes a canon of Westminster.

It is the power of the primatial opinion on moral issues, rather than on political matters, which has continued to the present day. In the abdication crisis of 1936 the whole world guessed what Lang's ruling would have to be on the marriage of King Edward VIII and an American divorcee. In the United States and elsewhere Lang was regarded as a villain, a bachelor archbishop who did not understand romance. Feeling also ran high in 1955 when Princess Margaret, wishing to marry a divorced man, found Fisher friendly but firm in upholding the indissolubility of Christian marriage.

For more than nine hundred years, when Canterbury was still tied to Rome, the archbishops had to handle the popes with the same patience and diplomacy required by the kings. At the outset the relationship with Rome was cherished. Theodorus was honored in 668 to be the first Archbishop of Canterbury consecrated by a pope. Aefsige froze to death in the Alps on his way to receive the pallium, the symbol of office. And Rome had a close interest in English affairs as illustrated by Urban IV's order in 1265 to the forty-seventh Archbishop: "Either repair the buildings at Lambeth or build new ones."

The popes bestowed the red hat of a cardinal on five archbishops between 1294 and 1558. Some primates fell into disfavor with Rome, the popes frequently mediating disputes with the monks of Canterbury. One, Archbishop John Mepeham, was excommunicated in 1330.

Mounting pressures for papal revenues from England caused much of the enmity between primates and popes.

The Vatican's last attempt to regain its bond with England was the offer after the Reformation to make Laud a cardinal if he would guide the return of the English Church to Rome. He later recorded, "Something dwelt within me which would not suffer that till Rome were other than it is."

Once free, the English Church took scant notice of Rome until 1897 when Frederick Temple issued, with the Archbishop of York, the *Responsio* to the papal bull, *Apostolicae Curae*, on the validity of the Anglican episcopate and apostolic succession. (Today more Roman Catholics than Anglicans use the Lambeth Palace library in continuing research on the same subject.)

As one of his last official acts, Fisher called on John XXIII in December, 1960, the first Archbishop of Canterbury to visit the Vatican since Thomas Arundel's meeting with Benedict XII in 1397. "I arranged the trip so that it would not be an out-and-out journey to Rome but a friendly, informal stop at the end of my trip to the Holy Land," Fisher says. The visit was hailed by many as the start of a new era of friendship between the Holy See and its "separated brethren."

Ramsey lives amid many reminders of his predecessors. Memorials are everywhere at Canterbury where fifty-two of the ninety-eight deceased archbishops are buried in the cathedral. At Lambeth, the London residence of Archbishops of Canterbury for more than seven hundred and fifty years, formal portraits of the primates line the halls, the dining room, and the big banquet hall known as the Guard Room.

Both Lambeth and the Old Palace, Canterbury, have seen archbishops who lived as grandly as kings and popes. The early primates clung to a monastic rule, but by the Middle Ages the Archbishops of Canterbury had become noted for their gracious manners and hospitality. In the 1590's John Whitgift paraded through Kentish towns with an elegant company of eight hundred horsemen. A primate of the early seventeenth century, George Abbot, enjoyed lavish hunting parties. (In 1621 he accidentally shot a gamekeeper, a tragedy that cast a cloud over the remaining years of his life.)

In the years from 1828 to 1848, William Howley, the last of the luxuriously bewigged archbishops, hosted banquets at which hundreds feasted on pig and turkey and venison. After his death the Church Commissioners reduced the archiepiscopal income and expense allowance to £15,000 a year—still a princely sum.

Today, the annual salary of the Archbishop of Canterbury is £7,500. The Commissioners have assumed most of the costs of running the palaces and of official entertaining. The extravagant Lang believed that palaces and servants, gourmet dishes and fine wines were a part of the dignity of the office. (Always mindful of his role, he never went into a shop or rode on a public conveyance.) He was sorrowfully aware that World War II had ended that era and upon leaving Lambeth in 1942 remarked that he probably was the last who would live in such stately splendor. So rigidly had Lang maintained appearances that he retired from the primacy with almost no personal savings and reluctantly accepted a friend's gift of £1,500.

The postwar years have borne out his prediction that the archbishops would live more modestly. When Lambeth was reconstructed from its bombed-out shell, plans were made for its increased use as a center for conferences and church administration. A private apartment for the archbishop was created on the second floor.

More spacious quarters are provided in the Old Palace at

Canterbury, sixty-two miles southeast of London. This is entirely his own residence. Here the archbishop comes to rest from the cares of Lambeth and to fulfill his more leisurely role as the bishop of the Diocese of Canterbury. The Old Palace also offers space for special guests and members of the archbishop's family. Frederick Temple, the last to remodel the house, had two sons. Fisher was the father of six sons and grandfather of four girls. ("We changed sexes," he explains.) Lang was a bachelor. The Ramseys, like the Davidsons and the William Temples, have no children.

The palaces did not know the presence of a wife, of course, until the Reformation. The subject of clerical marriages had long been in frequent controversy. Unaware that he was about to receive high office, Cranmer had wed only a year before he came to Canterbury. In the words of a contemporary, this created a situation that "was difficult to conceal and dangerous to disclose." The wife stayed entirely in the background, and when traveling from Lambeth to Canterbury, rode in a trunk marked "The Archbishop's Books."

As late as Howley's time, less than a hundred and fifty years ago, no woman was allowed in the official apartments of Lambeth Palace. In the evening, after the chapel service, the Archbishop crossed the courtyard to Mrs. Howley's lodgings preceded by footmen carrying torches.

Howley, primate at the beginning of the Victorian era, was a conservative High Churchman. A historian of the day wrote that Howley was "typical of the men generally chosen for ecclesiastical preferment: he carefully avoided any action that might have annoyed the comfortable and never expressed any convictions that might have disturbed the indifferent."

Since Victoria herself did not prefer the ritual observances, only one High Churchman was nominated to Canterbury during her long reign. This was Benson, who delighted in ancient forms of devotion and hymns from the Breviary and Missal. Many of these preferences were overlooked in the belief that, like other Englishmen, he loved ritual for ritual's sake but disliked it taking on deep spiritual significance. He skillfully avoided convicting the Bishop of Lincoln on charges of ritualism.

In the twentieth century the fluctuation between Low Church

and High Church has been something of a pattern. Ramsey describes it in this way: Davidson was Low Church, Lang was High Church, Temple was at once Catholic and liberal, and Fisher's churchmanship resembled Davidson's. Ramsey is High Church, but liberal too. "The Church of England remains comprehensive," says one observer, "and that is both its strength and its weakness."

The Archbishops of Canterbury have traveled throughout the world, their journeys many times longer than that first historic voyage undertaken by Augustine. In the early years, there were frequent trips to Rome. In the Middle Ages, they accompanied monarchs on the Great Crusades. Today the Archbishop travels often, visiting the far reaches of the Anglican Communion and participating in international meetings. The vast distances covered by Fisher and Ramsey in the age of air travel probably exceed the combined total of their ninety-eight predecessors. In the first year after his election, Ramsey made separate trips to Holland, India, Greece, and Russia and planned a coast-to-coast tour of the United States.

Davidson was the first Archbishop of Canterbury to visit the United States, and on a September evening in 1904 he dined at the White House with Theodore Roosevelt. Since that time all the primates have known the American presidents. Whereas Augustine knew only the King of Kent, his successors have walked with kings and rulers of many lands.

When Lang became the first Archbishop to go aloft in a plane, he insisted that an aide remain on the ground, wearing the archiepiscopal cloak, so newspaper reporters would not be aware of his daring and unconventional exploit. Temple's travel was restricted by wartime. Fisher was the first to fly regularly as part of the year's work.

The archbishops' evolving role as the honorary head of a universal communion requires their leadership in such meetings as the Lambeth Conference, the Anglican Congress, and the World Council of Churches. The dates of these meetings have, in fact, more or less dictated the retirement dates of recent archbishops. Davidson stepped down in time for his successor, Lang, to have eighteen months to prepare for the 1930 Lambeth Conference.

Fisher, too, felt Archbishop Ramsey should have ample time in office prior to the World Council assembly at New Delhi in 1961 and the Anglican Congress at Toronto in 1963.

It is not only the international responsibilities but also the demands of the Church at home which may well cause an archbishop to look forward to retirement. He is bishop of his own large Diocese of Canterbury ("the only thing that kept me human," says Fisher) and is head of an even larger province. He is expected to speak his mind on every important moral issue and, as titular leader of Anglicans in many lands, whatever he says is flashed around the world.

"Incredible, indefensible and inevitable" is the way Archbishop Lang described his daily routine. Later he wrote, "The job is really impossible for one man, yet only one man can do it."

Fisher, rather characteristically, takes a more philosophical view from retirement: "Our Lord said 'Be not anxious for the morrow, for the morrow shall take care of itself.' Each day gives you its job. You've got to have enough sense to know the direction. If you have long-range projects, you can only take it a day at a time. *Solvitar ambulando* means a step at a time. St. Paul told us that 'if we live in the Spirit, then walk in the Spirit' and walking is one step after the other."

Every Archbishop of Canterbury finds from the start that "there is no soft cushion in the Chair of St. Augustine."

The designation of the hundredth Archbishop of Canterbury had tremendous historical appeal in a history-conscious land. That Michael Ramsey's enthronement in 1961 should be recorded as the hundredth is due to the fact that his immediate predecessor is, in the words of the London *Times*, "a stickler for accuracy."

In view of the emphasis on direct succession from the missionary Augustine, it had seemed inappropriate to Archbishop Fisher that the exact order should be shrouded in the mists of history. The confusion had been borne in upon him during a trip to the United States when he heard himself introduced as "anything from the ninety-seventh to the hundredth Archbishop of Canterbury."

Fisher set scholars to leafing through the dusty records of

Church and State. They explored the books and registers of Canterbury and Lambeth, the British Museum, and the libraries of Parliament. Finally they determined that the discrepancy centered on the sixtieth Archbishop, Thomas Arundel, who was first made Archbishop in 1396, deprived for political reasons, and restored in 1399 with Roger Walden's term as primate intervening. It was decided that he should be counted only once.

There was some doubt, too, as to whether the list of archbishops should include two other men. Wigheard had presented his credentials in Rome in 665 as seventh Archbishop but died before being consecrated. Fisher reasoned that this monk "though elected to office should not be included in the list of archbishops since he died a priest." The same ruling applied to John de Ufford, who died in 1349 before receiving consecration. Both are omitted from Fisher's list.

The so-called "missing archbishops" are Aefsige and Beorhthelm. Their addition to the roster advanced Fisher from ninety-seventh to ninety-ninth. The tenth-century primate, Aefsige, died en route to Rome. His immediate successor, Beorhthelm, was forced to return to being Bishop of Wells when a new king favored another candidate, the brilliant Dunstan.

Two tests determine the right to a place in the list of archbishops. The first is election and confirmation (or papal provision, which would take the place of both). The second is occupancy of the see and being reputed as the Archbishop of Canterbury.

By those standards, both Aefsige and Beorhthelm may be admitted. When they are herded into the fold the list stands at ninety-nine, and Fisher says that should be official. He cautiously adds, "Much work is yet to be done in the investigation of Anglo-Saxon charters, and it is always possible that new evidence might be discovered."

On the day of the 1961 enthronement, the London *Times* devoted almost an entire column to an account of the doubts and disputes in the musty pages of history, happily concluding, "Such evidence, however, is unlikely to arrive to deprive the Most Reverend and Right Honorable Arthur Michael Ramsey of the distinction of being the hundredth Archbishop of Canterbury."

III MICHAEL RAMSEY

1. A CAMBRIDGE CHILDHOOD

Nightfall came gently to Cambridge. The mellow sunlight of an autumn day gave way to silky mists that drifted up from the River Cam and fell with warm dampness over the ornate buildings and quadrangles of the ancient university town.

Scholars bicycled along the winding streets, their black gowns caught up by the wind. In the colleges the dinner places were laid as they had been for centuries: crisp white napkins, folded in peaks, marched down the polished tables, and tapers in great silver candleholders sent shadows playing on the paneled walls and portraits.

In Chesterton Road, behind Magdalene College, an old lamplighter made his rounds, angling a long pole carefully to set the gaslights glowing in the evening dusk. In the stone house, No. 71, there was a new baby, a second son born to Arthur Stanley Ramsey and his pretty dark-haired wife.

Arthur Ramsey, the father—what a distinguished figure he was: tall, spare, balding, his austere features relieved by a luxurious mustache. Every day at exactly the same hour he walked along Chesterton Road on his way to lecture in mathematics at Magdalene College. He loved little Magdalene, always pronounced Maudlin, one of the oldest of the smaller colleges. He had studied there himself and, after graduating with honors in 1889, went to teach in Fettes College in the old gray town of Edinburgh. In 1898 he had come back to Magdalene. On a return visit to Edinburgh he had chanced to meet Mary Agnes Wilson, the sister of one of the masters at Fettes.

Agnes Wilson had taught for a few years before going to Edinburgh to keep house for her brother, Kenneth. She had grown up one of nine children in the busy, bookish atmosphere of a country vicarage in Lincolnshire. Everyone said her radiant cheerfulness was a perfect complement to the quiet, retiring manner of Arthur Ramsey, the son of a Congregational minister. They were married in 1902.

A son, Frank Plumpton Ramsey, was born the next year. The house in Chesterton Road echoed to his cries and squeals. Arthur Ramsey could hardly concentrate on writing his first book, a learned treatise on hydrostatistics. He scarcely finished before the arrival of the second baby.

The child was called Arthur, for his father, and to that was added Michael. It seemed a name of attractive simplicity in an era when the Royal Family popularized the custom of giving three and four and even five names to children. It was a name that rolled easily on the tongue—Arthur Michael Ramsey, the name of a professor, a doctor, a barrister, or even a bishop.

The Cambridge into which Michael Ramsey was born on Monday, November 14, 1904, was still thoroughly Victorian although the grieving widow of Windsor had been dead for nearly four years. It rejoiced in its reputation as "tutor of the world," the accolade it had earned from Uganda's prime minister, a man the newspapers called "the dark gentleman who came from over the seas to attend the coronation of Edward VII."

The dominant news of this Monday in mid-November was a state visit from the King and Queen of Portugal. A flotilla of Britain's naval might greeted them at the Isle of Wight.

But such affairs of London, fifty-seven miles away, seemed remote to Cambridge. There the motorcar had just begun to appear, stirring up dust and frightening the horses. One of the cars, traveling at the speed of three miles an hour, had killed a ten-year-old Cambridge boy. Another had collided with a buggy carrying a coffin, throwing the casket and body into the road.

The Independent Press & University Herald, conscious of the farmers of Cambridgeshire, editorialized on such subjects as "How much land should a man plow in a day?" It also noted Prime Minister Balfour's speech in Cambridge and his satisfaction that the address had been translated for a visiting delegation of German scientists. It reported, too, the remarks of a red-haired young man named Winston Churchill: "I make no secret of my belief that, as regards free speech, the House of Commons has lately adopted the attitude of a cannibal." The editor added a poetic thought:

> Though Master Winston's pleased to call
> The House of Commons "Cannibal,"
> It earns that accusation grim
> Because it cannot stomach him.

Six families paid for marriage announcements in the newspaper and eight for death notices that ran alongside an advertisement, "Garments dyed black for funerals in 48 hours." Only one couple, Kate and Harry Thrussell of Herbert Street, Cambridge, spent two shillings to record the birth of a daughter. The Ramseys were given to no such expense. The word got around quickly enough in the university circles.

"Arthur Michael, I baptize thee in the Name of the Father, and of the Son, and of the Holy Ghost . . ." said the Rev. Plumpton Stravenson Wilson as he stood at the stone baptismal font in Horbling Parish Church at Folkingham, a village near the town of Sleaford in Lincolnshire.

The old priest was christening yet another of his numerous grandchildren, and he reflected once again on how swiftly the years had passed since he left Oxford in 1855. Ordained by the Bishop of Lincoln, he had spent a half century as a rural vicar. In spare hours he tutored his children and those of his parishioners, and during the holidays he filled his house with nieces and nephews and tutored them, too. On an annual salary that rarely exceeded £150, he and his wife had managed to give college educations to each of their children. Two of their sons had become priests and one of their daughters married an Anglican priest.

Now and then Mr. Wilson went to visit the Ramseys in Cambridge. In the nursery he held Frank and Michael up to the window to see the River Cam on the other side of the road and the little waterfall that punctuated its placid course. He showed them the university men vigorously rowing their boats and storing them away in sheds painted with the colors of the various colleges. And in the distance, beyond the park called Christ's Pieces, he pointed out the towers and turrets of the town.

Michael was just a few years old when the family moved to the Castle Hill section of Cambridge. The new house was named Howfield, after an old estate which Michael's father had discovered as he pored, scholarlike, over the yellowed maps of the neighborhood. At Howfield a third child, Bridget, was born to the Ramseys in 1909.

Sundays at Howfield always saw several guests for luncheon and thirty or more students invited for tea. The nanny, Ethel, would bring in Bridget in a frilly white frock, and Frank and Michael in their sailor blouses, knee breeches, and black stockings. They were sandy-haired, chubby boys who liked to give their sister rides in the gardener's wheelbarrow. Unashamedly they would ask the university dons for "piggyback trots" around the garden.

Frank had his own room while Michael and Bridget shared the nursery. She called her brother "Mik," a nickname that sticks to this day. All too often the nanny ladled out a bland, almost colorless custard which Michael detested and always referred to as "slippy down." The best part of the nursery day was their father's stories about a character called Parker the Bear.

Not long after he started to school Frank began solving complex mathematical problems. Some of the dons considered him a genius. Michael was reticent in the light of his brother's brilliance. His mother found it difficult even to teach him the alphabet. But he was an imaginative child, and as he ran along

Huntingdon Road on his way to Miss Sharpley's kindergarten, he made up names for the women who stood talking in their yards. There was a certain muscular lady—Mrs. Bear Arms. There was another curious woman—Mrs. Antelope. Every day Michael stared at them openly. Then he would break into a run, certain that Bear and Antelope were chasing him.

When Michael did learn to read he became engrossed in a set of encyclopedias of the history of European nations. He studied them so hard and so long that he could, years later, identify each volume by its smell. At the same time he became earnestly devoted to a book of lurid ghost stories. He read the tales repeatedly by day and dreamed wildly of them at night. Finally, Mrs. Ramsey hid the book atop a tall cupboard. It was found there more than forty years later, across its cover scrawled, "Property of Arthur Michael Ramsey, Believer."

Ghosts, geographies, histories, stories he heard from his father —all of these fed Michael's lively imagination. He created for himself a world of fantasy in which he was a dignitary in a distant, exotic land. One day to his family's amazement he wrote his own epitaph: "Sacred to the memory of Arthur Michael Ramsey, for many years Bishop of Peking."

At least he was the bishop of his toy soldiers, and he gave them long and thoughtful sermons. Occasionally one died and Michael conducted the funeral. He wrote for this little army a long list of rules entitled "Roads to the City Bright," a guide for entering the Kingdom of Heaven. Letters, too, issued from his desk in the nursery. ("To King John, the High Street, Hell . . . Dear King John, You are a very bad man. Arthur Michael Ramsey.") His father's sister, Lucy Ramsey, recalls in what seems an understatement, "Michael was a quaint child."

He memorized long poems, serious and frivolous, and improvised on them as the occasion demanded. During a formal call on the family of a classics don, Michael began to repeat aloud a poem in which he had interpolated the name of one of the young daughters:

"Mary, Mary, stick, stick, starey. Ebo, ibo, bow-legged, Mary."

The Ramseys were as horrified as the hosts, and it took all of Mrs. Ramsey's tact to soothe over the incident.

Every summer the family spent a six-week holiday with their

Wilson cousins at Perranporth in Cornwall. Once on a train trip Michael confronted a woman in the compartment and demanded, "Do you know about John Gilpin?" She shook her head in the noncommunicative manner of passengers on English trains, affronted at having her privacy disturbed. Michael began in a singsong voice, "John Gilpin was a citizen of credit and renown. . . ." He repeated word for word the stanzas of *The Diverting History of John Gilpin* by William Cowper.

"Those summer trips were our only luxury," recalls Bridget Ramsey. "We were all to have expensive educations and there wasn't much money to spare."

In Cambridge the Ramseys had been one of the first dons' families to build a home in Buckingham Road on property bordering the estate of Charles Darwin's grandson, Horace. The neighborhood, known as Castle Hill, became "very donnish." Michael and Bridget played in the quiet street with the Elmslies, the Reddaways, and the Bulloughs, whose maternal grandmother was the actress Eleonora Duse.

On Sundays the family usually attended the Congregational Church. Occasionally, they went to the Church of England, St. Luke's or Holy Trinity. Mrs. Ramsey made her Communion there at Easter, Christmas, and other times during the year. Only rarely did they attend services at St. Giles. It was the parish church nearest Howfield and was considered "very High." The Ramseys had family prayers together and Bible reading at home every morning. Now and then in the evening they gathered around their mother at the piano to sing Gilbert and Sullivan. Michael's favorite was *Iolanthe*, and he was delighted when his father assigned him one of the solos.

Arthur Ramsey, fastidious and correct, unmarried until his middle thirties, had difficulty in understanding his children's propensity for untidiness. He was appalled to hear that one lad at Miss Sharpley's kindergarten had as his sole assignment the job of tucking in Michael Ramsey's shirttail. Later he puzzled over how his sons constantly replaced their collar buttons. "I've only had *one* all my life," he would say. "They *don't* wear out, you know."

Life was placidly pleasant: tea parties, dinner parties, boat races, picnics, perfect servants and better food than was found in most of England. Cambridge could not know that this gracious era would end forever with the assassination of an Austrian archduke and the outbreak of world war in August, 1914.

Michael spent the first years of the war in the sheltered routine of the Choir School of King's College, Cambridge.

"I was Michael Ramsey's first Anglican teacher," says Eric Milner-White, the Dean of York Minster, recalling his years as a Fellow and Dean of King's and its famous choir school established in 1441. "He followed his brother in the choir school in 1914. Michael had a great deal of charm, although not everyone saw it. I loved all my boys and they were to become my rather large family of distinguished churchmen. One of them was a future Bishop of Zanzibar who said he never understood the meaning of prayer until he came to my classes. I always started by teaching the boys how to pray. I taught by the Psalms. I would ask the boys to find in the Psalms all the verses pertaining to a certain subject. For instance, if I cited youth or education they would respond with the Psalmist's words, 'O God, thou hast taught me from my youth.'"

Michael was a day-boy at the choir school for two years. His favorite pastime was bicycling in the Cambridgeshire countryside to see old churches. He had developed a keen interest in architecture and sometimes made rubbings of the brass memorials in the churches. Often he took the train to Ely, the old market town where his uncle Archie Wilson was organist of Ely's Cathedral Church of the Holy and Undivided Trinity.

As the train approached Ely across the flats, Michael would press his face against the window to see in the distance the long hill, known as the Isle of Ely, rising from the River Ouse. The great quantities of eels had given the town its name centuries ago.

Michael went everywhere in Ely with Uncle Archie and his dog, Sancho. In the cathedral Michael peered down from the organ loft as Uncle Archie played for the colorful processions. Afterward he would explore with his uncle the great cruciform structure of the cathedral with its unique octagonal tower. More than once he earned a shilling by showing people around.

"My vantage point from the organ loft was quite plush," he recalls. "I came to know every stone of Ely Cathedral. Those visits opened my eyes to the beauty and pageantry of religion."

In the fall of 1916 he was sent away to school for the first time, to Sandroyd, in Surrey, about twenty miles from London.

"One of my uncles let me in 'on the cheap' or we couldn't have afforded it," he recalls. "My mother usually traveled as far as London with me. We would cross from Liverpool Street Station to Waterloo and someone from the school would meet a group of the boys there. Sometimes, between trains, we were taken to see Westminster Abbey or the Tower of London."

C. P. Wilson was the uncle who had founded the school with another master, W. M. Hornby, in 1905. The Tudor building was to shelter several boys whose names would become well known: Ramsey, Anthony Eden, and Anthony Armstrong-Jones.

Michael became the editor of the school newspaper, *The Sandroyd Times*, and wrote editorials about the fighting in France and the recent entry of the Americans. The war was close at hand, with troops on their way to the front passing often through the nearby villages of Cobhan and Oxshott. In Sandroyd's institutional environment Michael was not as aware of England's food rationing and power failures as he was when vacationing at home.

The war had left Magdalene and the other Cambridge colleges with a handful of students. Michael's father supplemented his dwindling income by tutoring men for the initial collegiate examination known as "the Little Go." Some of them were Siamese students who boarded at his home.

Another baby was born at Howfield, a sister, Margaret—or Margie, as the family called her—the last of the Ramsey children.

The two years at Sandroyd passed uneventfully. They fulfilled the two objectives of a preparatory school: accustoming a boy to being away from home and preparing him for a public school from which he could enter a university. As usual, Michael labored under the reports of Frank's amazing scholastic record. A master at the King's College Choir School said Frank had learned "all we have to teach in mathematics" and had enthusiastically recommended him for a scholarship to Winchester. Michael himself won a scholarship to Repton School in Derbyshire. It ranked below Eton, Harrow, and Winchester, but it was an old, respected public school. And Michael's father thought highly of Repton's young headmaster—a man named Geoffrey Fisher.

2. REPTON

It was September, 1918, when Michael walked, suitcase in hand, through the vast black and sprawling railroad terminals of London—first Liverpool Street Station, then Waterloo—but this time he took the train to the industrial town of Derby and from there he jogged along on another line that ran to Repton.

Here was the most English of English villages—an ancient church in a peaceful churchyard, a venerable cross in the market place, thatch-roofed cottages along the streets and lanes, and a thirteenth-century archway framing the mellow, mossy buildings of the school. Twenty years later it all would be the scene of the film, *Goodbye, Mr. Chips.*

The Rev. Geoffrey Fisher, beginning his fifth year at Repton, received the new boys one by one in his study. He had succeeded an archbishop's son, William Temple, who had gone on to become rector of the large London parish known as St. James's, Piccadilly.

There were four hundred boys at Repton that year, each of them called by his last name. Being addressed as "Ramsey" seemed rather gruff, as compared with Michael or Mik, but Ramsey it was for the next five years.

One afternoon in October the headmaster happened on young Ramsey as he was trying to open a gate.

"Oh, sir, this gate is locked," said Ramsey.

"It isn't locked, it's just jammed," replied Fisher—and pushed open the gate.

Today Fisher says, "Perhaps that little incident is symbolic of the whole Ramsey-Fisher relationship."

Ramsey was assigned to the Mitre, a prophetic choice among Repton's seven residential houses. An old building, the Mitre was remodeled as a "bedder" in 1865, and has seen generations of Reptonians. One of them was beginning to make a name for himself as an actor—Basil Rathbone. More than forty boys were crowded into the dormitory under the watchful eye of H. C. Hayward, the housemaster who lived with his wife and children in private quarters attached to the house.

Even on Sandroyd's starchy diet Ramsey had lost his little-boy pudginess. He was growing quite tall by then, and he wore his new uniform—flannel trousers and a short Eton jacket—with studied casualness.

Repton had been founded in 1557 in the ruins of an old monastery. Most of Ramsey's classes met in rooms with timber beams and huge fireplaces of centuries gone by. Here one day Ramsey heard a master explain the coat-of-arms and motto which every boy had on the breast pocket of his jacket. It was not the motto of the school's founder, Sir John Port, but dated only from the 1870's when one of the forms was translating the *Ovid* passage which describes the connotation attached to the Carmental Gate because through it the Fabii passed on their way out to disaster. "*Porta vacat culpa, Sed tamen omen habit*" was translated "It is not the arch's fault, but it has acquired an ill-omen." One master's sardonic humor had suggested the first part of the Latin sentence as an appropriate comment on some of the schools products, and with the additional pun on the name of the founder, the boys seemed to have chanced upon an amusing motto. And it was unusually appropriate because the ancient monastic archway was a symbol of Repton. The phrase was quickly adopted. "It is not the arch's fault." Repton had become unique among schools in having a motto with a derogatory reference to its alumni instead of the usual tedious prayer for its prosperity. (And it was a motto which could cover a variety of situations for archbishops.)

The Mitre had a reputation for good scholars just as some houses were noted for prowess in sports. Ramsey upheld the Mitre's tradition by winning the school's second highest award, the Douglas Marriott Exhibition for classical scholarship. He became a lifelong friend of the classics master, the Rev. Henry Balmforth, a kindly man whom the author-publisher Victor Gollancz has described as " 'Balmers,' a quiet little parson, as good a Christian as you could find."

But debate rather than the classics held Ramsey's real interest. The R.S.D.S—Repton School Debating Society—met three times a term in the school library. Ramsey and his colleagues were from sheltered backgrounds, the sons of business and professional men, but they chose subjects one might hear in a club of London sophisticates. In their teens these boys talked knowingly of a whole spectrum of political and moral issues—the League of Nations, the Labor Party, Bolshevism, socialism, private ownership of industry, and America's relationship with Russia.

The *Reptonian* records some of Ramsey's thoughtful remarks:

On the influence of the cinema: "Imitation is improbable as cinema plots are usually remote from English life. It is the fiction of the masses."

On the abolition of warfare: "The very word 'society' is a synonym for civilization which, in its ideal meaning, entails as a necessity the cessation of war."

On equal rights: "The women have never had a proper chance. Some public positions, such as management of workhouses, are better fulfilled by women's experience."

On the influence of surroundings: "The middle class is the backbone of our nation—and thanks is due the environment."

Ramsey spoke out in every weekly meeting of the debate society. (In a group of adolescents nobody much noticed or cared if one's voice was changing.) He won excellent reviews. "Mr. Ramsey made a buffoonish but telling speech," says one report. "He did not scruple to be bitter and personal."

Ramsey thrived on the debates. He read the newspapers from London with a new eagerness. Everything in his classes was grist for his speeches—a Latin phrase, a poetic quotation, an allusion to history. He discovered a definite gift for extemporaneous speaking and an ability to sort out the pros and cons of a sub-

ject. Increasingly he thought of studying law in preparation for
becoming a barrister or entering public life.

His father arranged through friends in London for Ramsey to
observe the House of Commons during one of its debates. More
than forty years later Ramsey mused over a Sunday luncheon,
"Just a little boy sixteen and a half, traveling to London by himself, to hear the House of Commons . . ."

Religion, too, was a growing interest for Michael Ramsey.
Fisher kept his boys spiritually primed, although one of them,
Canon Charles Smyth, wrote years later, "I have never met any
Old Reptonian except Michael Ramsey who realized at the time
how good Fisher's sermons were."

In the fall of 1920 Ramsey obtained his parents' permission to
become a member of the class which Fisher was preparing for
confirmation in the school chapel. On St. Andrew's Day, Ramsey
was confirmed by the Bishop of Southwell, Edwyn Hoskyns.

By this time the former headmaster, William Temple, had gone
on from St. James's, Piccadilly, to become a canon of Westminster. Repton still felt his influence and the lads quoted Temple-
isms to considerable advantage. A favorite was Temple's
sympathetic observation, "Boys are always reasonable: masters
sometimes: parents never."

Ramsey first heard Temple preach on Commemoration Sunday,
June 22, 1919. Less than two years later the school celebrated
Temple's consecration as Bishop of Manchester and sent him the
fine-wrought gold cross which he was to wear at Manchester and
as Archbishop of York and finally as Archbishop of Canterbury.
In 1921 he again came to Repton for Commemoration Sunday.

The following month Ramsey saw the famous Archbishop of
York, Cosmo Gordon Lang, for the first time. Ramsey was spending his vacation at a boys' camp in Yorkshire when that aristocratic
prince of the Church arrived on one of the Sunday afternoon
excursions he enjoyed. "He struck me as a very old man, even
then, and it was still seven years before he became Archbishop
of Canterbury," Ramsey says. "His sermon text was, 'Keep that
which is committed to thy trust. . . .' "

On Armistice Day, 1922, Ramsey and his classmates assembled
for the solemn dedication of Repton's war memorial. The Old
Priory had been restored and a garden had been created to form

an appropriate setting for a stone honor-roll and cross bearing the simple inscription, "These died for England, 1914-1918."

The participants included Headmaster Fisher, Bishop Hoskyns, Bishop Temple, and the aging Bishop of Hereford, Dr. Linton Smith, who had lived at the Mitre in 1883. Their white surplices and red hoods, set amidst the old gray walls, formed for the boys a link with the priors and canons who had trod this same ground centuries before when the buildings of Repton were at the heart of a thriving Augustinian monastery.

During his final year Ramsey added another interest, the Repton School Literary Society. He was inclined to listen rather than to speak in this group, although for the October meeting he prepared a thoughtful paper on "The Historical Novel." Here he struck up the acquaintance of the talented, soft-spoken C. W. Bradshaw-Isherwood who, in later years, would become famous as the novelist Christopher Isherwood.

The seniors talked more and more of their choice of a university. Both Fisher and Balmforth thought Oxford would be a good change for Ramsey, who already knew Cambridge so well. But Ramsey had been aware, ever since his brother was accepted by Trinity College, Cambridge, that his father longed for his other son to come to his own college, Magdalene. Ramsey sat for a scholarship and in December, 1922, awards were made to Ramsey, Isherwood, and two others. This continued a valued tradition dating back to 1568 when the first two Reptonians had been admitted to Cambridge.

At the Mitre the boys lined up in front of the ivy-covered building for the house picture, an annual event. The housemaster's wife and three daughters took their usual places in the front row with the house trophies—three loving cups and three silver plaques—at their feet. The picture shows Michael Ramsey looking unusually handsome—keen-eyed, intelligent, mature for his years. His light brown hair is neatly parted, his eyes deep-set. He is not the prototype schoolboy, pale and bespectacled, but he is undeniably English, a pleasant clean-cut lad. Whereas he had always been somber in other class pictures, now with a senior's prerogative he is wearing his tie loosely knotted and is smiling slightly. He achieves a man-of-the-world look when his nineteenth birthday is still four months away.

The entry of Ramsey's name in the school's official record book, *Valete et Salvete*, testified to five years spent in honorable study at Repton. He finished as a prefect of his house. He had listened to distinguished clerics and tutors and had perfected his own scholarship and oratory. Now he took his place in the category-conscious English society: he was an O.R., an Old Reptonian, an "old boy" of a good and ancient public school.

3. MAGDALENE COLLEGE: "THE MIND'S THE MAN"

As the fall's first frost silvered the Cambridge fens, Michael Ramsey waited eagerly, almost impatiently, to begin his university life.

Cambridge in the autumn of 1923 was considerably changed from the community he had known as a boy. Its colleges had graduated that year the last of the men whose educations were interrupted by the war. The slower pace of life appeared to have vanished with that war. Even Howfield was less quiet. The acquisition of a telephone (Cambridge 72) linked the family to numerous activities. Ramsey's father was president of Magdalene College in an era that would become known as "the resurgence of Magdalene." Mrs. Ramsey was active in half a dozen civic and charitable organizations, now that the youngest child, Margaret, was in kindergarten. Bridget was preparing to enter boarding school. And Frank was specializing in economics and philosophy in one of the most amazingly brilliant careers in the four-hundred-year history of Trinity College.

Yet Cambridge, even with motorcars, the cinema, and the wireless, was still at heart the old university town it had been for centuries, the Cambridge loved by generations of students—John

Harvard, Bacon, Byron, Darwin, Erasmus, Milton, Newton, Spenser, Tennyson, Thackeray, Walpole, and Wordsworth. The Cam flowed smoothly, black-gowned undergraduates strolling its grassy banks at the "backs" of the colleges. The pubs still offered a "pint" and a game of darts. Farmers displayed their produce under the shabby awnings of the market place. Ranks of bicycles were everywhere. And over it all there was the hourly benediction of chimes in the college towers.

The brick and stone buildings of Magdalene, first occupied by monks who came to study at Cambridge in the Middle Ages, awaited the new students. Through the fifteenth-century quadrangle, hard by the spot where Roman soldiers had erected one of their sturdy bridges across the Cam, Ramsey sauntered on a day in October carrying books and clothes to the room assigned him in the Pepys Library at the rear of the second court. Magdalene's gardens, shaded by old elms and fruit trees, made the college as peaceful and remote as a country orchard. A statue of the patron saint was serene in a gothic niche above the chapel door.

Within weeks Ramsey became fully absorbed in the stimulating life of the university which drew to its lecture platforms some of England's most celebrated personalities. He heard G. K. Chesterton, the author and historian, as well as the fiery Roman Catholic convert, the Rev. Ronald Knox, whose father had been succeeded as Bishop of Manchester by William Temple. T. S. Eliot came, too, to discuss his recent work *The Wasteland* for the Cambridge Literary Club's Saturday evening meeting in the Tea Shop. ("His notorious poem has occasioned nearly as many disputes as Prohibition," said the student newspaper.) And Edith Sitwell in a single lecture condemned the ranks of writers from Alfred Noyes to Noel Coward whom she denounced scathingly as "that writer of salacious reviews." She concluded with the words, "I've had a lovely grumble."

The Cambridge Union Society, venerable mother of more than a century of skilled speakers, was an irresistible attraction to young Ramsey. It was housed in an ugly Victorian building that raised its gables and peaks directly behind the twelfth-century Church of the Holy Sepulchre, the unique "Round Church."

In the Union's large and starkly furnished debating hall, the postwar generation was just coming into its own. The new group numbered several who would be leaders in public life, including two who would be cabinet members—R. A. Butler and Selwyn Lloyd. Ramsey's rooms at Magdalene adjoined Lloyd's.

"The freshman felt that he found in the Union a microcosm of national politics and not a little of its heat and fervor," Ramsey recalls. Before Christmas he made a fifteen-minute address in favor of a Liberal victory in the general election. Although he was not on the winning side, Ramsey's initial appearance established him as one of the most skilled speakers in the Union. The undergraduate magazine commented that Ramsey "bowled with a lengthy run 'round the wicket and broke rather cunningly. . . ." *The Cambridge Review* said, "Mr. Ramsey is a freshman speaker, with a distinctive style, who should go far." But an unsigned comment in *The Gownsman* is still quoted by Michael Ramsey four decades later: "For a freshman, Mr. Ramsey has had more encouragement than is good for him." (Ramsey believes the anonymous writer is today a well-known priest and writer in the Church of England.)

During the next two and one-half years Ramsey spoke with authority on a variety of subjects—strikes, legislative reform, academic freedom, and Marxism. He condemned government policy in Egypt, questioned the cabinet's wisdom on Singapore, and decried the lack of direction of British relations with the League of Nations—all of this from a young Englishman who had not been far beyond London. He could be highly amusing, too, as when he told with mock earnestness of a statesman who had lost his soul in the cogs of a political machine. Ramsey was a resourceful debater. Once to stress a point he sang in a high-pitched voice,

> My sweet Hortense, she ain't good lookin'
> But she's got some sense, my sweet Hortense . . .

Occasionally he spoke on some hypothetical subjects proposed by the less political-minded members of the Union: "This House would like to go back to Methuselah," or "This House hopes that steeplechasing, foxhunting, beagling, fishing, and all other sports of the field will ever flourish in England."

Ramsey, a heavy-set figure with a mustache that added to the impression of maturity, won more than half of the debates in which he participated. He championed the Liberal Party which lived on in the Cambridge Union, although the last election had reduced it to a remnant in the House of Commons.

It was his interest in the Liberals which carried Ramsey into community activities for the first time. Impressed with the speeches he gave at political meetings in the countryside, the party asked him to stand as a prospective Liberal candidate but the demands of his academic studies did not permit him to accept. He continued, however, to be an active speaker and, at a meeting in the Cambridge Town Hall, spoke from the same platform as the Liberal's chief, Lord Asquith. "We have in our midst a future party leader," declared Lord Asquith, turning to shake hands with young Ramsey as the audience applauded. The former Prime Minister's praise encouraged Ramsey to continue and in June, 1925, he participated in a Cambridge Union debate on the comparative merits of the Conservative and Liberal Parties.

One of the forceful speakers for the Conservatives was a parliamentary leader, Lord Hugh Cecil. His father had been foreign minister, his brother was president of the League of Nations, and Lord Hugh Cecil, then fifty-six, had served in Parliament since 1910 and had been a pilot in World War I. On this evening in early summer he caught Ramsey's attention and deep interest with a single remark. "After all," he said, "nothing in politics matters too much; it is men like Newman in the Church of St. Mary the Virgin, in Oxford, and Wesley, preaching up and down the country, *who do the most good.*"

The statement fell on Ramsey's ears with tremendous impact. In the year ahead he would ponder the words again and again. And ultimately he would consider them the passwords to a new life.

Summer holidays usually were spent with the family. One year Ramsey and his sister, Bridget, accompanied their parents on a vacation trip to France and Switzerland. But it is a trip to the English lake district that Bridget most readily recalls:

"We had hoped to see an eclipse of the sun, but the weather

was cloudy, and after going all that distance we didn't see a thing. On that trip I was allowed to drive the car for the first time. And my brother, Mik, would drive, too, but he scared us frightfully. It was just that he was thinking about other matters. He was that way at playing tennis, too, and I used to be very angry with him when he would get to thinking about something and wander off the court. There he would be, ambling all around the garden, talking to himself, while I waited for him to serve. The talking was something of a family trait; my mother talked to herself, too. We would see Mik pacing up and down, sometimes running, and still talking to himself. I'll never forget the time my mother insisted he take me to a dance during May Week at Cambridge. Mik was very sweet. He *did* dance with me. But the evening just wasn't a success and finally we went over to his rooms in the college and he fell asleep! But he was wonderful; he really did *try* to make it a nice evening."

Ramsey's oratorical skill won for him a place on the three-man Cambridge Union team to debate in the United States in the fall of 1925.

"It's a land of pep, punch, drive, and dash," he was warned by R. A. Butler who had led the previous year's team. Butler barely mentioned a rather humiliating defeat by the young women of Vassar College, but he spoke proudly of having been received at the White House by President Coolidge and of taking tea at the British Embassy—"That small English oasis amidst the hospitable desert of undiluted Americanism."

Ramsey and his two colleagues, Geoffrey Lloyd and Patrick Devlin,* spread out large maps in the Cambridge Union's library and traced their itinerary from New York through Pennsylvania, Ohio, Indiana, Illinois, Michigan, Wisconsin, and Iowa. Their eyes wandered on to California. For a few days they dreamed of debating their way across the United States, but the American University Union, which was arranging the trip, was firm, as it always had to be with undergraduates. It told Ramsey to adhere to the original plan.

* Like Ramsey, both men were destined for prominence in later life. Lloyd's activities as a Member of Parliament date from 1931, and he has also served as Minister of Information and Minister of Fuel and Power. Devlin was knighted in 1948 after becoming a Justice of the High Court.

After a summer of preparation the three men sailed from Southampton aboard the *Caronia*, a Cunard liner which also carried one hundred and fifty-five members of the British delegation to the Interparliamentary Union Conference in Washington. "Ramsey, Lloyd and Devlin were scrubbed of appearance and shabby of luggage," says a friend who saw them off. Tall Geoffrey Lloyd, who resembled a young Rex Harrison, carried Sinclair Lewis' recent books, *Main Street* and *Babbitt*, as a guide to American customs and character.

The *Caronia*, after ten days at sea, reached New York harbor on the chill autumn morning of September 28, 1925. As it docked at the foot of West Fourteenth Street, alongside the French liner *de Grasse*, police swarmed over the pier to protect the Interparliamentary delegates, guard a fur shipment, and keep a sharp lookout for the rumrunners who violated America's prohibition. A crowd cheered a passenger embarking for France, the Marquise de la Falaise de la Coundraye, whom the Cambridge team recognized as their favorite star of the silent films—Gloria Swanson.

The men taxied uptown to East Twenty-eighth Street and checked into the Prince George Hotel, the first of many hotels, dormitories, fraternities, boardinghouses, and day coaches in which they would live and sleep during the next month and a half in seven states. The first week took them to the University of Pittsburgh and on a wide circuit in Ohio—Western Reserve University in Cleveland, Ohio University at Athens, and Wittenberg College at Springfield.

"Our debate subjects vary from prohibition to the theme 'This house pities its grandchildren,'" said Ramsey in a letter home. "We pour scorn on the self-confident material prosperity of Americans, and predict dire menaces within a few decades—the Yellow Peril, the decay of moral energy through materialism, unpleasant applications of eugenics, and a host of problems before which our grandchildren will quail. Prohibition inspires Cambridge perorations on liberty."

Prohibition was, indeed, a subject which arose repeatedly in this era of bathtub gin, bootleggers, and hipflasks. For collegiate America it was a time of raccoon coats and co-eds with short skirts and bobbed hair. The nation was prosperous and its parents indulgent; in some colleges almost every student had a roadster with rumble seat, or at least a model-T Ford. Everybody talked about the Charleston—and danced it.

As for debating, it was Geoffrey Lloyd who first noticed the small metal boxes of indexed cards which the Americans brought to each debate meet. "They treated debate as a science, a subject of exacting study, whereas in England we had considered it a pastime," says Lloyd today in his London home in Lower Belgrave Street. "They spoke of having their debate presentations 'organized.' That was exactly what threw them off when a debate took an unexpected turn. We tried to be more flexible."

From Springfield the men pressed on to the University of Cincinnati and then into Indiana, for appearances at Earlham College, Indiana University, Purdue, and Culver Military Academy, which was the only secondary institution on the itinerary. In a letter to the Cambridge undergraduate magazine Ramsey spoke of himself as "an Asquithian [who] has too great a facility for being cynically amused during his speeches, and was on one occasion too weak with laughter at 'the whole thing' to be articulate. This was a debate before a military public school; the sight of a hall of uniformed boys was too much for him."

The second weekend of the American tour was spent in Chicago. The debaters stayed at the Drake Hotel where, to their embarrassment, Geoffrey Lloyd let his bath run over. They attended the opera and, at intermission, heard more talk of "a national baseball match called the World Series" than they did of music.

On Monday the men went to suburban Evanston for a debate at Northwestern University—"beside the inland sea"—and saw the North Shore in all the red-and-gold beauty of late autumn, the rolling gray waves of Lake Michigan a somber background.

The trip stretched ahead: the University of Illinois at Urbana and James Millikin University at Decatur, and then a swing into Michigan—Albion, Hillsdale, East Lansing, Kalamazoo—before going to Marquette University at Milwaukee, Wisconsin.

On his twenty-first birthday, during the team's visit to the University of Wisconsin, Ramsey wrote for a Cambridge undergraduate magazine a report which mingled historic detail with amusement at the unusual: "Between the Allegheny Mountains and the Rocky Mountains is the flat part of America known as the Middle West," he said. "This comprises those states which were added to the Confederation in the early years of the nineteenth century. The more northern of these states are the scene of activities for the Cambridge debating team. . . . The American teams appear on the platform exhausted by the rigorous training to which tyrannical coaches have subjected them. To ensure physical and mental fitness for the fray the professor of public speaking orders his pupils to take cold baths daily for a week, to eat no puddings, and to forego dinner on the night of the debate! The minutest gestures of their fingers are prescribed in text-books on oratory, and the coaches sit and shudder at the unscientific gesticulations of Cambridge. . . ."

In Iowa, the last state on the schedule, the tour's final days passed quickly. They traveled by train and bus from Coe College, at Cedar Rapids, to Cornell College, at Mt. Vernon, and on to the University of Iowa at Iowa City and to Iowa State College at Ames. There, half a world away from England, they read in a country newspaper of the death at eighty of the dowager Queen Alexandra.

After a final debate at Grinnell College in the town of Grinnell, Iowa, the men hurried to Des Moines and a train for Chicago and New York to catch the *Mauretania*. Again they went to the Cunard pier at the foot of West Fourteenth Street where the ship waited to sail at 1 A.M. on November 25.

The first day at sea was the American Thanksgiving. Ramsey remembers that a Negro trio called the Three Kings of Harmony played in the lounge.

There he found an old copy of *The Church Times* and was surprised at how eager he was for news of the Church of England. The books he had brought from England to read at sea were *Christus Veritas* by William Temple and *Belief in God* by the retired Bishop of Oxford, Charles Gore. They still interested him more than the book he purchased in New York to read on the voyage home, H. G. Wells' latest volume, *A Short History of the World*.

The American trip, he reflected, greatly broadened his knowledge of churches outside England. There was no "established" church in America, but it was obvious that religion had strongly influenced the country, particularly the founding of colleges. Ramsey learned that Earlham College had been opened in 1847 by the Society of Friends. Wittenberg was Lutheran, Marquette was Roman Catholic. Albion College and Northwestern had strong Methodist ties, while Hillsdale College and Kalamazoo College were Baptist. Coe College and James Millikin University were Presbyterian, and Grinnell had both Congregational and Episcopal backing.

In New York he had attended services at two of the leading Anglo-Catholic parishes—a choral Eucharist on Sunday morning at "the Little Church Around the Corner" (the Church of the Transfiguration) and Evensong at the Church of St. Mary the Virgin. In Chicago he attended the Church of the Ascension and "was deeply impressed." In smaller communities he heard references to the Episcopal church as "the English church." He had discovered Ames, Iowa, as the birthplace of the evangelist Billy Sunday, and he had learned, too, of another evangelist, Aimee Semple McPherson, who was combining glamour with hell-fire in broadcasts from her new temple in Los Angeles. As he sailed, he wondered if this land of diverse religious character would give a presidential nomination to Alfred E. Smith, the Roman Catholic governor of New York.

Three and one-half decades later Geoffrey Lloyd best summed up the trio's reflections on their youthful journey: "We went to America at a wonderful time—we were old enough to know what to be impressed about, young enough not to be constricted by opinions, and well in advance of the sclerosis of middle age."

Ramsey's rise to the presidency of the Cambridge Union was unparalleled. He advanced through the offices of secretary and vice-president, and was elected president in December, 1925, on returning from the United States. "Never before has anyone become president in the brief time of eight terms," said the undergraduate magazine in according Ramsey a place in its hall of fame.

One of his first official duties was to host a dinner at the Union for three men who were conducting missions to the city of Cambridge and the university community—an Irish evangelist, a Non-Conformist minister, and the Bishop of Manchester, William Temple.

"During dinner Temple commented upon a Cambridge mathematician's statement that scientists were renewing their interest in religion," Ramsey recalls. "I rather boldly said that we too often talked about the application of religion to this and that, when we needed to learn about the practice of religion itself."

Temple's mission was in the beautiful fifteenth-century Church of St. Mary the Great, usually called Great St. Mary's. Ramsey attended the mission several times during the week and also went to hear the other two ministers.

"I remember the Irish evangelist as a super-modern gospeler, a Billy Graham," Ramsey says. "I found him whipping the people into hysteria. He kept saying they should come to the Lord by standing up—'Stand up, sir, bless you!' . . . 'Stand up, lady, bless you!' People were bobbing up and down all over the place. I was holding tight to my seat. In the midst of all this we had another verse of the hymn 'Almost Persuaded' and then the evangelist called for all hypocrites to leave the church. 'You who came here to stare and maybe to laugh, you may leave the church now. Go back to your wine and your women and cigarettes.'"

Ramsey left the hall a few minutes later, thoroughly revolted by such revivalism.

The Easter vacation of 1926 was a time of great decision in Michael Ramsey's life. He withdrew to St. Augustine's Clergy House in Stepney, a poor and shabby section of London which embraces London Bridge, the historic Tower of London, Limehouse, and Whitechapel.

The hour had come, he believed, for choosing the Church or a life of law, government, and politics. Yet he knew, as he said years later, that his real contentment with politics had ended the night Lord Hugh Cecil said in the Cambridge Union, "After all, nothing in politics matters too much; it is men like Newman in the Church of St. Mary the Virgin, in Oxford, and Wesley, preaching up and down the country, *who do the most good.*"

Almost a year had passed since he heard those words. In the ensuing months he had read much of William Temple's writings and was deeply moved by his mission to Cambridge. Still, entering the ministry was not just a choice of career. It was a frustrating, heartfelt emotion all bound up with his real respect for his father and his father's own position as a Non-Conformist, a Congregationalist.

"My religious beliefs could not stand still," says Ramsey. "They either had to go forward or fall back. The Catholic movement in the Church of England fired my imagination. I knew my father would be tolerant. He *was* tolerant. Yet I had a deep regard for his beliefs. It was a great inner conflict for me and my interest in the Anglo-Catholic side of the Church made my feelings even more removed from my father's."

At the end of the vacation Ramsey went home to Howfield to tell his family he had decided to study for the Anglican priesthood.

A grueling series of academic examinations lay ahead in the final year of Ramsey's three years as an undergraduate. His university career had begun brilliantly. In the first term he had won the Magdalene College Latin Verse Prize. But what he later called "my political dissipation" in the Union, as well as the American trip, took its toll in his preparation for the "tripos" (examinations so named for the three-legged stools on which the scholars once sat). Ramsey did not place first. He emerged instead with what is called Second Class Tripos, and this doubtlessly was a disappointment to him and his family.

"Really the difference between a First and a Second didn't seem too important in Michael's case," recalls a man who was studying at Cambridge in 1926. "His switch to theology meant he wouldn't be Prime Minister after all. We simply considered that he'd found another way to eminence."

On May 4 Ramsey made one of his last addresses in the Union, speaking brilliantly against a proposition that declared "the youth of today is degenerate." The motion lost 145 to 77 and the meeting adjourned in time to hear the BBC news bulletins on the General Strike sweeping over England.

The strike eventually involved three million workers. It closed down the railroads, iron and steel mills, construction, and newspapers. Cambridge read mimeographed editions of the student newspapers and the few copies that could be obtained of the *British Gazette,* the newspaper the government had begun publishing when Fleet Street was paralyzed. Women students volunteered to take over bed-making in some of the colleges, and members of the Union and other debating societies, the Magpie and the Stump, operated the gas works. (Some said it was quite appropriate.)

The Union, which always took itself very seriously, met in a grave session on May 14. It approved a motion that "notwithstanding anything in the laws of the society, the officers be empowered to suspend debates, private business meetings and elections during the national crisis and that the present officers and trustees be empowered to carry on the business of the society until the normal life of the university be resumed."

The routine of Cambridge and most of the nation was as still as if it were in the frozen grip of a winter blizzard. Ramsey believes his view of the situation was "very anti-government." He kept to his room, reading assiduously to compensate for his late decision to study theology.

Meanwhile, a group of Magdalene men and other university students volunteered to unload ships and help run trains and buses in London. At night the undergraduates slept in a London warehouse in which bathroom fixtures were stored. Indeed their jokes about life among the plumbing were the only bright features of an exhausting time. But as the days wore on the men played street ball with the strikers and later invited them for a visit to Cambridge.

By the end of the summer the last holdouts of the strike, the miners, had been starved into submission. The new university term began. Ramsey's old friend, Patrick Devlin, came to the presidency of the Union, but Ramsey had little time for it. He gave himself completely to theological studies. Occasionally he spoke in favor of a missionary movement known as the World Call, and frequently he attended the Friday evening "open house" maintained by his boyhood tutor, the Very Rev. Eric Milner-White, then Dean of King's College.

"I discussed religion but I never allowed the boys to talk it," recalls the Dean. "You know why? Because undergraduates almost always get into the question, 'Does God exist?' I gave them their tea before they could get started talking."

When members of this Friday evening group became ordinands (candidates for ordination), Milner-White usually asked them to join his secret society, "The Diocese."

"I was its archbishop, known as 'the Arch,'" laughs Milner-White. "When Ramsey became an ordinand I asked him to become a member. He did come in and I was *his* archbishop for many years."

Ramsey's twenty-second birthday passed quietly. How different it was from the year before when he had been in the United States, a member of the debate team, speaking to crowded auditoriums, seeing a fresh campus and city almost every day, questioned, complimented, and traveling thousands of miles. The tripos had been, in a way, a humbling experience. The retreat in London had been humbling, too, bringing him face-to-face with truth and faith and ambition and all the qualities of which he had spoken so glibly in debates.

He read countless books in preparation for the weekly tutorial sessions sometimes referred to in Cambridge as "two men, two chairs, two pipes and a fire." The student would read his essay aloud, afterward defending it against the tutor's criticisms. Indeed, the tutorials suggested the truth of the motto on the front of Magdalene's library: *Mens cujusque est quisque*—"The mind's the man." Ramsey was especially impressed by the lectures of the New Testament scholar, Edwyn Clement Hoskyns.

On February 23 Magdalene held its annual dinner celebrating the birthday of its alumnus and benefactor, Samuel Pepys. Afterward in the mellow light of the Combination Room the men lifted their glasses beneath Pepys' portrait.

When the tripos came up again Ramsey did brilliantly, achieving a First Class for his year of graduate study in theology. Now he prepared to move on to a seminary for a final year of preparation for his ordination. He chose Cuddesdon College, an Oxfordshire seminary founded in 1854.

Years later he characterized the 1920's in Cambridge as "a St. Martin's summer [Indian summer] of liberalism with at least a small 'l' in a world more cold and stormy than any of us could know."

4. CUDDESDON: THE MAKING OF A PRIEST

From the moment he saw Cuddesdon College, serene and remote across the plowed fields of Oxfordshire, Ramsey knew it was a place apart.

Here, a few miles from Oxford, the country lane levels out, with woodlands to the left and farmlands to the right. The college buildings stand hard by the roadside across from a gray stone gatehouse that guards an estate which since the seventeenth century has been the home of the Bishop of Oxford.

"There is of necessity a certain severity belonging to a theological college where men come to recognize the sternness of life," an alumnus has written, "but nothing could be farther away from what is supposed to be the seminary spirit of narrowness and obscurantism than the spirit which is bred in Cuddesdon. The place itself, open to every wind of heaven, and founded on a hill, standing rock-like, looking, as it were, from the present upon the past and the future in one survey, seems to be a parable of the life of the English Church. Faith in the fixed foundation has never faltered, but always there has been welcome for new light on old truth and an eager readiness to accept all that should come daily from the providence of God. Cuddesdon has shown how the Church of God is ever bringing from her treasures things new and old."

The main entrance at Cuddesdon formerly was from a courtyard by the main road. Ramsey opened this door on July 30, 1927, and signed the college register:

No. 1804, Ramsey, Arthur Michael, Magdalene, Cambridge, B.A., Classical Tripos, Pt. I, Class 2; Theological Tripos, Pt. I, Class 1; born November 14, 1904; attended Repton School.

In this register the college secretary later makes the notation of a student's ordination to the Diaconate and the Priesthood, and of his assignment to his first parish.

The register indicates that the majority of Cuddesdon enrollments was from Cambridge and Oxford, for whose students the seminary was founded when the ancient universities passed from Church control. Ramsey's registration followed that of another Cambridge man, Egerton Edward Farrar Walters. After Ramsey came Eric Henry Knell from Trinity College, Oxford, who would one day be the Bishop Suffragan of Reading. A total of sixteen new men entered Cuddesdon that month, swelling the enrollment to thirty-eight. All wore the scholar's black gown.

Late in the first afternoon of that new term, Ramsey and the others strolled around the bend of the road, past thatch-roofed cottages, to the parish church, All Saints, for the service of Evensong. The principal of Cuddesdon College is also vicar of the parish church and Evensong is traditionally held there rather than in the college chapel.

The men passed under the peaked wooden roof of the lich gate, walked along the paths of the old churchyard, and assembled before the beautifully carved altar of the country church.

"*My soul doth magnify the Lord. . . .*" The words of the *Magnificat* rose in the stone tower of the ancient church.

"*. . . and my spirit hath rejoiced in God my Saviour,*" their voices continued, strong with the enthusiasm of new ordinands.

"*For He hath regarded the lowliness of His handmaiden.*" Not a few of the new students were unsure of the plain-song they would come to know so well.

"*For behold, from henceforth all generations shall call Me blessed.*" These words from St. Luke they would say every day of their lives, as ordinands and priests, in the obligatory reading of Evensong.

Ramsey and a few of the new ordinands had a chance after Evensong to see the village, finding there a few homes where an overflow of Cuddesdon men lodged, a scattering of shops, and the local pub, The Bat & Ball. Beyond the village, in the valley that dropped off below the college grounds, women and children were picking blackberries in the hedges and horses were grazing on the brown hillsides. There were no street lights in Cuddesdon and in an hour, when darkness fell and the mists moved in, the shadowy stillness was as deep as it would be at midnight.

Dinner at eight that evening in the refectory was served by a new head butler, David Davie, who had trained under George Belcher, a faithful servant of fifty years. On his retirement earlier that month, Belcher had been given a gold watch in a presentation made by Cuddesdon's most distinguished living alumnus, Cosmo Gordon Lang, Archbishop of York.

At the high table sat the Rev. James Buchanan Seaton, the principal, or "Princeps" as the office traditionally is known at Cuddesdon. He had seen the college through the war years when Serbian theological students had been quartered in the buildings. Next to him was the vice-principal, the Rev. Edward J. Bicknell, who had arrived in 1919 when the college was reopened for Anglican ordinands. A newcomer to the high table was the chaplain, the Rev. Terence Leslie Manson, a member of the Society of St. John the Evangelist and the first religious to hold a post in the college.

Over after-dinner coffee in the Common Room, the men had their best opportunity to become acquainted and to study a large world map showing where Cuddesdon alumni were serving throughout the Anglican Communion.

At 9:30 P.M. a bell rang for Compline* in the chapel. It was dimly lighted, a candle flickering in a crimson bowl beneath an icon given by the Serbian students of the war years. Ramsey

---

* "Compline?" asks a curate who lodges with Ramsey family friends in London. "*We* always said *we* didn't hold Roman Catholic services in the theological college *I* attended. We called it the last service of the day."

found before him the *Cuddesdon Office Book,* devised through the years for the college's special use.

Then began the service that sealed the seminary day. The name Compline stems from the Latin *Completorium,* and marks completion of the day's work with a perfect form of night prayers, a preparation for death or for the night's sleep.

After Compline there fell over Cuddesdon College the rule of silence—the Great Silence, as it was called—during which no one spoke until breakfast the next morning. The halls of Cuddesdon became as quiet as the village.

As the day ended, so the next began, in the chapel. Prime was at 7:15, Matins at 7:30, and celebration of the Holy Eucharist at 8.

Ramsey found that the seminary set before her sons certain regulations on the basis of which they would frame themselves for a professional life of service and devotion. "The College desires each man to approach the College rules with the sincere desire for self-discipline," says an early history of Cuddesdon. "The obedience which it asks is the free and hearty consent of the full-grown man, who takes on trust (at first) rules which the experience of others has shown to be helpful in the training of character, and imposes them upon himself as his own rules of life."

The beginning of the 1927-28 year at Cuddesdon is well remembered by a close friend, Dr. Austin Farrer, now warden of Keble College, Oxford.

"Some of us found Cuddesdon very mild after the stimulating atmosphere of our undergraduate colleges," he says. "It was obvious that Ramsey was the man with real, first-rate academic ability. Oh, there were many clever people who knew their fields—music and so on—but Ramsey was my only sparring partner. And he was a teasing gossip, too; knew everything that was going on, all the details. At the same time he was an intellectual eccentric. No one thought he could possibly administer anything. At times he could be an *extreme* eccentric. He was an odd young man and I felt, 'Well, sometime this chap will be *his own age,* as young as he is or as old as he acts.' He talked to himself some and he had a great, witty sarcasm. I remember a pretentious theologian who came to speak to us, and Ramsey composed a limerick:

> 'We've heard the great ———,
> Who aspired to the established Church.
> But they found his D.D.
> Was a bogus degree,
> So they left Dr. ——— in the lurch.'

"Then I remember, besides Ramsey, some other fine men— Hugh Lister, who did outstanding work in London's East End before he was killed in World War II. And there was Neal Russell from the Episcopal Church of Scotland. We used to find him praying in the chapel, standing upright with face shining. We thought he would establish the religious life in Scotland, but instead he gave himself to the Universities' Mission to Central Africa."

Ramsey, Farrer, Lister, Russell—it was a remarkable class. In the afternoon "free periods" from two to four the young men walked in the orchard (*"O beata solitudo,"* they called it), went swimming in the river, watched the beehives one student had begun, and played croquet or tennis on the lawn.

"Ramsey was accomplished at croquet," says Farrer. "He had control over the ball, strategy, and surprising skill. Croquet *is* a don's game."

The first term at Cuddesdon passed rapidly for everyone. Ramsey was content except for missing the celebration of his parents' silver wedding anniversary.

"I was at Howfield that day," says an old family friend, F. R. Salter. "Only the master of Magdalene called Arthur Ramsey by his first name. The rest of us, the Fellows, referred to him as A. S. R., his initials. We talked about A. S. R.'s new portrait, painted for the Combination Room at Magdalene, and A. S. R. said, 'If I outlive my wife—which I intend doing, as the Scotsmen say—I may have my portrait painted again.' We talked cars too —the Ramseys had a new one, an open car, a Morris Oxford."

Others at the anniversary tea were the pastor of the Emmanuel Congregational Church, the Rev. H. C. Carter, his wife, and their house guest, Miss Marguerite Lindberg of Copenhagen. The

Ramseys invited the Carters and Miss Lindberg to accompany them the next day on a drive to Stafford, near Godmanchester.

At Cuddesdon, Ramsey began his third week. At Communion that morning he felt for the first time that he was a member of the college, a part of the life. The summer day wore on with the classes, the noontime chapel service of Lauds, and luncheon. About an hour later he received a telegram from his brother, Frank. Their mother had been killed instantly in an automobile accident near Cambridge.

"It's such a little thing. I was trying to put my coat right," Arthur Stanley Ramsey said to the first man to reach the scene of the accident.

The sixty-year-old don, in that moment of restlessness, had lost control of the car. It left the pavement, swerved to the other side of the road, missed a telephone pole, and overturned. Mr. Carter, also in the front seat, was thrown clear and was uninjured. But the three women in the back seat were pinned beneath the car. Mrs. Ramsey died instantly; Miss Lindberg was critically injured; and Mrs. Carter had a broken arm.

At Howfield, Bridget learned by telephone of her mother's death and went immediately to tell Frank Ramsey, married now and living in Bridge Street. Their father was at Huntingdon County Hospital under treatment for broken ribs, internal bruises, and shock. A jury which assembled that day to investigate the fatality returned within twenty-four hours a verdict of accidental death.

"I went into Oxford and took the train to Cambridge," says Michael Ramsey in a quiet, grieved voice, his eyes filling with tears as he speaks these many years later of the tragedy. With the other members of the family he attended the funeral service in Holy Trinity Church. The vicar officiated, assisted by Mrs. Ramsey's brother, the Rev. C. P. Wilson.

Thus there began for each member of the Ramsey family a "dark night of the soul" that would deeply influence each of them in the years ahead.

The father never again drove a car. He tended to blame himself for his wife's death, but in the words of another don, "He bore his grief in a way that was gallant beyond words."

At Howfield, Frank and his wife, Lettice, moved in to help look after Bridget and Margaret. For Bridget, especially, it was a difficult time. She was just beginning a pre-medical course at Cambridge. And at Cuddesdon, Michael Ramsey paced the corridors, deeply grieved at the loss of the mother who had bade him good-by less than a month before at the Cambridge Station.

The tragedy caused him to enter into the spiritual life of the college with deeper feeling. Although sad and depressed he continued to be well liked among the other men and on October 24 was elected secretary of the Common Room.

In December the college watched with lively interest and then disbelief as the Church's recommended revision of the Prayer Book was rejected in Parliament by a vote of 238 to 205.

Ramsey saw in the newspapers the face of the man who had so influenced him in the Cambridge Union—Lord Hugh Cecil. Many felt that Cecil had failed to move the Parliament as he could have done.

The whole situation spoke to Ramsey's foremost interests, religion and politics, but he could not focus upon it. His grief at his mother's death was still very much with him. The shock persisted, never lifting by day or night.

"I had a mental breakdown," says Ramsey. "I did not go back to Cuddesdon for the next term."

Christmas season of 1927 was a melancholy time at Howfield and, once it had passed, Ramsey went to London to consult a psychiatrist.

Only a few friends know of his acute depression. His family speaks of it guardedly. Ramsey himself says only that he saw the psychiatrist several hours a week over a period of months. He adds that he was so impressed and helped that he has not hesitated to recommend the counsel of qualified psychologists and psychiatrists.

Certainly it was an unusual occurrence in a life that had been, to that moment, confined by propriety and tradition. Psychiatry was in its infancy, a new science in England, and it is remarkable that such therapy was suggested to Ramsey.

By the spring term Ramsey was back at Cuddesdon. A notation in the Common Room record of April 25, 1928, reads, "Mr. Ramsey made a dramatic return to public life, together with the long-lost minutes book and his own remarks therein. . . ."

Cuddesdon's routine continued at a gracious pace. There existed a minimum of austerity and self-denial, but the era of many servants had not quite passed away. David Davie's staff of six men and five women called the students in early morning, cleaned the rooms, shined shoes, posted letters and ran errands, brought in coal, built fires, and served up generous teas.

"The men were waited on," says Davie. "Miss Ada Boyes, the cook, had six in kitchen help, and they made Cuddesdon known for its food. At a single meal the men could have their choice from two steaks, four chickens, and two legs of lamb. They could have 'seconds' too, and for anyone who didn't feel well there was always a nice milk pudding. At Sunday breakfast there were three helpings of ham, and Sunday dinner always had five or six desserts to choose from as well as biscuits with butter or cheese."

Davie and his wife, who remember all the Cuddesdon men as vividly as they recall the customs, live in retirement in "Woodsleigh," the same college-owned house they have occupied for more than forty years. Only the top of their new television set is reserved for pictures of their nieces and nephews; the rest of the room—the walls, the tables, the top of the piano—is covered with pictures of Cuddesdon men at all stages of ecclesiastical progress —from seminary to enthronement as bishops.

"Oh, the boys I've known who became bishops!" says Davie with pride. "The only thing I like better is when one of their sons comes to study at Cuddesdon. There's Henderson, the son of the new Bishop of Bath and Wells. His father lived in my house thirty years ago, and now his boy is here.

"Ramsey? Ramsey had a reserved manner, but he was well liked. He was always in the library. So was Austin Farrer. Both of them studied all the time."

That was true, indeed, for Ramsey, having lost a term, felt more than ever that he had a great deal of reading to do. But there was time for laughter, too, among Ramsey, Farrer, and their friends. One of their favorite amusements was the Ramsey limerick about a theological college principal named Burn. Ramsey would say the lines aloud:

> Quoth the Rev. Principal Burn,
> "I should like all my young men to learn,
> It does no great hurt
> For a student to flirt,
> Since its better to marry than burn."

Both Ramsey and Farrer attended the fortnightly evening classes conducted by Dr. Albert Mansbridge for the laborers of Cuddesdon.

"Old Dr. Mansbridge was a layman and an eccentric," says Dr. Farrer. "He was a Socialist, the founder of the Workers' Educational Association. Ramsey took a leading part in his classes."

Dr. Mansbridge liked the two young men from Cuddesdon. The Rev. John Brewis, rector of St. James's, Piccadilly, remembers that he was visiting the "Princeps" when Dr. Mansbridge came in and said with the Cockney accent he was to keep all his life, " 'Ere 'r two outstanding young men in 'e generation now in 'e College—one is Ramsey and 'e o'er is Farrer."

In their regular classes Ramsey and the others studied "parochialia," the whole spectrum of the duties of a clergyman both in his church and among his flock outside. They learned to conduct services by reading aloud in the chapel and delivering their own sermons in the church on Mondays and Tuesdays after Evensong. The nearness of the Bishop's Palace with its old stone chapel made it convenient for the men to familiarize themselves with ordinations, confirmations, and other services.

As a final chore before leaving Cuddesdon students discarded most of their old clothes, a custom regarded now as another extravagance of the era. The "good suit" which they took home, a new gray flannel or black worsted, would be their clerical dress for traveling and street wear.

The class picture made in the early summer of 1928 shows the twenty-three-year-old Ramsey in the dark suit and tie of a seminarian. He is tall and slim with shining hair and the mustache he had first affected as an undergraduate at Magdalene. In the picture Ramsey stands next to D. J. Chitty. ("An eccentric but clever country rector: Ramsey always likes eccentrics," says one of their classmates.) At Ramsey's left stands John Tenbruggenkate who later changed his name to Rouse and migrated to Australia.

There were thirty-six men in this seminary class. All of them before the year ended would be ordained deacons, and in another year, priests. Most would later serve as diocesan clergy, one would be deposed, another would go over to Rome. From this class would come two foreign missionaries, a leading educator, two bishops, and an archbishop.

"How do we describe what Cuddesdon meant to us?" asked Ramsey in a sermon at the college in 1956. "It was here that we came to know and to love, each in his own time, One who taught, guided, and inspired us. It was here that the ideal of what it means to be a priest came vividly home to us. It was here that we faced the truth about ourselves before the cross of Christ, and with the painful shattering of our pride discovered that we have no sufficiency of ourselves to think anything of ourselves. And, with memories solemn and searing, there mingle memories light and ludicrous, since, for all the seriousness of the purpose which brought us here, we were here as human beings with our absurdities and our sense of the absurd. Learning to laugh at ourselves, we did not lack other things to laugh about. How should we, if the Christian life is indeed the knowledge of Him who is the author of laughter as well as tears?"

5. LIVERPOOL: THE FIRST YEARS

Liverpool's black streets glistened with rain on the morning of September 23, 1928, when Ramsey was ordained a deacon at the Church of Our Lady and St. Nicholas. He would remain here for two years, first as a deacon, then as a priest.

His assignment to St. Nicholas, a parish on the Liverpool docks, was a complete break with the sheltered academic life he had known at Cambridge and Cuddesdon. Looking out on the River Mersey as it flowed to the open sea, the old church had since 1257 drawn to its altars the great variety of souls who lived and worked in England's second largest port city.

On this wet September Sunday only two young men presented themselves for ordination at the hands of the Bishop of Liverpool, Dr. Albert Augustus David, the former headmaster of Rugby. Ramsey was to be a curate at St. Nicholas, a post he had learned of from his Uncle Archie, at that time the organist of Manchester Cathedral. The other ordinand was Harry Arrowsmith, of St. Aidan's Theological College, who after several years as a curate would devote his career to a hospital chaplaincy in the Diocese of Birmingham.

The ordination of Ramsey and Arrowsmith to the Diaconate was briefly reported on page twelve of the next day's *Liverpool*

Post & Mercury. The city's major religious event on that particular weekend, however, had been the visit of Cardinal Bourne for the consecration of Dr. Richard Downey as Roman Catholic Archbishop of Liverpool.

"I found lodgings in a house at 13 St. James's Road, just across from the Cathedral," Ramsey recalls of his two years at Liverpool. "I had to get up at 6:30 to get a tram before 7 to say Matins in the church by 7:10."

The rector of St. Nicholas was Dr. J. C. H. How, later the Bishop of Glasgow and Primus of Scotland. He saw to it that his curates were busy throughout the day. Ramsey particularly remembers being given a great number of funerals. Also there was a large amount of parish calling. (The shifting population of Liverpool had caused a half dozen parishes to be merged with St. Nicholas in the years between 1898 and 1928.) Ramsey found his parishioners by going up and down stairs and in and out of mews and dark courtyards. There were many families to see, even though 50 per cent of the dock area was Roman Catholic, the decendants of those who had come from Ireland in the huge migrations of the nineteenth century. Father Ramsey, as he was called, was well liked. A few observed, "The new curate's not chatty." Others admired him the more for his quiet and affable manner. He smiled readily, and when he laughed a shock of light brown hair fell over his forehead.

At the end of every day, Ramsey took a dingy tram up the hill to St. James's Road.

The young curate was always fascinated by the massive structure he could see from his window. This was Liverpool Cathedral rising stone by stone in an age when most people thought cathedral building was long passed. The foundation stone had been laid by Edward VII the year Ramsey was born, and part of the new Cathedral had been ready for use by 1924. Now Ramsey saw the work going forward every day as a glorious eight-sided tower took shape over two Gothic arches believed to be the largest ever built.

Ramsey's years at Liverpool passed quietly, although the Church was experiencing an eventful time. The recently retired Archbishop of Canterbury, Randall Davidson, took an unusual but friendly step in accepting an invitation to address the newly reunited Scottish Presbyterians. Meanwhile, three branches of British Methodism—Wesleyan, Primitive, and United—formed one society. And in Rome the Lateran Treaty set free "the prisoner of the Vatican," Pius XI, in whom the British had a special interest as a modern Pope who had visited England and even knew a bit of the language.

The Anglican clergy appears to have been a lively, articulate group in the waning summer of 1929. The Bishop of Birmingham was umpire at the annual cricket match, "Parsons vs. Police." The Bishop of London went golfing. The Vicar of Highcliffe denounced "cuddling couples on the beach." William Ralph Inge, "the gloomy Dean of St. Paul's," was better known to many than even the Archbishop of Canterbury. "No one talks about war now," he said in a sermon that summer. "A generation of young people is growing up who knows nothing of it."

One of that generation was the three-year-old Princess Elizabeth, daughter of the Duke of York, who was spending a holiday near Liverpool with her maternal grandmother, Lady Strathmore. The little girl in the green frock was cheered by Liverpool crowds. No one imagined that in seven years she would be heir presumptive to the throne and in twenty-three years would be Queen.

On Sunday, September 22, 1929, Ramsey and Arrowsmith again knelt before Bishop David, this time for ordination to the priesthood. Twelve young men were ordained deacons during the same service.

As had the service of St. Nicholas, this ceremony at Farnworth Parish Church in suburban Widnes followed a custom of holding autumn ordinations in parish churches so that congregations might witness, at least once every few years, one of the Prayer Book's most significant and moving acts of faith. Afterward the newly ordained were recorded in the Farnworth parish's "Register Book of Chrystenyngs, Maryages and Buryalls." In its parchment pages were listed the names of several men who had received baptism in this obscure parish and who went on to positions of great prominence. Among them was Richard Barnes, who became Bishop of Durham in 1577, and Richard Bancroft, who from 1604 to 1610 was the seventy-fourth Archbishop of Canterbury.

Ramsey celebrated his first Eucharist on Tuesday, September 24, 1929, and entered into a schedule of parish work even busier than that of the previous year.

Another blow, as shattering and shocking as his mother's fatal accident, struck Ramsey early in the new year, 1930—the sudden death of his brilliant brother, Frank. Only a month before his twenty-seventh birthday Frank died of jaundice. His young wife was left with two baby daughters. The whole university community in Cambridge mourned his death—a loss, an unfulfilled promise.

Who would have believed, Ramsey wondered, that two such joyous, energetic persons as his mother and brother would be taken in death in less than three years. Ramsey studied a picture of Frank on a summer holiday in the Austrian Tyrol—a snapshot of him there on a mountainside, biting into an apple as he leafed through a book, his white shirt open at the neck, a sweater thrown over his shoulders. So typical of Frank! And his childhood recollections, his first memories, were of Frank, only twenty-one months older. In the long watches of the night and in his vigils at the altar, he thought of Frank's bulky Johnsonian frame, his spontaneous laugh, the simplicity of his feelings and reactions.

There swept over Ramsey a feeling of deep sorrow for the loss of his mother and brother. Remembering his earlier breakdown, his family was thankful he had come to ordination before this second blow, for now there would be some refuge in his work, some peace and escape in his responsibilities as a priest in a busy parish.

Bridget visited her brother later in the spring and was happy to find his grief somewhat subdued. He had an acquaintance with a dwarf who also had a room in the house in St. James's Road. They shared a mutual and active dislike for the landlady. The dwarf referred to her as "It." Bridget was amused at the "conspiracy" between her brother and the dwarf.

In confirming this recollection Ramsey adds, "I quarreled with that landlady, Miss Young, and moved away. Since there had been no Liberal candidate in that year's election, I voted for the Labor Party. The landlady was a strong Ulster Conservative and didn't like my views. That was the beginning of tension, and after a while I went to live at a small hotel, the Eggleston."

Ramsey stayed at the Eggleston for the remainder of his time in Liverpool. As unemployment swept over England and America in 1930, especially in the industrial areas, Ramsey and his parishioners faced new problems. The docks near St. Nicholas that had been so busy importing thousands of tons of grain and raw materials, and exporting steel, textiles, and pottery, were quiet. As many as one hundred thousand of Liverpool's citizens were unemployed. At the altar rail Ramsey saw the worn gray faces of depressed men and women. From the pulpit he saw fear and hunger. Now and then he heard angry demonstrations at the Town Hall in the neighboring block.

Out of this misery and unrest the Liverpool city council eventually devised a plan for municipal employment that has served as a model for many other cities. But it was not fully perfected until 1936, and Ramsey did not see the relief that finally came to Liverpool.

In the summer of 1930 he heard from a friend at Cambridge that the post of sub-warden was open in Lincoln Theological College. For all his love of parish work, he felt he could better serve the academic life. He accepted the call to Lincoln.

But in the experience as curate, that period of very hard work and humble service which the Church in its wisdom exacts from the newly ordained, he had learned much of the spiritual and practical sides of being a priest. "It is not easy," he once told a group of ordinands. "Not only will the round of ceaseless business in Church and Parish hinder you, but—and here is the more subtle danger—the devoted practices of prayer and office and penitence can themselves be twisted into a sort of busyness which can hide you from yourself in an aroma of professional piety. So the need is for spaces of quietness in which you see yourself as you are, in the presence of the Creator who made you and the Lord who ordained you. Take heed to thyself, that self which can deceive itself unless it is revealed in naked simplicity before its God. It is in this taking heed that a true devoutness, simple, generous, Godward, has its root and its renewing."

6. LINCOLN'S "SCHOLAE CANCELLARII"

The eleventh-century Cathedral Church of the Blessed Virgin Mary of Lincoln commands a sweeping view of the plains and heaths of eastern England, the town of Lincoln tumbling away down the steep hillside. Almost in the shadow of the cathedral is the Lincoln Theological College, or *Scholae Cancellarii*, as it is often called after Lincoln's ancient scholastic foundation that pre-dated the universities of Oxford and Cambridge. Here Michael Ramsey arrived in the summer of 1930 to take up his new duties as sub-warden of the seminary.

The warden, the Rev. Leslie Owen, had a house adjoining the college, living there with his wife and their small children, John and Faith. The family ate with the men in the college dining hall, for life at Lincoln was more informal than at Cuddesdon. Then, as now, Lincoln had a reputation for being less High Church and less "high-brow" than Cuddesdon. It is the only theological college which always has admitted married students.

Ramsey's duties as sub-warden were overseeing the library and directing the intellectual life of the college. His sitting room was as drab as any in the college, but it was larger and had a glorious view of the Cathedral. The men who gathered after dinner in the Common Room soon became familiar with Ramsey's habit of pacing back and forth as he threshed out a problem in his quarters directly above them. In the chapel he could tear a handkerchief to shreds while deeply absorbed in prayer; some wondered how many handkerchiefs were destroyed each week.

Two students who went to him for a tutorial found that as he read their papers he moved his eyebrows up and down in a characteristic gesture, now and then nodding in agreement, "Yes, yes, yes." He put the papers aside and sat thinking for a long while. No one spoke, as indeed no one had spoken since the beginning of the hour. Finally the bell rang for chapel and Ramsey arose with the words, "Yes, yes, Lincoln is a very quiet place."

Hearing such reports, the ordinands joked about Ramsey. But they soon learned that he was a brilliant theologian who could quickly turn the tables when they asked teasing questions. In lectures and classwork he prepared them extremely well for the G. O. E., the difficult General Ordination Examination sometimes called "God's Own Exam."

Brother Edwin, a stout, cheerful monk of the Society of the Sacred Mission, recalls Ramsey from the thousands of men he has tutored in plain-song in the chapel at Lincoln. "He wasn't bad; he was Ramseyish," says Brother Edwin. "That means he would try intently. He was the most co-operative pupil you could have. He was a 'wheelbarrow baritone.' I've never forgotten how quickly he was on his feet the time I dared to say Latin was a dead language."

Ramsey is remembered as "one of our intellectual heavyweights" by Hugh Edward Ashdown, later to become the Bishop of Newcastle. And Eric Abbott, now the Dean of Westminster, recalls Ramsey's tennis matches under the willow trees at the front of the college: "He didn't play tennis very well, but he strode brisk about and enjoyed himself. All of us knew he would be great. We were not sure just how, perhaps as an academic man. The thing to remember about Michael is that he is a man of spirituality and above all a great priest. He is as spiritual as he is theological. For him theology is always the central thing. He doesn't call in theologians as some people call in lawyers when they can't manage otherwise."

A sense of humor was not obscured by the serious study of

these years. Ramsey's classmate from Cuddesdon, Dr. Austin Farrer, recalls that Ramsey attended a conference at St. Deiniol's, the theological library endowed by Prime Minister Gladstone on his estate in Wales. "I saw the sardonic Ramsey humor I'd known at Cuddesdon," says Farrer. "I mentioned to Ramsey that there was no cross on St. Deiniol's altar, and he replied, 'Well, the sub-warden, Noel Davey, has been reading some of Karl Barth's theology and has decided that *Nothingness* is the symbol and meaning of the crucifixion. He has removed the cross from the altar and left Nothing there.' Years later when I mentioned this to Noel Davey he cried, 'Nonsense! I had sent the cross to be repaired!' "

There was also a thoughtful, gentle side to Ramsey's character which showed itself in many ways. He often asked to take the two Owen children for walks. And when Miss Lucy, his father's sister, talked to him about being received into the Church, he arranged for her to stay at Lincoln during the instruction period and to be confirmed in the college chapel.

That same year when Ramsey was visiting at home in Cambridge, his sister Bridget told him of her plans to marry Henry Barcroft, a young doctor who had been at the King's School with Ramsey. "Of course, Michael knew both of us very well," says Bridget. "Our views differed from those of the Church, and he was aware of that. He knew we had not been to Communion in a long while. He asked us what we thought he should do, and we had to agree it would be against his principles to marry us, knowing our feelings as intimately as he did. We were married in the Church of England, however, by the vicar of a country parish. We were deeply touched when we received from Michael as a wedding present the magnificent sum of £50. Think how long it took him to save £50! It was a substantial part of a year's salary. We were overwhelmed."

Lincoln Cathedral saw several memorable ceremonies in Ramsey's years as sub-warden in the theological college. On November 3, 1932, the staff and students attended a service of thanksgiving for the preservation of the Cathedral. Modern engineering had saved the old building, strengthening it against the ravages of earthquake and time. In jubilation, "Great Tom," the five-ton bell in the central tower, tolled over the college and the town. It was a joyous day for Lincoln and for Ramsey with his lifelong interest in cathedral architecture.

Another solemn ceremony honored Edward King, Bishop of Lincoln from 1885 to 1910, dramatically indicating the Church's growing regard for Anglo-Catholic observances. Whereas Bishop King had in 1890 been tried before the ninety-fourth Archbishop of Canterbury, Edward White Benson, for ritualistic practices in the celebration of the Holy Communion, the ninety-seventh Archbishop, Cosmo Gordon Lang, now came to Lincoln to lead a service of thanksgiving for King's witness to the Catholic heritage in the Church of England. It was an occasion of personal significance to Archbishop Lang, who in 1889 had been confirmed by Bishop King in Lincoln Cathedral. "Lang was at his best in reminiscences of this nature," says Ramsey. This was the second and final time he saw the Archbishop, though he was often to hear of him in the ten remaining years of Lang's primacy.

Ramsey in time knew Lincoln Cathedral almost as well as he had known Ely as a boy and Liverpool as a curate. But not until 1933 did he see that great edifice which many consider the most glorious of all the English cathedrals—Canterbury. He roamed its nave and chapels with his former master, the Rev. Henry Balmforth, who had become headmaster of St. Edmund's School, Canterbury. The next year he accepted an invitation from the Dean of Canterbury, Hewlett Johnson, to preach in the Cathedral.

In 1934 Ramsey had an opportunity to become sub-warden of a theological college in a university community. He refused the offer, preferring to remain at Lincoln and to finish writing his first book, *The Gospel and the Catholic Church.* Accepted for publication in 1936 on agreement that the author would not expect any royalties until the publisher had realized his own investment, the volume gained wide acclaim for the thirty-one-year-old author. It was regarded as one of the few Anglo-Catholic treatises to deal with Martin Luther with sympathetic fairness and to show enthusiasm for a nineteenth-century theologian and Christian Socialist, F. D. Maurice.

In this first book Ramsey wrote that "the Church exists for

something deeper than philanthropy and reform, namely to teach men to die to self." He added that "the Church points men to a unity and a peace which men generally neither understand nor desire."

It was the promise foretold in this book that plucked Ramsey from relative obscurity to prominence in the Church of England. In his pigeonhole mailbox at the college Ramsey began finding letters of comment from the clergy, among them one from William Temple, Archbishop of York. He invited Ramsey to Bishopthorpe, the archiepiscopal estate near York, for a three-day theological planning session for the Oxford Conference on Church, Community and Society, a forerunner of the World Council of Churches.

"This was my first meeting with eminent persons," says Ramsey as he looks at his faded photograph of the twelve men and two women standing on the steps of Bishopthorpe in the bright morning sunlight of July 18, 1936.

Archbishop Temple came striding out in gaiters to meet his guests at the gatehouse. The tallest, and perhaps the best known, was Reinhold Niebuhr, forty-four, a professor at Union Seminary in New York.

Other participants were J. H. Oldham, a veteran of the ecumenical movement that had begun at Edinburgh in 1910; Bernard Lord Manning, a Congregational layman and Cambridge don; Herman Sasse, a professor in a small German university; Emil Brunner of Zurich; J. S. Bixler of Harvard; Dwight Bradley of Andover-Newton Seminary in Massachusetts; and a Dutchman of scrubbed appearance, Willem Adolf Visser 't Hooft, a leader in the Student Christian Movement in Holland and destined to become General Secretary of the World Council. The youngest man present was a husky, black-haired Episcopal priest, Edward R. Hardy, a substitute for Professor Frank Gavin of the General Seminary in New York, who had become seriously ill in London.

"Ramsey was presented, indeed correctly, as a young man of whom more would be heard in the future," recalls Hardy, now a professor in Berkeley Divinity School, the Episcopal seminary at New Haven, Connecticut. "I suspect that Temple was the only person present who had read Ramsey's book. As for me, I had published nothing in those days but a recondite thesis. Ramsey's appearance, especially his complexion and build, gave an impression of middle-age. I was twenty-eight at the time, and did not realize that he was so slightly my senior."

Of the meeting Ramsey recalls little but imagines that he expressed "rather critical opinions." (He later wrote of Brunner as the somewhat ineffective translator of the Swiss theologian, Karl Barth.)

"Whatever was produced could as well have been done by Temple, Oldham, and Niebuhr," says Hardy. "The rest of us mainly sat around drinking in their wisdom and enjoying the privilege of Archbishop Temple's hospitality. The moments I remember are prayers in the chapel, dinners, Niebuhr telling stories over barley water and other harmless English drinks, and the afternoon when Temple took us all in to Evensong in York Minster."

In the evenings the group permitted its discussions to go beyond theological issues. Oldham arrived proudly with a complicated hearing aid, involving a box and crank rather like an old-fashioned telephone, and said that now he could again be a real member of a committee. Temple frequently referred to his visit earlier that year in the United States. Sasse held everyone's attention when he told of Germany's religious opposition to Adolf Hitler. Bixler sprawled in a chair, beside it the crutches he was using since a recent accident. The only professedly liberal theologian in the company, he was regarded as an interesting survivor from a previous generation.

Miss Olive Wyon, prim with dark shell-rimmed glasses, acted as secretary. A translator of many theological books, she had come prepared to serve as an interpreter but found instead that Brunner, Sasse, and Visser 't Hooft spoke excellent English.

On the last evening Frances Temple asked the group to sign her guest book. Looking at the list today, in her home in Winchester, she recalls the diffident compliment of one of the Americans: "Bishopthorpe has the only decent coffee I've been able to find in England."

Ramsey's first book not only brought him into contact with "eminent persons" but also made him better known to the clergy of his own diocese. In September, 1936, he addressed their annual Quiet Day in the Lincolnshire coastal town of Boston.

"I scarcely knew Michael Ramsey but he had written a new theological book of some importance and the diocese was beginning to recognize that his work in Lincoln was something out of the ordinary," says Canon A. M. Cook, the former vicar of Boston Parish Church, who extended the invitation. "He stayed the night and that evening I asked whether he could recommend any young priests as a possible lecturer or senior curate. We had just lost our lecturer and the other three curates were as yet too immature for promotion. To my surprise Ramsey said he would like to come and, needless to say, I accepted the proposal with gratitude. A few days later I was at some meeting in Lincoln and the bishop, Nugent Hicks, came across to me, saying he had been urging Michael to join my staff. The bishop said that the whole church has a responsibility over the training of a man of unusual abilities, and he was eager to see that Michael Ramsey was not confined to academic spheres."

So it was arranged that Ramsey, after an interlude of six years as a teacher, would return to parish work. It was not an altogether drastic change, for he was going only a few miles away and would remain in touch with ordinands as Examining Chaplain to his former headmaster, Geoffrey Fisher, who had become Bishop of Chester in 1932.* Moreover, he would have time to continue his writing. ("Michael is *always* writing a book," friends would say in future years.) He was encouraged by the success of *The Gospel and the Catholic Church* and the plans for it to go into a second printing in February, 1937. "The book was hailed for its new and creative approach to the conflicts of [Roman] Catholics and Protestants and to the problem of Christian unity," a reviewer recalls. "It quickly came to have an influential place in discussions between different Christian traditions both in England and on the Continent."

Eric Abbott, the new warden of the theological college, was one of the first to learn of Ramsey's appointment to Boston. "There are sixteen thousand people there and also much cattle," Ramsey said, smiling at his reference to a passage from Jonah which tells of a city "wherein are more than sixscore thousand persons . . . and also much cattle."

* Ramsey was Examining Chaplain to the Bishop of Chester, 1932-38; to the Bishop of Durham, 1940-50; and to the Bishop of Lincoln, 1951-52.

7. THE LECTURER OF BOSTON

The noble tower of Boston Parish Church, fondly called "the Boston stump," has been a guide for travelers on land and sea for more than five hundred years.

This tower was the last bit of England seen by the Pilgrims as they sailed for the new world in 1629, and it was this town they remembered in choosing a name for the capital of the Massachusetts colony. In so doing they continued to honor St. Botolph, whose name is anglicized to Boston, a pilgrim himself when he established a monastery on the Lincolnshire coast in the year 654.

The Pilgrim fathers, before sailing to America, had established the lectureship of Boston Parish Church to insure the preaching of the gospel should the vicar neglect this duty. It was to this post, in England's largest parish church, that Ramsey came in the fall of 1936. He took a room a short distance from the church in a brick, semi-detached house at 8 Thurold Street.

Meanwhile, the Bishop of Bradford—whose name was, appropriately, Bishop Blunt—made a reference at a diocesan conference to the monarch's "duty to his people." It was then Britain learned that the former Prince of Wales, so recently come to the throne, wished to marry an American woman twice divorced. The ensuing course of events held keen interest for the clergy as they

81

saw the Archbishop of Canterbury, Cosmo Lang, among those at the very center of the storm. It was a situation of wide repercussions, involving the Church's delicate relationship with the Crown, and reminding the people of the Church's teachings on the remarriage of divorced persons. On the night of December 11, 1936, Ramsey listened to the abdication address broadcast from Windsor Castle.

Canon Cook speaks at length of the years when he was Ramsey's vicar at Boston. "In age Michael was a sheltered thirty-two when he came to Boston. There were traces of the boy still about him but he soon began to get in touch with all sides of life. He understood why his book had not caused much stir in Boston. The people don't read things like that. He preached on the average of three times a month, usually in the evenings. He was simple, straightforward and good. He soon realized we were not an intellectual congregation. I can see him now, squeezing up his eyes and saying, 'Let us make a picture . . .' as he re-created some Biblical scene. He demonstrated a great aptitude for extemporaneous speaking with guts in it. His words came out in a slow way, but his sentences were absolutely beautiful."

Once again Ramsey ministered to the parishioners of a seaport, but Boston was not a great industrial city as was Liverpool. Here he found simple country people, and he got along with them extraordinarily well. "Mr. Ramsey," they called him, not being inclined to titles.

Canon Cook continues, "I put him in charge of the Sunday schools and the confirmation classes. He made a deep impression on our young people, only mitigated by his inability to recognize them in the street. Nonetheless, his sheer goodness attracted an immediate response from people. I can think of homes where he was always welcome. Above all there was his work in the evening classes. I was determined to try and use him for lecturing on theological affairs as well as preaching. We had built up a good group of churchfolk and Non-Conformists for the evening classes and Ramsey continued this success with a group of teachers with whom he studied the new *Agreed Syllabus* for religious teaching in schools. It really laid the foundation of work that still continues at Pilgrim College."

Ramsey made his parish visitations on bicycle, and occasionally he played on the parish hockey team. But his favorite relaxation was a solitary hike in the flat countryside. Often he took a packet of sandwiches and strolled for several miles along the footpath of an old canal. His usual destination was a pub, the Malcolm Arms, in the village of Anton's Gowt. The cream-colored stucco inn stood at the crossroads of the village, and here Ramsey would have a beer or an ale with his bread and cheese.

Continuing his friendship with Archbishop William Temple, Ramsey in April, 1937, was invited by Temple to address the diocesan clergy school at Scarborough. During the trip back to Boston he purchased a Bible with a wide margin. He remembers the Coronation Day of 1937, for it was a holiday which gave him an opportunity to read the newly acquired Bible. Ramsey made many marginal notes on the Gospel of St. Luke, and he still keeps this Bible within reach of the armchair in his study.

A group of women dusting Boston Parish Church were surprised one day when a priest from another town remarked to them that Mr. Ramsey was a wonderful preacher. The women agreed but one added, "Well, we don't queue up to hear him." The visitor replied, "Perhaps not, but the people don't mind queuing up when he comes to my place."

The years at Boston must have been almost totally absorbing, for Ramsey's reputation for absent-mindedness flourished as it had in no other place he had lived. It carried over to church services where, if a cleric's hood was missing, one might find Ramsey was wearing two hoods. When a monotone hum accompanied a hymn, anthem, or organ solo, it was known to be Ramsey.

Bicycling about the town, Ramsey inevitably signaled right before turning left, and left before turning right. "He was forever misplacing that bicycle," says one Bostonian. "Couldn't remember where he left it. He was a *bit* tangential."

The landlady at 8 Thurold Street was either remiss in her duties or had given up any attempts to keep Ramsey's wardrobe in reasonable repair. He often had holes in his socks. (Once she was shocked to notice that he was wearing pajamas under his cassock.) As she straightened his room one day, hoping to make some order of the books and papers spread over the desk and bed, she heard a knock at the downstairs door and supposed it was someone seeking the lodger.

"Mr. Ramsey's not here. He's gone out," she called.

"Oh, yes, yes, yes. Thank you very much," came the reply.

The voice was Ramsey's, the landlady realized. She reached the door just as he was turning away.

Ambassador Joseph P. Kennedy's visit in July, 1938, brought Boston Parish Church briefly to international attention. The American financier and prominent Roman Catholic layman accepted, as United States Ambassador to the Court of St. James, an invitation to attend a festive service of thanksgiving for the safe restoration of the church's ancient tower and nave.

Kennedy was himself a native of Boston, Massachusetts, whose citizens had contributed generously to the repair fund. The parish appropriated £250 of its own budget for broadcasting the service directly to the United States. It was heard in America over the facilities of the Columbia Broadcasting System.

Canon Cook and his curates, headed by Michael Ramsey, lined up with Mayor Tom Mountain to greet Ambassador Kennedy. They proudly showed him the chapel furnished by American Bostonians in 1857 in memory of five Lincolnshire men who had become governors of Massachusetts. Afterward the townspeople, the clergy, and the Ambassador dined by candlelight in the fifteenth-century Guildhall where the Pilgrims had once been imprisoned.

The clergy of Lincoln and Boston spent frequent holidays or weekends at the motherhouse of the Society of the Sacred Mission at Kelham, one of the Anglican Communion's largest and most active monastic Orders for men.

The manor house, built originally by the Manners-Sutton family, had been admirably adapted for use by the Order which has as its main work the training of seminarians. A tiled court, originally the conservatory of the country house, had been turned into a refectory, and here the monks and seminarians ate in silence.

Ramsey has a warm regard for Kelham: "Just outside Newark

in Nottinghamshire you look across the fields for a mile or two and you see a great big country house of rather odd neo-gothic architecture. It looks for all the world extraordinarily like St. Pancras Station in London. But it is not all that kind of architecture, which the friends of Kelham both laugh at and love so dearly, for Kelham also has its very beautiful chapel. . . ."

On arrival at Kelham, Ramsey and his friends from Lincoln often found Brother Edwin, the master of plain-song at Lincoln Theological College, walking down the lane to meet them. The old manor house would be almost overflowing, then as now, with the monks and the seminarians, all wearing over their cassocks scapulars of light blue denin. "Our pinafores," laughs Brother Edwin.

Kelham offered the monastic routine Ramsey so much admires —the discipline of regular prayer, the deep peace of the Great Silence, and the long periods of uninterrupted time for reading and meditation.

"During recreation one could see Michael playing tennis more strenuously than skillfully," recalls Brother Edwin. "And if he was thinking of his books, he might occasionally forget his partner. In the early evenings when Michael walked with the others, you could almost follow the conversation by watching his head nodding in agreement or disagreement."

It was the great domed chapel that attracted Ramsey as it does every visitor to Kelham. Its altar stands supreme before a broad concourse. High above, bridging over the sanctuary, an arch of bare bricks supports a powerfully scaled crucifix. Ramsey has described it as "a chapel which, as a piece of architecture, seems wonderfully to escape the different conventionalisms in which church architecture gets itself involved through the centuries, and to be something both touching the modern age and wonderfully timeless in its representation of the great austerity and at the same time the great tenderness of our Christian faith. And that is Kelham."

These peaceful moments on retreat gave Ramsey strength and inspiration for the pastoral care of a flock which, in its own small way, was part of a nation reluctantly preparing for a war it prayed would not materialize.

On December 28, 1938, he left the house in Thurold Street,

almost two years to the day that he had first entered it, to become vicar of St. Benedict's Church, Cambridge. He had served a long apprenticeship—six years as a teacher, four as a curate—and now, ten years and three months after his ordination, he was to have his own parish.

Out of this decade of experience evolved strongly reasoned opinions woven into much of what Ramsey said and wrote in future years.

On the work of parish priests: "Many people are frightened about the world we live in, about the insecurities of life, about guilty fears which they do not always face or admit; and lives are battered like vessels without a course. The message of the Church, sharing in the world's pain and perplexity, and sensitive to all that men and women feel, is the sovereignty of God, a faithful Creator. And the parish priest again and again brings the serenity of faith to those who are torn and tossed; and when consciences are troubled by tempests of guilt he speaks the word of absolution, 'Peace, be still.'"

On preaching: "There is a simplicity born of shallowness, and falsely so called; and there is a simplicity which is the costly outcome of the discipline of mind and heart and will. Simplicity in preaching is properly the simplicity of the knowledge of God and of human beings. To say of someone 'he preaches simply' is to say 'he walks with God.'"

On the return of the Eucharist as a central feature of Sunday worship: "If the Eucharist were to be the one service which a congregation attended, I should like to see a liturgical revision allowing a rite wherein Psalms and Canticles were given their place in Introit, Gradual, and Sequence; and revisers should consider the possibility of an Old Testament lection. . . . I [have] great thankfulness for the revival of the Holy Communion in the life of so many of our parishes. In the long run it will be its own interpreter and teacher. For the supreme question is not what we make of the Eucharist but what the Eucharist is making of us, as (together with the Word) it fashions us into the way of Christ."

Enthroned as the hundredth Archbishop of Canterbury and Primate of All England, Arthur Michael Ramsey occupies the ancient marble Chair of St. Augustine in a supreme moment of colorful ceremony in Canterbury Cathedral, June 27, 1961. He wears cope and mitre of cloth-of-gold and holds a richly carved pastoral crook, symbol of his role as chief shepherd of the Anglican Communion. Chaplains in attendance are the Rev. John Andrew, holding ornate Primatial Cross of the See of Canterbury, and the Rev. Simon Ridley.

Mason & Basevi, Cambridge
Courtesy, Margaret Ramsey Paul

The Ramsey family posed for this picture about 1909 in a Cambridge studio. Michael Ramsey perches on the back of a chair in sailor suit identical with one worn by his elder brother, Frank, who was destined to become a brilliant economist and philosopher before his death at the age of twenty-six. Their father, Arthur Stanley Ramsey, was a Cambridge don who wrote numerous textbooks on mathematics, and became president of Magdalene College, Cambridge. The mother, Agnes Wilson Ramsey, was prominent in Cambridge civic and charitable activities prior to her death in an automobile accident in 1927. She holds daughter Bridget Mary, now a physician in London. A second daughter, Margaret, was born a few years later.

Courtesy, Bridget Ramsey Barcroft

At play during one of the Sunday afternoons when their parents invited dons and students to tea, Michael and Frank give Bridget a ride in a wheelbarrow in the garden of Howfield, the neo-Gothic family home the Ramseys built in the Castle Hill area of Cambridge. Bridget wears a lacy white dress while her brothers favor the long black stockings and sailor suits reflecting influence of the Royal Navy. One of Ramsey's first memories is the sodding of the garden at Howfield. His favorite house on the quiet street was St. Giles' Vicarage, at the corner of Buckingham Road. The nurse who dressed the children so carefully was living in Yorkshire more than half a century later when her young charge became Archbishop of York.

In the spring of 1923, Ramsey was completing five years of study at Repton School, in Derbyshire, where Geoffrey Fisher was headmaster. He finished at eighteen as prefect of his dormitory, The Mitre, and holder of a classics scholarship to Magdalene College where his father had studied.

Early in 1926 an undergraduate magazine used the picture above with a report on Ramsey's student activities. He was president of the Cambridge Union, a member of a university debate team that had toured the United States, and an active campaigner for the Liberal Party led by Lord Asquith.

Ramsey's picture as a young priest in "dog collar" and black suit was taken by one of his father's sisters in the leafy shadows of the garden at Howfield. The layout of the carefully tended grounds was retained after the sale of the house years later to the Dominican Order.

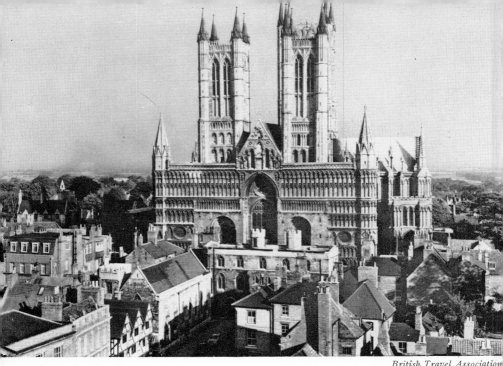

British Travel Association

Ramsey had this view of the unusual façade of Lincoln Cathedral from the window of his sitting room at Lincoln Theological College where he was sub-warden for six years in the 1930's. In World War II, the spires of the cathedral were often the last sight of England for many RAF and American bomber crews flying from nearby bases on missions over the Continent.

Courtesy, the Most Rev. Michael Ramsey

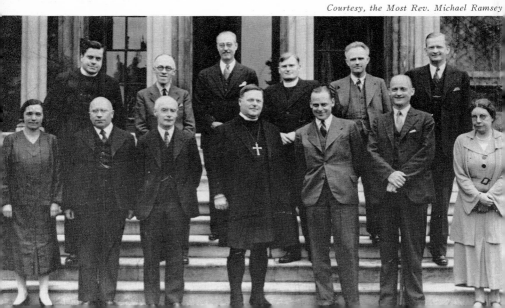

At Boston Parish Church in Lincolnshire from 1936 through 1938, Ramsey held a preaching post originally established by the Puritans. The ornate tower, completed in 1450, saw the Pilgrims set sail for the New World and in 1940 witnessed the exodus of many small boats speeding to the rescue of Allied troops at Dunkirk. A landmark for travelers forty miles distant, the "Boston stump" is dedicated to St. Botolph who founded a monastery in the area about 654.

LEFT: Impressed by the promise of Ramsey's first book, the Archbishop of York, William Temple, invited him to attend a conference in July, 1936, that contributed to the organization of the World Council of Churches. Photographed on the steps of Bishopthorpe, the archiepiscopal residence, were (left to right, front row) Mrs. William Temple, Herman Sasse, J. H. Oldham, William Temple, W. A. Visser 't Hooft, Reinhold Niebuhr, Olive Wyon; (back row) Edward R. Hardy, Jr., Bernard Manning, Dwight Bradley, Michael Ramsey, Emil Brunner, and J. S. Bixler. Ramsey regards the photograph as a memento of "my first meeting with eminent persons," and still had it among his effects in 1961 when he moved to the Old Palace, Canterbury.

British Travel Association

Durham Cathedral was a focal point of Ramsey's life from 1940 to 1950, when he was Canon Theologian of Durham University, and again when he was Bishop of Durham from 1952 to 1956. The Ramseys were married in the Galilee Chapel (at front of Cathedral, far left).

Canon Ramsey leaves Durham Cathedral on April 8, 1942, hand-in-hand with his bride. The men of the wedding party wear their everyday black cassocks in this wartime ceremony. The couple is followed by the best man, Eric Abbott, now Dean of Westminster; the bridesmaid, Faith Owen, daughter of the late Bishop of Jarrow; and a groomsman, the Rev. Stephen Dennett.

Photo by Northern Echo; Courtesy, Bridget Ramsey Barcroft

In Westminster Abbey on June 2, 1953, Ramsey stands reverently at the side of ElizabethII moments after her crowning by the ninety-ninth Archbishop of Canterbury, Geoffrey Fisher. For centuries the Bishop of Durham has held this position of honor during the long and solemn Coronation service.

York Minster, a majestic cradle of the faith in the north of England, was built over a period of 250 years from 1220 to 1470. Its eleven-ton bell pealed for Ramsey's consecration here as eighty-ninth Bishop of Durham in 1952 and for his enthronement as ninety-second Archbishop of York in 1956. Delicate tracing inspired name for center window: the Heart of Yorkshire.

At the royal wedding in York Minster on June 8, 1961, Katharine Worsley on the arm of her father, Sir William Worsley, for her marriage to the Duke of Kent, in uniform (center), standing next to his brother, Prince Michael. Guests in the front row are (left to right) Anthony Armstrong-Jones, Princess Margaret, Prince and Princess Paul of Yugoslavia, Princess Alexandra, Princess Marina, Queen Victoria Eugenie of Spain, Queen Mother Elizabeth, Prince Charles, the Duke of Edinburgh, and Elizabeth II. Directly behind the Queen is her uncle, Duke of Gloucester. At left is the Dean of York, Eric Milner-White.

George Bruce's 1958 portrait of Ramsey "mingles formality and informality with conspicuous success," reported the London *Times* art critic. It hangs at Bishopthorpe.

Courtesy, Dr. Paul Anderson

An Anglican delegation in cassocks holds attention of passengers on a Moscow subway train in July, 1956. Ramsey raises his hand in a typical gesture as the late Bishop of Derby, the Rt. Rev. A. E. J. Rawlinson, listens at his side. Smiling priest at right is the Rev. Harry Williams of Trinity College, Cambridge, seated with a bearded bishop of the Russian Orthodox Church.

Under brooding skies Ramsey lays the foundation stone of All Saints Church, Temeke, Dar es Salaam, Tanganyika, near end of trip marking the one hundredth anniversary of the Universities' Mission to Central Africa. Music was by bandsmen of King's African Rifles.

British Information Service

Lambeth Palace, situated between Surrey banks of the Thames (foreground) and rail approach to Waterloo Station, was vulnerable to wartime bombing. Large structure with peaked roof (left) houses library. Courtyard, centered by Davidson memorial cross, has fig tree Cardinal Pole planted in 1556. Financier J. P. Morgan gave six hundred tons of rich soil for the gardens.

Ramsey and wife arrive at Lambeth a week before Canterbury enthronement. In background are press officer, Colonel Robert Hornby (left), and the Archbishop's secretary, Robert Beloe.

Dr. Sarvepalli Radhakrishnan, who became Vice President of India in 1952 after four years as Ambassador to Russia, greets Ramsey at garden party in New Delhi, November 21, 1961.

The six presidents of the World Council of Churches, seen here in New Delhi, are (left to right) Sir Francis Ibiam, Dr. Martin Niemoeller, Archbishop Iakovos, Archbishop Ramsey, the Rev. Dr. David Moses, and Charles Parlin. They gathered outside Vigyan Bhavan assembly hall.

At London dinner with his predecessor, Geoffrey Fisher, Ramsey wears formal evening dress and the Order of the Holy Sepulchre conferred by Benedictos, Orthodox Patriarch of Jerusalem.

His velvet Canterbury cap at a rakish angle, Ramsey listens to the Primate of Greece, Archbishop Chrysostomos (left) and the Bishop of Achaea, on his arrival in Athens in May, 1962.

An atmosphere of informality prevails in the Archbishop's study when he sinks back "encased in purple" to talk slowly and thoughtfully from the depth of a favorite wing-chair.

8. THE VICAR OF ST. BENET'S

The spirited, eloquent preaching of Michael Ramsey in the Church of St. Benedict, Cambridge, gained attention for the ancient parish in a community where it had no particular rank or role. With the affectionate familiarity the British have for venerable institutions, the old church's name long ago became a contraction—St. Benet's. Its stone tower dating from about 1050 is considered the oldest structure in Cambridge. For several centuries St. Benet's served as the chapel of Corpus Christi College which it adjoins. Today it is wedged into a tiny plot of ground on a narrow street in the heart of Cambridge and is in the care of the Society of St. Francis, an Anglican monastic Order founded in 1921.

Since St. Benet's had no vicarage (most of its vicars had been Fellows of the colleges), Ramsey took a house in Owlstone Road. He made his rounds by bicycle as he had done in Boston, a prototype of countless English vicars who pedaled along on errands and calls. Often he stopped at Howfield to see his father and aunt, and at the Cambridge Union, once the scene of his oratorical triumphs. He liked to browse in the University's new library. Dinner at Magdalene remained the gracious ritual he had known as an undergraduate.

Cambridge pursued the same calm existence it had known for centuries. Meanwhile, Hitler and Mussolini blustered about Europe threatening war, then talking peace, then threatening war again. The French boasted of their Maginot Line. This troubled background increased the interest in the visit which King George and Queen Elizabeth made to the United States in June, 1939, for everyone knew America's alliance would be vital if war broke out. Many refugees from Nazi Germany came to lecture at Cambridge and occasionally one of them filled the pulpit at St. Benet's. They were far from optimistic about the prospects of peace.

On August 27, less than a year after Prime Minister Chamberlain's fruitless negotiations at Munich, there was read in the great cathedrals and in the parish churches, including St. Benet's, the Archbishop of Canterbury's solemn call to prayer: "In all places of worship throughout the country may there be special and united acts of prayer; prayer that even now the crime and horror of war may be averted and time given wherein nations may try to settle their differences by peaceful means; prayer for all to whom the tremendous responsibilities of government has been committed. . . . Prayer that through all these confusions God's will may be done."

The fervent words of Archbishop Lang were the subject of an editorial in *The Cambridge Chronicle* of Friday, September 1: "To those who reflect on the deeper trends in our national life, few signs can have been more encouraging than the way in which, both in the crisis of last September and in this crisis, the nation has turned to prayer. . . ."

That September 1 was the day on which Cambridge received its first group of children evacuated from London—some four thousand eight hundred docile but frightened youngsters in a milling contingent that was expected to increase to six thousand within a few days.

During air-raid alerts, sirens shrilled over St. Benet's and Ramsey's house in Owlstone Road, over Magdalene and Howfield and the Union and all the places he loved. Protective sandbags were placed around many of the old buildings. Citizens were given instructions on the use of gas masks and on driving in "the black-out."

A member of Parliament spoke at Newmarket, near Cambridge, declaring, "Our country is supremely ready," and the townspeople answered, "Hear! Hear!"

On Sunday, September 3, 1939, Ramsey conducted an early celebration at the ancient altar of St. Benet's. The day had begun peacefully, but at 11:20 A.M. Neville Chamberlain broadcast to the nation, "This country is at war with Germany."

As the Prime Minister spoke, there occurred an event that has always been a symbol of the future, a reassurance that life would go on—the birth of a boy to a woman living in Glebe Road.

In the early hours of the following day Cambridge and other towns of East Anglia and the Midlands had their first air-raid warning. The sirens sounded at 2:45 A.M., sending thousands to the safety of their cellars.

"I volunteered to be a chaplain to the forces," says Ramsey, "and would have been called up in a few months if I had not been offered an important teaching post in Durham University."

Ramsey's appointment came at a time when Durham wanted an able preacher as well as a good theologian. A new relationship had arisen between the Cathedral and the small industrial city. Credit for this change was due largely to Dean Cyril Alington, who, when vacating the Deanery for a much smaller house, left it to be used for many civic and social purposes, and who made deep friendships with some blunt-spoken miners' leaders. Congregations in the Cathedral grew, and old estrangements gradually faded. Yet the Cathedral, to hold these larger numbers, needed a compelling speaker. The choice of Ramsey seemed providential indeed.

9. DECADE AT DURHAM

The year at St. Benet's in Cambridge may be regarded, in a backward look at Michael Ramsey's life, as a brief prelude to an eventful and satisfying decade at Durham.

Ramsey arrived in Durham, in the north of England, on a bitter-cold day in January, 1940, and promptly fell ill with influenza. To make matters worse, his house was not ready for occupancy and he had to stay, sick and alone, in the gloomy old Durham Castle in the shadow of the brooding Cathedral. ("Half church of God, half castle 'gainst the Scot," the rocky mount has been called.) When his boyhood friend, James Duff, vice-chancellor of Durham University, called on Ramsey there and found him wearing a shabby overcoat for a dressing gown, Duff said, "Michael, it's time you were married."

He had come to Durham to take the Chair of Divinity in Durham University and to be a canon of the Cathedral, a position for which he had been recommended by the Bishop of Durham, Dr. Alwyn Williams, who had liked Ramsey's book and reports of his work. The Durham newspaper commented that "the new canon is comparatively young for the post. . . ."

Ramsey was installed as canon professor in a ceremony in the Cathedral on Saturday, January 27, 1940. Later, in his inaugural lecture, he remarked that "it was for me a rather moving discovery that I was the first Cambridge man for over a century to come to this, the oldest of Durham's chairs. I can only do my best not to discredit either the rock on to which I have come, or the hole of the pit whence I was digged."

The title of his inaugural lecture was *Jesus Christ in Faith and History*. In it Ramsey said that "the historical structure of Christianity seemed, like Durham Castle not long ago, to be in danger of slipping down, and the energies of scholars were devoted to protecting the structure stone by stone and to fighting on the ground chosen by historical criticism. . . . Now, Durham Castle is safe; and we do not want to spend our days nervously poking about its foundations, asking if this stone or that stone is really secure. We want to go in and out and enjoy what it offers us and teaches us. And so with the New Testament."

The address was well received, not only for the endearing knowledge of local history, but for the fact that here was a probing scholar, a champion of the classics who could also quote Quakers and Methodists. It revealed extraordinary skill at defining the progress of human thought and placing it in a proper relationship to ancient scripture.

Ramsey's house at Durham was a tall tower-shaped structure standing at the center of the close that was joined to the Cathedral by an ancient cloister. Next door to Ramsey lived the Bishop Suffragan of Jarrow and his family—the same Leslie Owen who had been the warden at Lincoln Theological College a decade previously.

The Rev. John Brewis, principal of St. Chad's College of Durham from 1937 to 1947, remembers those first years of the war as "a time when Durham University was reduced from a small university to a *very* small university with what was called 'a high degree of intimacy.' It made staff members closer to the Cathedral. More like a family. And there was a great deal of planning for the future without any assurance of implementation. Ramsey was very much involved in that planning as well as his lectures of the day. He was worshiped by his students as students always worship good teachers."

In the governing body known as the University Senate were the professors of science, economics, education, medicine, music, law, agriculture, and divinity. James Duff recalls his surprise "at seeing this rather odd-looking theology professor from Cambridge making himself well known. He quickly became the Senate's most persuasive speaker, the one who was most certain to get his way. He jumped me once when he wanted a longer holiday —and he got it. 'These poor scholars need more time for their own work,' he told us, and so the vacation period was extended."

In December, 1941, Ramsey addressed the ordinands' retreat at Bishopthorpe. During the recreational periods the principal subject of conversation was the surprise Japanese attack on Pearl Harbor and America's subsequent entry into the war.

Ramsey and the ordinands were unaware of a drama of a different nature that was unfolding behind the closed doors of Archbishop Temple's study at Bishopthorpe. On November 27 the Archbishop of Canterbury, Cosmo Lang, had told the Prime Minister that he wished to retire after thirty-three years as an archbishop, first at York and then at Canterbury. Consequently, arrangements were quietly being made, in discreet telephone conversations between Bishopthorpe and London, for the announcement that William Temple would be the next Archbishop of Canterbury. The nomination was disclosed in January along with the fact that the Bishop of Winchester, Cyril Forster Garbett, had been nominated as Temple's successor at York.

In the Cathedral close at Durham, Ramsey often had tea with his neighbors, the Leslie Owens. Here he met Joan Hamilton,* an attractive woman in her early thirties, who had been a social service worker in Durham before becoming secretary to Bishop Owen.

Frequently Miss Hamilton brought Ramsey a message or a sheaf of papers from the bishop. She was tall and thin with shining eyes, light brown hair, and a sense of humor very much like

---

* Burke's Landed Gentry of Ireland lists Joan Alice Chetwode Hamilton, born September 16, 1909, one of two children of the late Ouida Mary Tryon Hamilton, a relation of Ireland's Stafford-O'Brien family, and the late Colonel Francis Alexander Chetwode Hamilton. Her uncle, the Rt. Rev. Eric Knightley Chetwode Hamilton, was in 1940 consecrated Bishop of Shrewsbury, suffragan to Lichfield, and from 1944 to his death in 1962 was Dean of Windsor.

Ramsey's. Soon they began having tea together or walking down
the hill to look in the shop windows. They announced their engagement on his thirty-seventh birthday. The prospect of a
Canon's wedding was almost unprecedented in the annals of Durham.

"It hadn't occurred to us that Michael would ever marry. It
was quite a surprise," says his Aunt Lucy, recalling a visit the
young couple made to Cambridge a few weeks before the wedding. Bridget Ramsey, too, recalls that "as soon as possible I
hurried to Durham to look over Joan."

The wedding day, April 8, 1942, dawned cold and gray. Ramsey's father and aunt came up from Cambridge and the bride's
parents arrived from their home in Tinwell, Stamford. "The regular choir was on holiday, after Easter, so we had a choir of
friends," recalls Ramsey. "And my Uncle Archie was there to
help with the music."

The *Durham County Advertiser* reported, "The Galilee Chapel
of Durham Cathedral was adorned with arum lilies, narcissi, and
palms for the wedding on Wednesday of Canon Michael Ramsey,
Professor of Divinity in the University of Durham, and Miss Joan
Hamilton, until recently secretary to the Bishop of Jarrow. . . .
The bride, given away by her father, wore a gown of pink brocade, with lace veil, and carried lilies. The bridesmaid, Miss Faith
Owen, was gowned in white net over green silk and carried
narcissi. . . . The Bishop of Jarrow, wearing cope and mitre,
officiated. . . ."

Accompanying the report was a picture of the bridal party
leaving the Cathedral. The bride and groom walked with hands
tightly clasped, the wind whipping Ramsey's black cassock and
the bride's veil. In the background were Faith Owen and the best
man, Eric Abbott.

"Michael was an unusual bridegroom," says Abbott, who was
still the warden of Lincoln Theological College. "He wasn't
nervous. The ceremony went smoothly. It was just that it was
Michael getting married, the *academian* getting married."

The war years dragged on. Ramsey was an air-raid warden and
later was chief fire watcher on the Cathedral during the period of
"Baedecker raids," when the German attacks appeared to follow

the famous Baedecker guidebooks to English cathedral cities.

For the Ramseys, as for everyone in England, the devastating air raids threatened the landmarks of a lifetime. Ramsey read with sorrow that his first parish church, St. Nicholas, had been demolished in the heavy raids on Liverpool. Boston Parish Church had been damaged, too, on the morning of Good Friday, 1941. Coventry Cathedral was almost completely destroyed. In June, 1942, German bombs leveled much of Canterbury but providentially missed the Cathedral. Lambeth Palace was hit repeatedly. In Cambridge, a bomb fell in Huntingdon Road, near Howfield, and shrapnel and fire badly damaged the Cambridge Union.

England's cathedral cities experienced another kind of invasion in those wartime years—American servicemen who came from bases nearby to see the cathedrals. At Durham, one of the stories of "the eccentric Ramsey" concerns a group of American soldiers whom he admitted to the Cathedral after its closing hours. He dutifully locked the door, saying he would return. He forgot to come back. The soldiers had to climb out a window, adding to their wartime experiences a tale of being locked in a vast cathedral by a forgetful canon professor.

As classes dwindled in number and the nights of black-out stretched endlessly into the future, Ramsey worked away on his second book, *The Resurrection of Christ*. It was published in 1944 a few months before his fortieth birthday. Meanwhile, the success of his first book had made him something of a legend at the Lincoln Theological College. The students perpetuated a story that Ramsey had written on the walls of his room in his enthusiasm for putting his thoughts on paper. Ramsey's successor at Lincoln, Eric Mascall, celebrated the story in a poem published in the college magazine:

> Of Michael Ramsey now the Muse must sing.
> He lectured upon almost everything,
> Conducting the most erudite research
> Upon the Gospel and the Cath'lick Church.
> In knowledge deep, in judgement most discerning,
> A veritable prodigy of learning,
> In such a paragon what flaw could dwell?
> He had but one, and this I blush to tell,

Let truth be spoken, though the welkin fall!—
He stripped the paper off his bedroom wall.
His failing came to light one fateful day,
And in disgrace our *Michael* went away.
Within a grey and distant northern town
Through Norman aisles he paces up and down.
No paper decks the walls of Durham's fame,
So he can never write a book again.

In the autumn of 1944, as Britain braced itself for another winter of war, Archbishop Temple died unexpectedly at the age of sixty-three. Geoffrey Fisher, who had been translated from Chester to London in 1939, became Archbishop of Canterbury. The end of one primacy and the start of another was watched by Ramsey with deep personal interest since he knew both men for years. At Durham he continued his reorganization of the theological faculty in anticipation of the university's postwar growth. By 1947 there had assembled "a strong team of six"— Ramsey, S. L. Greenslade, and Reginald Cant, all Anglican priests; Kingsley Barrett, a Methodist minister; W. A. Whitehouse, a Congregationalist; and J. S. Wilkie, a Presbyterian.

One of the precentors at the Cathedral gives an excellent picture of Ramsey's years at Durham: ". . . It was inevitable that the longer he stayed the more his influence was felt and the more the demands made on him, demands that were always met 'gladly and willingly,' and always with a leisured consideration that a busy man does not always seem able to give. Canon Ramsey, I think, had mixed feelings regarding my job as a Precentor, one who keeps the Cathedral's machinery turning over smoothly. But my visits never seemed unwelcome. He would raise his eyebrows in the typical way that we all knew and rejoiced in, and point an admonitory finger: 'Now, what have I done wrong?' or 'Where have I to go this time?' He had some quite distinctive mannerisms which those who were here with him are not likely to forget and which endeared him to all. His progress in a procession left the picture of a large man—he is that in every way—with his head in the air, striding up the aisle with his arms folded beneath the sleeves of his surplice—hardly the recognized procedure! But, though his head may have been in the air, his feet were very firmly on the ground. He was by no means like many saintly men (he is one), impractical, nor is he the typical 'professor in politics.' On the contrary, he is very much *au fait* with all that is going on and the implications involved, has a very inquiring outlook, and is a singularly shrewd observer. One who knew him well has described him as 'a great saint, but devilishly shrewd!'

"The Cathedral close in Durham is delightfully informal: doors are always open and the residents go in and out without the formality of ringing or knocking. Towards the end of the war, when fuel was rationed, my wife and I were sitting hugging the kitchen fire awaiting the visit of a member of the Choristers School staff. When we heard someone enter, we called to the unseen visitor to bring himself a chair and come in. And he came in, complete with chair—Canon Ramsey, as always a welcome and informal visitor.

"It is only natural that a 'character' should attach to himself anecdotes of various kinds. For instance, one afternoon Mrs. Ramsey had dispatched her husband to a meeting of a university committee. The next news she had of him emerged from the loud speaker of her wireless set—a familiar voice reading one of the lessons at Evensong, which was being broadcast from the Cathedral! On his way to the meeting he had found in progress a BBC rehearsal, and not having broadcast before, thought that it might be a matter to which he should give some attention.

"Whether this story is true or apocryphal, it is illustrative of his lively interest in all that is going on. In this respect Mrs. Ramsey is in no way behind her husband, for she has a warm and practical concern alike for causes and people. One remembers her walking leisurely through the College yard, complete with basket, to do the shopping, calling perhaps on old Mrs. Burton, the widow of a cathedral verger; sometimes driving the old car that had somehow been persuaded and caressed into holding out through the war years, as she went to visit the tenants on a large housing estate on the outskirts of the city where she was greatly loved, or drove her husband to a Sunday service in one of the parishes of the diocese. Durham has twice had to regret their departure, and each time the regret was deeper. In their house in Durham they were charming and delightful neighbors and friends—always the same, full of good fun and good works, friends with everyone, and never forgetting their friends."

In the mid-1940's Ramsey's friendship for and interest in the Eastern Orthodox Church became well known, especially through an Anglican-Greek organization called the Fellowship of St. Alban and St. Sergius. His statement, "The Church of England and the Eastern Orthodox Church: Why Their Unity is Important," was circulated by SPCK (Society for Promoting Christian Knowledge). "The reunion of Christendom is a subject which calls for the urgent prayer and endeavor of every member of the Church of Christ," he wrote. "Nothing in the world matters more than the fulfillment of the prayer of our Lord 'that all may be one.'

"In the Church of England the passion for unity has expressed itself specially in two directions," he continued. "Some, of whom the late Lord Halifax was the most saintly example, have been filled with a longing for a reunion with the Church of Rome. 'To Rome we were once united, and with Rome we must one day be united once more.' Others have felt that the first claim upon us is to seek reunion with the Non-Conformist Christians of our own land, for they are our immediate Christian neighbors and share with us in the use of the English Bible. Without wishing to criticize either of these longings, and without raising any questions of priorities (for Christ's prayer is that *all* may be one), I ask my readers to hearken to the less familiar cause of unity with the East. I shall not shrink from making some very big claims: namely, that our familiar divisions have their root in the original schism between East and West, that in unity with the East there lies a remedy for many of the problems and perplexities of the whole Church, that the Church of England has a special debt and obligation in this matter, and that the present crisis in the Church and world summons our thoughts *Eastwards*."

Long in the formative stages, the World Council of Churches met for the first time at Amsterdam in 1948.

"I have never forgotten the sight of Michael Ramsey and Karl Barth, the famed Swiss theologian, seated together on a bench on the conference grounds, in animated discussion of the most minute points of theology," says Henry Pitney Van Dusen, for many years president of Union Theological Seminary in New York.

Reginald Cant also recalls Ramsey's meeting with Barth: "I was impressed with Ramsey's lucid and persuasive manner of speech. He had immense skill at choosing his words and presenting his case, making it seem utterly reasonable."

A short while after the Amsterdam meeting Ramsey's third book, *The Glory of God and the Transfiguration of Christ*, was published. Like his first two volumes, the book gained considerable attention. Ramsey's name began to be mentioned whenever high-ranking appointments were under consideration. He reportedly rejected an opportunity to become rector of London's famous old Anglo-Catholic parish, All Saints, Margaret Street, and did not respond to suggestions that he be made Bishop of Edinburgh.* In 1939 he had turned down a chance to become warden of St. Augustine's, Canterbury, the recently reorganized Central College of the Anglican Communion. However, the year 1950 brought an invitation that appealed to Ramsey for manifold reasons. He was asked to become Regius Professor of Divinity in Cambridge University, succeeding Canon Charles Raven, the preacher at Ramsey's ordination in 1929.

From a prosaic point of view, the opportunity to return to Cambridge was a dream come true. At long last Ramsey would be a don, and more than that, a professor, a title reserved in Cambridge for the head of a faculty or department. It was, sentimentally speaking, quite wonderful to return to his boyhood home as a professor in his alma mater and a colleague with his father on the governing board of their old college.

"The departure of Professor Ramsey to Cambridge has been a great loss to the University and to the colleges," wrote Canon T. S. Wetherall, principal of St. Chad's College at Durham. "When Oliver Chase Quick went from Durham to be Regius Professor at Oxford in 1939, he had set a standard of scholarship and lucidity which might have alarmed any successor. Michael Ramsey had also to face the difficulties of the war years, when numbers were small and enthusiasm might have disappeared, and the difficulties of the post-war years, when the University was expanding in many directions. He was successful beyond praise. . . . He used the quiet years to reorganize thoroughly the theological teaching at Durham, especially the Diploma course: and in the

* In 1962 Ramsey termed both reports "inaccurate."

second part of his time here, when other departments were
rapidly increasing, he kept Theology firmly in the center of the
picture. . . . Add to all these solid achievements much that is the
proper equipment of the genuine character—his slow, rumbling
laugh, his roll, his relish over his dinner in the Hall, his erratic
progress through the Cathedral, his formidable patience in argument, the equanimity and friendliness of his wife. We shall miss
him and Mrs. Ramsey very much."

Canon Wetherall's words, read years later, are more perceptive
than the routine observations usually made on a man's departure
for another job. They reflect the subtle changes the years had
brought in Ramsey's life. His physical appearance was so elderly
that strangers, at first glance, sometimes mistook his wife to be
his daughter. His venerable presence was increased by the
Biblical phrases and words he favored. It was a matter about
which he felt strongly, explaining to his students his belief that
"by sophisticated attempts to be contemporary at all costs, we
blunt the force that lies in the universal imagery of the Bible:
bread, water, light, darkness, wind, fire, rain, hunger, thirst, eat,
drink, walk. . . ."

At the time of his arrival he had written one book, and though
it was highly regarded, the scholars still waited to see what would
follow. Ramsey had obliged with two more outstanding books.
In 1940 his teaching experience had been limited to his few
years at Lincoln where he lectured to students already well
along the road to ordination. At Durham, Ramsey had reached
students of various denominations, some of them puzzled and
undecided about theology and careers. He had not lost the opportunity to give direction and purpose to many of those students. And the stories of his personal eccentricities were well
behind him now, for in every way possible Joan Ramsey had
seen to it that her husband was less forgetful or absent-minded
or too often carried away in his scholarly musings. Those who
knew Ramsey felt he was coming to a position in which he
would influence several generations in the great tradition of a
Regius Professor of Divinity.

10. REGIUS PROFESSOR

Ten years had made a great difference. In 1939, as the vicar of a small parish, Michael Ramsey was not in the mainstream of Cambridge life. Now, returning from a decade of hard work at Durham, he assumed an important role in the university.

As Regius Professor he continued many of the traditions of Edwyn Hoskyns, stressing the relevance of theology to contemporary affairs. "His lectures on the Atonement were distinguished by an impressive clarity of exposition and judicial balance," a colleague recalls. "They commanded a very large and enthusiastic undergraduate audience, and even the extreme Evangelicals regarded them as unexpectedly sound." In 1951 Ramsey received the scarlet hood of a Durham University doctor of divinity, his first honorary degree. Later that year he published his fourth book, *F. D. Maurice and the Conflicts of Modern Theology,* which he describes today as a study of "an Anglican theologian of the last century, unpopular in his day but of increasing influence in recent times."

In February, 1952, there occurred one of those events which are landmarks of time in England, the death of a monarch and the ascension to the throne of a new sovereign. When George VI died peacefully in his sleep, Princess Elizabeth became Britain's first reigning queen since Victoria. Had Ramsey reckoned time back to the year of her birth, 1926, he would have found that she was born in London during the same month he had been on retreat there, that decisive retreat when he resolved to seek Holy Orders.

The Ramseys did not readily find a home they liked in Cambridge. They "moved house," as the English say, three times in two years—from Latham Road to a large house in Wordsworth Grove and finally to a tiny house near the Fitzwilliam Museum. One of the difficulties was Joan Ramsey's health. There was a recurrence of the loss of equilibrium which, at Durham, had sometimes confined her to a wheel chair or forced her to walk with one or two canes. She spent long periods resting in Devon and Torquay.

At No. 3 Fitzwilliam Street the Ramseys thought they were settling in for life. They sold some of their larger pieces of furniture that did not fit in and were having bookcases built and carpets put down when, on the first Saturday after moving, Ramsey decided to bicycle over to Wordsworth Grove to pick up any letters that might have arrived at the house. He found some tucked under the door, among them an envelope from No. 10 Downing Street. It crossed his mind what this might concern. He opened it and began to read, "As you know, the See of Durham has recently fallen vacant. . . ." It was a letter from the Prime Minister, Winston Churchill, expressing the hope Ramsey would permit him to submit his name for nomination as Bishop of Durham.

Ramsey bicycled back to Fitzwilliam Street and put the letter before his wife. "There are stories that he didn't read the letter until he came back home and had comfortably settled himself in his favorite chair in the house we'd just put in order," says Mrs. Ramsey. "But it really wasn't like that."

Ramsey began the round of calls that customarily fall in the wake of such a letter from the Prime Minister. First he went to consult Geoffrey Fisher, who was staying in the Old Palace, Canterbury. This was Ramsey's third visit to the cathedral city but his first to the archiepiscopal residence where so many archbishops had lived.

The factors discussed by Fisher and Ramsey in their meeting at the Old Palace are not, of course, a matter of record. There are strong indications that Church leaders may well have been looking ahead to the time when the second highest post, Archbishop of York, would fall vacant. (Its incumbent, Cyril Forster Garbett, was then seventy-five.) In the words of one clergyman, "Ramsey had to be got ready, by being a bishop first, before he could be in the running for archbishop." Other men thought that Ramsey would not have given up his professorship—whatever the episcopal post—had his wife been well and happy in Cambridge.

In a few days after his trip to Canterbury, No. 10 Downing Street announced, "Her Majesty the Queen has been pleased to nominate Dr. Arthur Michael Ramsey, Regius Professor of Divinity in the University of Cambridge, to be the eighty-ninth Bishop of Durham, succeeding Dr. Alwyn Williams who has been translated to Winchester. . . ."

The following Sunday an item appeared in an unsigned column, "Pendennis," in *The Observer*, the highly respected weekly newspaper published in Tudor Street, London:

WEIGHT AND SEE

The anonymous author of the celebrated annual Preface to *Crockford's*, the clerical directory, recently attacked the bench of Anglican bishops for their poor intellectual quality. Last week's preferment of Canon Michael Ramsey, the Regius Professor of Divinity at Cambridge, to the bishopric of Durham, is partly an answer to that charge. Ramsey is the first really weighty scholar to have been made a bishop for a long time. He learned his theology twenty years ago at the feet of Hoskyns, the legendary Cambridge figure who revolutionized New Testament studies. Primarily, Ramsey remains a scholar. But he is also an outspoken man who believes strongly that theology is worth nothing unless it is related to its social context. The Church of England in recent years has suffered from loquacious bishops who, if they have not been heretical, have been platitudinous. Ramsey, both in the pulpit and in the House of Lords, could give the episcopacy a new standing. It is even being said that with his promotion the gap in the Church of England left by William Temple's death is, if not filled, at least partially closed. Ramsey is not yet fifty.

Ramsey spotted the item himself, at breakfast that Sunday, and clipped it out.*

---

* Rose Macaulay, the novelist, also clipped the item for her friend, the Rev. John Hamilton Cowper Johnson, SSJE. Enclosing it in a letter she sent

It was considered a splendid appointment, an excellent choice matching the right man with the right job. Not only did Ramsey know the Diocese of Durham, but he was, as *The Observer* noted, a scholar of weight. He would continue the grand tradition of learned bishops in the See of Durham.

The date chosen for Ramsey's consecration as a bishop was his name day, the Feast of St. Michael and All Angels, September 29, 1952. The consecration would take place in York Minster and would be followed on Saturday, October 18, by Ramsey's enthronement in Durham Cathedral.

Ramsey asked his former master at Repton, Canon Henry Balmforth, to preach the consecration sermon. From Ely Theological College, where he was principal, Canon Balmforth happily sent his acceptance, which Ramsey forwarded on to another of his former schoolmasters, Eric Milner-White, who as Dean of York was co-ordinating arrangements for the ceremony. Ramsey added a personal note July 16, 1952, from 3 Fitzwilliam Street: "If the Michaelmas hymn, 'Stars of the Morning, So Gloriously Bright,' were included, I should count it happy. . . ."

Magdalene College asked for the privilege of presenting Ramsey with his episcopal ring, the time-honored symbol of a bishop's fidelity to his diocese and the Church. The college chose a massive amethyst in shanks of heavy gold. Lincoln Theological College claimed the privilege of giving Ramsey the other symbol of a bishop's office, the pectoral cross.

These splendid gifts reminded the Ramseys that they should consider the matter of cope and mitre to be worn at the enthronement and later for ordinations, confirmations, and other ceremonies. They gave the assignment to Mrs. Mary Wilde Ozanne, a skilled vestment maker in the village of Sawbridgeworth in Hertforshire, not far from London. A rich purple (known as Murrey Purple in the colors of heraldry) was chosen for the cope and mitre.

---

to him in Cambridge, Mass., she wrote, ". . . a rather anti-episcopal comment from *The Observer* on Canon Ramsey's appointment to Durham. I believe it was inspired by——who obviously doesn't care for most bishops. I'm not sure how fair it is; they are surely rather less scholarly than that? Not that at the moment I recall many works by them. But after all their main business is to direct and administer, not to study." (*Letters to a Friend*, Atheneum, 1962.)

"The height of the mitre is determined by two factors," explains Mrs. Ozanne. "One is the over-all height of the man—how tall he stands—and the other is his frame of mind, his Churchmanship. Ramsey asked for a tall mitre."

Meanwhile, there appeared in the *Durham Evening Chronicle* a "portrait of Durham's new bishop" written at the newspaper's request by Ramsey's boyhood friend, James Duff, who had recently been knighted for his long service to education. "What sort of man is our new bishop?" asked Sir James after outlining Ramsey's career. "He will, I hope, forgive me for saying that he is unusual in appearance. A huge frame, a rolling gait, a trick of looking twice his real age—even as a small boy he looked quite elderly—eyebrows that shoot up and down in a manner that might be disconcerting but for the acute and kindly face below them. Asked a difficult question, he seems to go into a trance, repeating, 'Yes, yes, yes . . .' with closed eyes while thinking out the answer. But if anyone supposed from these appearances that he was absent-minded or gullible, or unbusinesslike, he would soon realize his mistake. . . . He can speak to the industrialist and the pitman, the farmers of Weardale and the shipyard workers of Sunderland as well as to the students. We who know him believe that as our Bishop he will, with God's blessing, prove equal to the greatest of his predecessors."

The remainder of the summer in Cambridge went quickly for the Ramseys. They sold the house in Fitzwilliam Street, moving to the West Hotel for the final weeks before returning to Durham.

"On August 12, 1952, I made a visit to Little St. Mary's in Cambridge and that was the last time I rode my bicycle," says Ramsey, as if he were ticking off the priviliges of anonymity given up for the episcopacy. He was, for all practical purposes, already a bishop and was so listed in the directory of an international meeting which he was to attend the next week in Lund, Sweden—the third World Conference on Faith and Order.

The two years as Regius Professor had been lived quietly, most of it within the circle of dons and their families. In Durham there waited the busier life of a bishop—administering a diocese, looking after clerical appointments, ordaining and confirming.

After the custom of bishops taking the ancient names of their sees, Ramsey would sign himself "Michael Dunelm:". He would be addressed as "My Lord Bishop" or "Milord," but since it was a spiritual rather than a temporal title, his wife would not be called Lady Ramsey. As for a coat-of-arms, he did not seek a grant from the College of Arms. "My family has never had its own heraldry, I shall not ask it now," he said.

Two special prerogatives were attached to the senior See of Durham. One was a seat in the House of Lords, an immediate privilege not contingent on a place falling vacant with the death of another bishop. The other was the Bishop of Durham's prominent part in the coronation of a monarch. This was a role which, with the crowning of Elizabeth II, would fall to Ramsey in the first year of his episcopate.

"In a sense, Dr. Ramsey came into his own with his appointment as a bishop," says a phonetics specialist in London University. "Anyone hearing his voice for the first time would say *at least* a bishop was speaking. On the whole, it is a completely unbelievable voice, (almost a caricature) a voice out of a play about the Church in the eighteenth or nineteenth century. He has an occupational accent, decidedly clerical. If it is regional at all, it is Cambridge donnish. And it is consciously studied for the effect it has. One would hope the younger clergy would not be too imitative, although a few try. (Listen to them saying 'com-passionate.') When he is framing a reply, Ramsey often gains time by repeating an interviewer's words, a habit which contrasts his accent with the faceless, neutral English of the BBC. His murmured 'yes, yes' is verbal nervousness. I have counted seventy-six 'yes's' in a half-hour television interview. The clarity of his 'stops' are remarkable: he explodes his 'p's' and 't's' with extreme precision. He pronounces his 'a's' as 'o' and his 'u's' as 'e.' But he spits out a word and projects to the back row. His cadences are so musical I find it difficult to take him seriously. Most people speak twice as rapidly. If religion is to be mystical, this voice is part of it. If the Church is to be as modern as it says it wishes to be, this voice may be out of place. But it goes with ritual and high ecclesiastical position."

11. PRINCE PRELATE

Four colorful ceremonies steeped in the traditions of Church and State introduced Michael Ramsey to the full possession of the See of Durham: consecration in York Minster, homage to the Queen, a formal welcome at the border of his new diocese, and finally enthronement in his own cathedral.

Three thousand persons gathered in York Minster for the consecration. In the slow procession that moved up the wide center aisle, Ramsey walked behind the guest preacher, Canon Balmforth. After them came twenty bishops who would join the Archbishop of York in the act of consecration. Last of all was the Archbishop himself, Cyril Forster Garbett.

At the high altar the old Archbishop began the ancient ceremony which the Church provides for the consecration of a new bishop of its flock. During the singing of the Nicene Creed, Canon Balmforth was escorted to the pulpit where he began a sermon that movingly revealed his Biblical scholarship as well as his knowledge of the man who awaited consecration.

"The generations come and go and the original apostolic group is constantly being enlarged," said Canon Balmforth. "As the Church lives on through the years, so the apostolic ministry lives on, continued by the same process of commission and delegation as the Lord himself used and commanded: 'As my Father hath sent me, so send I you.'"

Looking ahead a few weeks to Ramsey's enthronement in Durham Cathedral, Canon Balmforth added, "The word 'enthroned' may sound very prelatical to democratic ears, but the bishop's throne is not in its true meaning and primitive intention one of the trappings of prelatical pomp; it is the chair of the teacher; the chair occupied by him who, in the grace of his episcopal office and consecration, speaks authoritatively to the people in the name of God and His Christ, building them in our most holy faith. We know well that when the Archbishop and his assistant bishops lay their hands on Michael Ramsey's head they will be sending forth one who is eminently equipped as scholar and teacher for this great work of a bishop."

The ceremony that followed saw Ramsey leave the sanctuary twice to be vested in St. George's Chapel in the robes of a bishop. First was put over his robe a white rochet and a chimere, then he stood before the Archbishop to hear the Queen's mandate and to take the oath of canonical obedience. The second time he returned to the sanctuary wearing full episcopal vestments, the final step toward consecration. The hands of twenty bishops joined the Archbishop's in imparting the authority and power of a successor to the Apostles. Among the group was Ramsey's cousin, Roger Plumpton Wilson, who had been consecrated in York Minster in 1949 as sixth Bishop of Wakefield. The others were the bishops of Sheffield, Newcastle, Southwell, Carlyle, Manchester, Edinburgh, Lincoln, and Ely, and the Bishops Suffragan of Grimsby, Whitby, Selby, Lancaster, Warrington, Kranesborough, Pontefract, and Jarrow, and Bishops Hubbard, Gerard, and Weller.

Ramsey rose a bishop, and from the crowded nave came the hymn he had chosen for the occasion.

> Stars of the morning, so gloriously bright,
> Filled with celestial resplendence and light.

"Out of the dim recesses of York Minster yesterday walked 47-year-old Arthur Michael Ramsey, joining the long and illustrious line of Durham bishops who have spanned nearly nine centuries of episcopal history," wrote the *York Journal* of the two-hour ceremony.

Ramsey was the first newly consecrated bishop to pay homage to Elizabeth II, who had ascended the throne only a few months before and would in another year be crowned by the Archbishop of Canterbury. According to custom, only the Home Secretary was present with the Queen when Ramsey was received at Buckingham Palace. He was accompanied by the Clerk of the Closet bearing an open Bible upon a cushion. Ramsey knelt, placing his hands between those of the young Queen, repeating the homage sentence by sentence after the Home Secretary, and kissing the Bible at the conclusion. Elizabeth may well have regarded this fatherly figure with some interest for, as the new Bishop of Durham, he would be at her right side throughout her coronation ceremony in June. For a moment she caught his eye as if to say with twinkling amusement, "We are both new at our jobs."

In the days of old the Bishop of Durham had the rank of a quasi-independent prince. He was an earl palatine, holding all the rights and exercising all the power (even the coining of money) which could be claimed by the Crown in County Durham. Although these rights reverted to the Crown in 1836, many traditions persist, including a ducal coronet on the coat-of-arms and mitre and the presentation of a medieval sword, the falchion, on arrival in the diocese.

It was the observance of this latter ceremony, the bestowal of the falchion, that took the Ramseys to the large industrial town of Darlington, at the border of County Durham, on a lovely fall afternoon, October 10, 1952. Ramsey recalled in his acceptance address that one of his predecessors, William Van Mildert, had entered the diocese in 1826 in a carriage drawn by six horses and followed by his wife in another carriage, drawn by four horses, with fifty carriages of the gentry following and outriders waving wands. "My stable is not quite equal to that at the moment," he said, "and it must be admitted that the equestrian skill of bishops has very sadly declined."

Ramsey might have added that a bishop's customary black gaiters, which he was wearing for the first time, were a holdover from the days when bishops made their rounds by horseback.

They remain the traditional dress for bishops of the Church of England, completed by a frock coat worn over a knee-length cassock, sometimes called an apron, another adaptation to horseback riding. The "uniform" is completed with black shoes, often worn with silver buckles.

From the castle where he had stayed as a young canon professor more than twelve years before, Ramsey walked confidently to his enthronement on October 18, 1952. He wore the deep purple cope and tall mitre which had as its base a small and exquisite coronet, the symbol of the Bishop of Durham's ancient rank as a Prince Prelate. He carried in his hand Bishop Cosin's 280-year-old pastoral staff especially regilded for the occasion.

Except for a small BBC microphone, the scene at the great north door could have been any medieval enthronement. Four thousand persons waiting inside the Cathedral listened as he struck the door with the pastoral staff, saying in a clear voice, "I, Michael, by Divine Providence Lord Bishop of Durham, elected and confirmed, do ask entrance to this Cathedral Church. . . ."

The procession stopped under the central tower; an eighteen-year-old King's Scholar, Colin Hindson, came forward, carrying on a red cushion the priceless eighth-century Bede Gospels. On these Ramsey took his oath of allegiance.

After fanfares of trumpets and the singing of a festive *Te Deum,* Ramsey climbed the steps to his pulpit and spoke for the first time as the newly enthroned eighty-ninth Bishop of Durham.

" 'The love of Christ constraineth us,' " he read from Second Corinthians as the text of his enthronement sermon. ". . . Finding myself called to be your Bishop . . . I want only so to rule, so to teach, so to minister the mysteries of grace, that the love of Christ may be not hindered but spread abroad. . . . Let me therefore charge you, it is my first counsel, to serve Christ in his Church above all else with *joyfulness.* Members of the *Clergy,* rejoice that you are privileged to teach his truth, to care for his people, to celebrate the mystery of his body and blood, and to know perhaps his patience and his suffering as you serve him. Let the source and the spring of your joy come—not from your environment, not from the way things go—but from him. Members of the *Laity,* rejoice that you are privileged to worship a Creator who made you for himself, to enjoy all the gifts of Christ in his Church, to do all you can in the building up of the common fellowship and the worship of the Church in days of trial, to bear the reproach of Christ before men. Rejoice that he asks the whole of your allegiance, that he honors you with the most complete demand upon you. So rejoicing we know that the Durham we love and the heavenly pattern are not strangers one to another; and near to us always is the constraining love of Christ, Enthroned as the Prince of Life and the Bishop of our Souls."

The Ramseys' new home was Auckland Castle, a rambling two-story structure of blackened stone about twenty-five miles from Durham. Although many people regarded great country houses as outmoded, gloomy, and costly to maintain, Ramsey was eager to use Auckland Castle as a residence and center for diocesan life.

St. Peter's Chapel within the castle contains the tombs of three of Durham's most distinguished bishops—Cosin, and Lightfoot, and Westcott. At Auckland Castle the twelfth-century Bishop Pudsey had built his banqueting hall and gorged himself. More than a century later Bishop Bek had ruled in the same hall, attended by a hundred knights. From here the English army had marched to Neville's Cross, saving Durham from the Scots. In one of the drawing rooms Sir Walter Scott had spun stories for Bishop Barrington as they sat drinking port wine. And upstairs, Princess Victoria stayed overnight—and left behind her nightgown, still a treasure of the castle.

That life in an episcopal palace can be expensive, indeed, was acknowledged by Bishop Ruthal, who once complained to Cardinal Wolsey that entertaining three hundred people a day "is the way to keepe a man poore." Later Wolsey himself held the house as part of the bishopric of Durham. Cinnamon-scented rushes were planted that they might be strewn on the floor of his chamber. Wolsey never came to Auckland Castle, but the rushes planted for him still flourish in its grounds.

In a letter for the diocesan bulletin Ramsey acknowledged the disadvantages of living in the castle, but added, "I believe that

its abandonment by the See of Durham would be a tragedy for
there can be few houses more filled with associations of past
religious history and with possibilities for present and future use-
fulness."

Joan Ramsey began at once to plan the refurbishing of the
castle. A small kitchen was improvised to serve the private dining
room. Care was taken to save the castle from further damage
from dampness and dry rot. Bright wallpapers and gallons of
fresh paint provided an atmosphere of cheerfulness.

A second-floor room, used for storage and as a meeting place
for children who sewed for the poor, was designated as Ramsey's
private chapel. As Bishop Cosin's study in the seventeenth century it had been given beautiful oak-paneled walls painted with
the coats-of-arms of distant countries and episcopal sees. A shrine
to Thomas Becket, long ago made into a console table, was restored as an altar. St. Peter's, the large chapel built in the 1660's,
was reserved for diocesan assemblies.

The canopied bed in which Victoria had slept was placed in
the Ramseys' bedroom. In a chest in the same room was kept the
quaint nightgown that had belonged to the royal visitor. "It's a
little cotton-and-lace affair with an embroideried 'V,' " says Mrs.
Ramsey. "I doubt that it was forgotten. The servants probably
left it out of the luggage on purpose."

The biggest job of renovation was St. Peter's Chapel. The
marble altar steps were repaired and a linoleum wainscoating
was taken off so that the bishops' shields would stand out on the
freshly whitewashed walls. Dry rot was removed from the choir
stalls and several dangerous beams from the roof. This led to
the discovery on the ceilings of intricate heraldic emblems that
had been varnished over in years long past.

"We were fortunate in having a painter named Bobby who
took the greatest trouble with details of wallpapering, plastering,
and painting," Mrs. Ramsey recalls. "We had to go slowly on the
chapel ceiling, painting in every detail, because once the scaffolding came down we didn't want to find that some of the lions on
the shields didn't have red tongues."

Auckland Castle's devoted head butler was Ernest Alexander.
Tall, impeccably dressed, correct but friendly, he was more

knowledgeable of the castle's history than almost anyone. There was an initial embarrassment when he asked for the Ramseys' silverware only to be told they had none. But he soon became quite fond of the new occupants.

"Yace," he would say in the north-country accent which delighted the Ramseys, "it was in October of 1905 that I first came here. I had planned to enter the service of the Duchess of Bucculeugh but chose instead to become first footman at Auckland Castle. Bishop Moule was here in those days. He died in my arms in 1920. Then came Bishop Henson, and he was succeeded in 1939 by Bishop Williams. We had many of the Lambeth Conference overseas visitors here in 1908. And in 1910 we had some of the delegates to the international conference in Edinburgh. After five years as footman I was promoted to butler, and in 1913 I served tea to Queen Mary. We had another royal guest the same year—King Dawdi of Uganda, a tall and handsome lad of seventeen wearing a flowing blue robe and a magnificent headdress. He was accompanied by five native attendants in white cotton suits. They ate steadily from noon until three o'clock and would have continued if we hadn't taken the food away."

Alexander did his best to adapt to the changes in decor and routine inevitable with each new bishop. One of the Ramsey innovations was early morning celebration of the Holy Communion in the private chapel. Alexander never had been accustomed to this observance, but he turned up regularly. He was a devoted communicant and, too, he couldn't have the new Bishop doing something in the castle that he wasn't in on. The moment the service was over Alexander would rush downstairs, quarrel hurriedly with the cook, and have hot toast on the table by the time Ramsey came from the chapel.

The old butler was extraordinarily kind to Mrs. Ramsey who was still in poor health, going out very little. He brought her every detail of events in the village. But Alexander could not accustom himself to the breakdown in social barriers that permitted the townspeople to be guests at the castle. He was amused at the notion of town councilmen having tea in the Bishop's parlor and thought them awkward. Once he got the giggles so badly he almost had to be sent from the room.

Proud of his knowledge of the castle, Alexander refused to be surprised at the discovery of the elaborate decorations on the chapel ceiling. "Yace, I knew about that," he said. "They were painted over because they detracted attention from his Lordship's sermons."

On his fiftieth anniversary in service Alexander was called into the Bishop's study for the presentation of a Westminster chiming clock inscribed, "To Ernest Alexander, a friend of four Bishops, Auckland Castle, 1905-1955." A small group of photographers and friends heard Ramsey's words of appreciation: "He has looked after four Bishops of Durham with infinite kindness, and many of the clergy and the laity will long have him as part of their memory of the place. May his help and presence long continue."

The monthly magazine of the Diocese of Durham is known as *The Bishoprick* (the ancient spelling for bishopric). It might have been another of the gray, trite church publications that clutter the mails—hardly more than a dull listing of routine announcements—except for the fact that Ramsey's skill as a writer is almost equal to his eloquence as a speaker. His enthusiasm for editing this magazine was one of the first indications of the vigor he would display in reaching both the clergy and the people.

The feature which attracted most attention each month was Ramsey's sophisticated and often sagacious book reviews. In discussing H. Richard Niebuhr's new volume, *Christ and Culture*, Ramsey wrote that "it sometimes happens with a pair of brothers that the one who is less distinguished and loquacious is really the more able of the two; and I incline to think this is true of the Niebuhrs. For every hundred people who have heard of Reinhold there is perhaps one who has heard of Richard: but it is doubtful whether Reinhold has written a book of such penetration and balanced judgment. . . ."

In almost every issue Ramsey's reviews ranged from humility to biting sarcasm. He wrote of Dr. Raven Gifford's *Science and Religion* that he had read it "with the gratitude of one who is very ignorant." But of another he said, "The most important thing about books is that nine-tenths of them may be neglected." When he wrote kindly of *The Christian Duty of Happiness* by the retired Dean of Durham, Dr. Cyril Argentine Alington, he received from the old Dean a postcard of poetic thanks:

> What happiness and even pride
> A Dean must feel, confessing
> His pleasure at a (qualified)
> Episcopalian blessing.

Briefly reviving the splendor and pageantry of ages gone by, Britain prepared in the winter and spring of 1953 for the coronation of the youthfully beautiful Elizabeth II.

Centuries of history were bound up in the ceremony in which almost every role went to the holder of some ancient office or title. Custom held that the Bishop of Durham should stand at the sovereign's right hand while the Bishop of Bath and Wells, the Rt. Rev. Harold William Bradfield, should stand at the left. Accordingly, in the Bishop's Palace at Somerset in Wells and at Auckland Castle, the chaplains brought out the special coronation copes of heavy white brocade embossed with golden sunbursts. Ramsey's was bundled off to Mary Ozanne for a handsome navy-blue lining to replace the one stitched in for Edward VII's crowning in 1902.

In May the two bishops joined other prominent figures for meticulous rehearsals in Westminster Abbey. A sense of excitement and informality prevailed. ("I heard Robert, Lord Salisbury —Lord Hugh Cecil's nephew—referred to as 'Bobberty,' although *I* never called him that," Ramsey says.) One duke wagered that the Bishop of Durham was the oldest of the clergy. Ramsey laughed when he heard the report, amused as he has always been when his age is misjudged. In this group of bishops, some nearing eighty, he was a mere forty-eight.

The long ceremony was rehearsed until everyone taking part knew his role perfectly. Ramsey noticed from day to day that the Abbey grew in its readiness to receive the Queen. He saw rising in the nave elegant galleries covered with fine blue material emblazoned with golden crowns and national emblems. Just before the Queen's dress rehearsal a broad new carpet, woven in one piece, was stretched out the length of the nave.

Ramsey's bulky figure under the magnificent cope made him

an impressive subject for an artist sketching nearby—the Polish-born Felix Topolski, commissioned by the Duke of Edinburgh to capture the coronation in a huge mural to hang in Buckingham Palace. Topolski painted Ramsey as a benevolent father symbolizing the wise and kindly comfort the Church stood ready to offer the Queen.

After the dress rehearsal Ramsey went to visit his father in Cambridge. He hoped to get a haircut he badly needed before the coronation. A few minutes after he had left his bag at Howfield and walked down to the center of Cambridge, a police car stopped at the family home and an officer asked the old gentleman in slippers and black skullcap if his son was there.

"I think you might find him in a barber's shop," said the father, "but look in the bookshops, too."

The policemen cruised the Cambridge streets and finally spotted Ramsey just as he came out of a bookshop on his way to the barber's. They gave him the urgent message that the Queen had requested another rehearsal and that he should return to London immediately.

For those who collect anecdotes of Ramsey's forgetfulness the episode with the police constituted a story frequently told: Bishop Ramsey had gone browsing in a bookstore in Cambridge and had forgotten the rehearsal at Westminster. Reportedly, even the Queen was very amused. Alas, the delicious gossip was unfounded, for it was the Earl Marshall who had neglected to notify Ramsey of the extra rehearsal. (Ramsey never got his haircut.)

On June 1, 1953, the day before the coronation, the streets of London were festive with Union Jacks and masses of flowers. Ramsey left the hotel where he had been staying during the rehearsals and, joined by his wife, became the house guest of Canon Charles Smyth, rector of fashionable St. Margaret's Church next to Westminster Abbey.

Almost everyone in London rose early on Coronation Day. Joan Ramsey, wearing a formal gown and a treasured tiara left to her by an aunt, took her seat in the Abbey, as directed, hours before the ceremony began. As the lords and ladies and other dignitaries waited, there was passed around the church a bit of whispered news that swelled the day's pride in nation and empire: a British team had successfully scaled Mt. Everest.

Ramsey stood just inside the door of the Abbey, now joined to a glistening white annex that had been built to accommodate the formation of the long procession. In the distance was heard the muffled sound of the Queen's escorts approaching Westminster. Within a few moments there echoed from the rain-streaked pavements the clatter of hooves of eight white horses drawing the Queen's golden coach. They came to a gentle stop in front of the pristine cupola that marked the royal entrance to the annex.

The great west doors of the Abbey framed for Ramsey an unforgettable view of the monarch's arrival. He heard behind him a scuffling of feet on the stone floor and a deep mumble, "This is too good to miss!" The words were coming from Winston Churchill.

A resounding fanfare of trumpets announced the Queen's entrance. She began her slow procession down the nave—on her left the Bishop of Bath and Wells, and on her right the Bishop of Durham. Every eye upon them, the Queen and her two supporting bishops moved through an abbey filled with the splendid color of uniforms and robes. The Queen went first to the Chair of Estate, then to the Coronation Chair, and finally to a throne on a platform facing the high altar. Ramsey stepped momentarily aside as four Knights of the Garter approached with a canopy to shield the Queen during her anointing with holy oils. He took his place again as the ceremony continued toward the climax of crowning. Ramsey held one side of the Queen's cape as she was handed the jeweled scepter. The Archbishop of Canterbury, Geoffrey Fisher, lifted high the heavy crown and placed it on the head of the young Queen, declaring her sovereign of the realm and of the lands beyond the seas, *and defender of the Faith.*

The development of television, still so new it seemed almost unbelievable, enabled thousands throughout the British Isles—and, indeed, the world—to share in the coronation. Repeatedly they asked each other, "Who is that kindly old Bishop at the Queen's right hand?"

What Ramsey had done as he stood reverently at the throne amounted to little more than a few gestures of helpful protectiveness. Yet his was the most memorable countenance among all who passed in homage. Many would always think of the coronation of 1953 when in future years they saw that face—"the kindly old Bishop at the Queen's right hand"—in the newspapers and newsreels of the new Elizabethan era.

The armistice of the Korean War came in July, 1953. It was welcome news, for men of the Durham Light Infantry had been in the front lines for many months fighting what Ramsey called "two enemies—the cold and the Communists." Preaching in Durham Cathedral, he expressed his thankfulness that "the United Nations, the only instrument of international justice which exists in the world, have brought to a halt an aggressor in a critical test of their power to do so."

When the Ramseys prepared for vacation in August they found it hard to believe that only a year had passed since they left Cambridge. The busy months had seen the meeting in Sweden, the consecration at York, enthronement at Durham, diocesan conferences, settling in at Auckland Castle, a mission at Oxford, the coronation, and the unending round of ordinations, confirmations, and other episcopal duties. These were the memorable milestones of Ramsey's transformation from Cambridge don to Christ's bishop.

Ahead in his second year as Bishop of Durham lay another appearance on the world stage—a meeting of the World Council of Churches. Held at Evanston, Illinois, in August, 1954, it was an event which Ramsey has always remembered with lingering disapproval. Only two years before at the Faith and Order Conference at Lund, Sweden, he had questioned the merit of reports produced by mass assemblies working in sections. At Evanston his displeasure turned to disgust and anger as he saw the same mass procedures again dominating the World Council.

"It might have been possible for the five hundred delegates to have had good discussions in a hall by themselves, but they sat in a place vast enough to house a fleet of Zeppelins, with crowds of the 'hangers-on' of the conference and the general public included," Ramsey reported to his diocese. "I have rarely known such stultifying of the personal touch between speaker and audience; and as the main speeches were in the hands of all of us in typescript, their recital into a machine served no practical purpose and created no personal contact."

He was repelled by the atmosphere as well as by the size of the conference. "It was accompanied from the first to the last by the sort of publicity which can only be called vulgar 'boosting.' The American public had to be prepared for great pronouncements, and great results; and the delegates were being 'staged' as a performance. This is not the atmosphere in which spiritual results are most likely to ensue."

Finally, Ramsey attacked the whole planning of the conference program. "It was overloaded," he declared. "For over a fortnight the whirl of oratory, discussions, committees and typed documents continued without pause. Great matters of religion need thought, and thought requires spaces of quiet and leisure. The profoundest matters of theology cannot be illuminated by high-pressure drafting. Why should such procedures be the medium through which the Holy Spirit speaks to the Church?"

Angrily, then sadly, Ramsey wondered if the European delegates and certainly most Anglicans had not felt frustrated by the whole affair. "The weaknesses in the conference may have struck a blow at the tendency to claim far too much for what great congresses can achieve, and at the naïve conference mentality which is a growing evil in the Church."

His disappointment in the meeting was apparent at Evanston. He frowned on the streamlined methods of parliamentary procedure that lumped motions together. On at least one occasion Archbishop Fisher had walked over to him to quiet his protests.

Ramsey's vigorously expressed opinions and his personal appearance combined to make him one of the most picturesque personalities of the conference. He wore the purple cassock of an Anglican bishop—not ostentatious by any means, but his large frame and fringe of white hair made him conspicuous on the conference floor and on the streets. He regarded Evanston as something of a seaside resort town, and more than once walked clad in a bathrobe from his hotel to Lake Michigan.

The visit in the United States lasted from August 5 to September 13, 1954. The greatest change Ramsey noticed between the United States in 1925 and in 1954 was the progress in transportation, the remarkable swiftness with which trains and planes traversed the broad land.

In retrospect, he found considerable good in the Evanston meeting: ". . . The intercourse of Christians from every continent brought fresh understanding of what it means to *hope in Christ* in the different settings in which the Christian communities live. What does it mean to hope in Christ, if you are a Church in India amid a vast non-Christian culture, or a Church in South Africa amid an *apartheid* forced by the government, or a Church in Hungary under a regime which lets you preach the Gospel only under restrictions which create an agony of conscience? That is what the delegates were enabled to think about more closely, and to carry back to their Churches. . . . The oneness in Christ apparent at Evanston cries out for the realization of the unity of the Church for which Christ prayed."

In addition to expressing himself on the spiritual issues, Ramsey proved an astute observer of the undercurrents of thought inherent in any large council. "The familiar contrasts between different beliefs about the unity of the Church were to be seen, but one particular ideology of unity made itself more felt at Evanston than at the preceding conferences," Ramsey noted. "This may be called the American Federal Protestant World Council ideology, not confined to Americans but especially vocal through them. This is the belief that division into denominational sects is not an evil to be cured, but is a good thing according with divine purpose: and what is needed is for the sects to remain sects but to be embraced within the World Council as a sort of super-Church or Protestant Vatican. This ideology is really held, and it is from it that the extravagant claims for the World Council come. In these circles the slogan 'we intend to stay together' means 'we intend while remaining separate denominations to be over-arched by the World Council as a sort of Jerusalem above.' It was against this tendency that the Faith and Order section of the Conference pleaded for actual uniting of separated bodies, and the will towards this is most apparent in the younger churches of Asia. But can deliverance from denominationalism come except by the acceptance of a totally different 'dimension' in the meaning of the One, Holy, Catholic, and Apostolic Church, a 'dimension' of which the historic Church order is the effectual sign and instrument? Here the Anglican Communion can exercise a unifying role, but it can do so only if we commend the principles entrusted to us by putting ourselves alongside others in the give and take of fraternal intercourse."

Now in his eighty-seventh year, slippered, bearded, and deaf, Arthur Stanley Ramsey lived on at Howfield. He could look back on fifty-eight years of service to Magdalene—as lecturer, tutor, bursar, president, and member of the governing board. In these retirement years he enjoyed keeping abreast of the well-chosen books circulated among members of a book club run by and for university dons. He liked to keep a volume of the classics by his bedside. One day he announced that he had thus finished reading the whole of Shakespeare.

The elder Ramsey's sternness had mellowed, although he still was faithful to the austere standards of a lifetime. "I have never called anyone by his first name outside my own family," he would say in a deliberate mode of speech that lent relish to his pronouncements. Long ago he had given up his customary seat at the right of the fireplace in the Combination Room at Magdalene. He could no longer climb the stairs at the college or at Howfield. He turned his downstairs study into his bedroom. Here his son, as Bishop of Durham, administered to him the rite of confirmation in the Church of England. "It was a very moving thing," says Ramsey. "My father was old and lonely and wanted the comfort of the sacraments."

On the last day of 1954 Arthur Stanley Ramsey died, full of years and good works that had inspired each of his children and generations of men in his beloved Magdalene College.

"His gifts as a teacher of mathematics on the highest level were exceptional, and as bursar and tutor he made an even more notable contribution," said an appreciative, anonymously written obituary in the London *Times*. "It is no coincidence that these years marked the rise of Magdalene to a prominent position among the smaller colleges in the university. . . . There was something in the glance of his finely cut features that struck awe in the most light-hearted culprit. On such occasions he became, in the words of one Magdalene president, 'all eyes and moustache,' as indeed he was apt to appear when his combative liberalism was aroused. But beneath the mellow candlelight of the Combination Room, and especially in the reminiscent vein of later years, none would suspect the caustic capacity of this kindly, albeit redoubtable, don. . . . His domestic circle was a perpetual benediction to him until it was broken by two successive tragedies. . . . But it was given to him to see his younger son, Canon A. M. Ramsey (now Bishop of Durham), become Regius Professor of Divinity in 1950, and to serve with him on the governing body of the college which had produced them both."

When the Christmas vacation ended and Magdalene was again in session, a memorial service was held in the college chapel. Ramsey and his sisters then turned to a sad task—disposing of Howfield. It was a tender, sentimental decision, for the house had been built by their parents and never occupied by another family. Yet it was too large for Miss Lucy Ramsey who had so well looked after her brother in the twenty-seven years since his wife's death. A smaller house was found for her, on a nearby street, Mt. Pleasant, the very street in which friends of Ramsey's mother had erected a memorial bench in a small park.

The whole neighborhood of Castle Hill was changing. It was not so much a place of dons' families anymore. One or two commercial garages had been built. One house had become a hostel for Magdalene students. (Ramsey's father had contributed £750 toward its purchase.) Another house, the Bullough home, had been willed to the Dominican Order and this led to the Order's request that it be allowed to buy the Ramsey property.

"Michael Ramsey was very kind in seeing that we were able to acquire the residence," says Father Bullough, a towering monk who grew up in Buckingham Road and returned to found in his mother's former home the first Dominican priory in Cambridge since the Reformation. Many changes were made in the two houses. The Bulloughs' garage became a chapel while the Ramsey parlor and dining room were made into a refectory. The upstairs rooms were turned into monks' cells. (In 1962 the two structures were connected by a yellow-brick building that is the monastic library.) Where once the Ramsey children raced in and out, white-robed monks now moved quietly. In Howfield's gardens they walked at twilight, reading the Daily Office. It was a curious but peaceful fate for the old house of so many memories.

Twice during 1955 Ramsey presided over the York Convocation when Archbishop Garbett was ill. In November the aging prelate announced his retirement. There was a flurry of speculation that Ramsey would be his successor, but it was pointed out that he had been Bishop of Durham for only three years.

In the late afternoon of Christmas Eve, 1955, the Ramseys drove from Auckland Castle to Durham for a carol service in the Cathedral. When they returned home Ramsey ambled into his study to thumb through a bundle of Christmas cards that had arrived in the final post before the holiday.

He was startled to find on top of the stack a letter from Prime Minister Anthony Eden. It asked permission to submit Ramsey's name to Queen Elizabeth for nomination as Archbishop of York.

As events turned out, the Prime Minister was wise in his swift dispatch of business, for Archbishop Garbett died at Bishopthorpe on New Year's Eve, 1955 (a year to the day after the death of Ramsey's father). The public announcement of Ramsey's nomination to York was made on January 4.

The unofficial but widely circulated *Church of England Newspaper* commented almost immediately that many people had reacted with "shock and disappointment" to the news of Ramsey's translation to York. The *Yorkshire Post* and other influential newspapers quoted the report. "It is to his disadvantage as he mounts his new throne that he does so as the candidate of a group and, what is more, a group that is known for its intolerance and for its suspicion of comprehensiveness," said the *Church of England Newspaper*. "Indeed, it is a group that has always valued liberty more for itself than for others. The canvassers have been out on Dr. Ramsey's behalf ever since he went to Durham. Scarcely within living memory has there been such a campaign for any candidate to high office. Long before he had given any proof of his capacity the idea was sedulously nourished that he was the only possible candidate for York whenever it should become vacant; that nobody else even began to be in the running; that he was a giant beside whom all other churchmen were minnows; that after a brief tenure of York he must with the same inevitability succeed Dr. Fisher at Canterbury, who should hardly with decency refrain from stepping aside to let him. All that has been said may be perfectly true. As at present advised there is no evidence."

After reviewing Ramsey's career the newspaper continued its dubious observations: "Dr. Ramsey has yet to prove himself. To many who have watched his career closely his appointment has come as a shock and a disappointment. It is for him now to demonstrate that they have underestimated him. Nobody will be more happy than they to confess as time goes on that their fears were groundless and acknowledge greatness if they see it."

The newspaper also registered its displeasure at Henry Montgomery Campbell's nomination. "If anything could ensure that there shall not be an alternative candidate for Canterbury when the time comes for Dr. Fisher's retirement it is the translation to London of the Bishop of Guildford, Dr. Montgomery Campbell. Already aged sixty-eight and rumored not to be one of the strongest of men it is fairly obvious that short of dramatic events, the selectors will not be able to look in that direction for a successor."

An Anglican correspondent for the *Manchester Guardian* wrote, "Among the more extreme Anglo-Catholic elements in the Church of England Dr. Ramsey's appointment will be welcome. Some others may tend to regard him as a party candidate. Fears have been expressed that his appointment to such a leading position as that of Archbishop of York will be a setback to the cause of Christian reunion; in particular his interventions at the Evanston conference caused dismay in some quarters concerned with the ecumenical movement. On the other hand, it was noted that in the recent debates of the Convocations on the subject he supported the resolutions bringing about closer relations between the Church of England and the Church of South India."

In the United States *The New York Times* gave the news prominent treatment and printed with it a picture of Ramsey and Queen Elizabeth at the coronation.

The British weekly *Time and Tide* printed a recollection of Ramsey in Cambridge in the early 1950's: "The name of Michael Ramsey conjures up at first thought a genial figure, even then looking venerable, bicycling along Trinity Street to the Divinity

School to give a lecture to a room packed to the windowsills with an enthralled audience. Then came the transition from Regius Professor to Bishop. The Bishopric soon became aware that it had a scholar and a pastor in the Durham tradition. The Bishop knew the history of his See and has guarded it enthusiastically. Whether audiences have been learned, juvenile or the ordinary people of the Diocese, his brilliant preaching has revealed his understanding and friendliness. Auckland Castle, which he and his wife have done so much to repair and preserve, has been a center of hospitality for the Diocese and the Church beyond. But the Bishop of Durham proved very soon that he was more than a scholar and a pastor. There is no committee in the Diocese which has not been aware of his quick grasp of detail or, especially, when things have gone a bit wrong, his great gales of laughter. Amongst his many achievements has been to prove that although in theology he followed the Catholic tradition, he coupled with this a profound understanding of those who take a different line. Already his approach has been of great value in talks about reunion. Intellect, hard work, human concern, an immense sense of humor and a deep personal piety are the qualities which the Bishop of Durham takes with him to the Primatial See. There can be no doubt that another great Archbishop has been found for York or that the Church of England will benefit greatly by his wise counsel."

Within his own diocese there was far more praise than criticism of Ramsey's appointment. Canon Wetherall of St. Chad's College in Durham wrote in the college magazine: "Up in Durham we have known Michael Ramsey's stature and though we would have liked him to stay as our Bishop, the Church plainly needed him at York. The curious cry in parts of the Press that he was a party man showed simple ignorance of what he has done in Durham. Ecclesiastical statesmen are apt to confuse charity and woolliness, and it will be good for the Church to have a spokesman who can speak his mind and hold all kinds of people together in his large-heartedness."

Criticism of Ramsey's nomination to York only gave rise to speculation that he had not been Archbishop Fisher's first choice for the post. Ramsey had his champions, of course, although most of his contemporaries were not sufficiently high placed to wield strong influence in his behalf. Nonetheless, his capabilities were plain—the scholarship which had recommended him to the See of Durham, the traditional post of a scholar, and the administrative ability which he had evidenced in the years at Durham. His work with the World Council of Churches had given him the kind of experience, regardless of how distasteful it may have been, that would make him more than a narrow provincial archbishop. At fifty-two he was fairly young, as archbishops go, and could undertake large projects. Moreover, a High Churchman at York was an excellent counterbalance to Fisher's preference for the Low Church tradition.

Ramsey became the seventh Bishop of Durham to be translated to York. The first was Laurence Booth, who spent nineteen years there before appointment to York in 1476. The second, Christopher Bainbridge, was at Durham only one year before going to York in 1508. Matthew Hutton spent seven years there before succeeding to the archiepiscopate in 1595. His immediate successor, Tobias Matthew, followed him to York in 1606. George Monteigne served less than a year before translation to York in 1628. The last translation from Durham to York had been in 1860 when Charles Thomas Longley was named Archbishop of York and then in 1862 became the ninety-second Archbishop of Canterbury. Like Ramsey, Longley was Bishop of Durham for less than four years before going to York.

The Archbishop-designate had two and one-half months before he legally ceased to be Bishop of Durham, and he used the time fully. One issue on which he took a stand was the increasing influence of the American evangelist, Billy Graham, who had been preaching in Britain.

Ramsey's dislike for evangelistic preaching and emotionalism had not declined since he had abruptly left the revival meeting in Cambridge thirty years before. Now he wrote of "the menace of fundamentalism," describing it as "a phenomenon well known and possessing certain very clear characteristics, a phenomenon which was becoming more conspicuous in religious circles in this country before ever Billy Graham crossed the Atlantic.

"I am not certain how far Billy Graham, a man of utter humility and simplicity, is completely at one with our English fundamentalism," Ramsey said. "He comes from a milieu which is very similar to it, but he has tried to disassociate himself from particular movements and he claims to preach the first steps of Christianity and to say 'Now, for the rest, go on to one of the Churches.' There is evidence that he has genuinely done this. There is also evidence that he has taught the grossest doctrines and flung his formula 'the Bible says' over teaching which is emphatically *not* that of the Bible. . . .'"

Ramsey's criticism, coming as it did from one of the highest prelates in the Church of England, was newsworthy. The Associated Press located Graham preaching in New Delhi, where, on the day Ramsey's comments were quoted in England, he had persuaded seven hundred persons including a Hindu holy man to "receive Christ."

Billy Graham, on hearing Ramsey's charges, said he could only respect Ramsey's right to say what he wished. It was a wise reply that did not further publicize the charges and enabled their friendship to remain intact.

On March 6, 1956, Ramsey appeared before a group of County Durham clergy to speak to them for the last time. "There is always a strong link between a Bishop and those whom he has ordained to the sacred ministry. . . . Their ministry means much to him, more sometimes than they may realize and more indeed than he can easily express. And if he should have to cease to be their Bishop he will want to join with them in thankfulness for things for which he and they together owe gratitude to Almighty God."

The day was approaching when Ramsey did, indeed, have to "cease to be their Bishop." A total of forty-one months had passed since his consecration—an extremely short episcopate in the annals of Durham, yet embodying a rich experience. His long years as canon at Durham had given him the advantage of many friendships that aided him in his task as bishop.

Those who had feared that Ramsey was "too High Church" found he was keeping an even balance. He had, however, done much to develop appreciation of Catholic traditions. Almost always he wore cope and mitre when visiting parishes. A miner's son, seeing a mitre for the first time, asked boldly, "Be those *jewels* in the bishop's hat?" At another country church, the tall mitre had tipped over the sanctuary lamp, spilling the hot wax down the back of the beautiful cope.

In the village outside the gates of Auckland Castle, Ramsey was greatly liked for his interest in restoring the old palace. He was fond of the village operatic society, especially its presentations of Gilbert and Sullivan. He liked to listen to the "cheap-Jacks" hawking their wares in the market place. And when the children saw him on the street they skipped along beside him, a jolly group making its way to Woolworth's where the Bishop bought sweets for the whole lot.

When the clergy wives and other women of the diocese met in Auckland Castle, Mrs. Ramsey poured countless cups of tea as her kitten, Pudsey, named for a twelfth-century Durham bishop, played at her feet. In the summer she was often hostess at large garden parties for the diocese. "After the widow of the Headmaster of Eton, I always heard that Joan Ramsey was the most loved woman in County Durham," says Mrs. William Temple.

Ramsey, working in his study at Auckland Castle in the last days as Bishop of Durham, bundled together his favorite addresses and sermons for publication in a book called *Durham Essays*. In the introduction he wrote, "A Bishop of Durham lives in the daily consciousness both of the ancient tradition of Christianity which, reaching back to Aidan, Cuthbert, and Bede, has a genuine continuity through the centuries and an inescapable impact upon the contemporary Church. . . . The dedication of this little book ['To the clergy of the Bishopric in gratitude and affection'] gives a hint of the depth of my feeling towards them as I look back upon my time among them as their 'Pastor Pastorum.' Amid the strain imposed upon them by the smallness of their number, the want of variety in the types of parish to which they can move within the limits of the diocese to which they are devoted, they work on; and whatever blemishes they have are the scars of battle."

12. PRIMATE OF ENGLAND

On the Feast of St. Mark, April 25, 1956, a timid spring day with cold rain hanging in the air, Michael Ramsey went in splendid cream-colored cope and mitre to his enthronement as Primate of England and ninety-second Archbishop of York.

The ceremony took place in York Minster where, only three and one-half years earlier, Ramsey had been consecrated Bishop of Durham. Now he returned as chief bishop of the Church's northern province and the second highest ecclesiastic in the Church of England.* Twenty-four bishops and six hundred clergymen marched in the colorful procession which moved in three sections from the Church of St. Michael le Belfry to the steps of York Minster. Above them rose the Minster's massive towers shrouded for a prolonged renovation in timber and steel scaffolding.

Much of the ancient history and tradition of the Church was symbolized in the enthronement rite. Those age-old customs inspired Ramsey's first sermon from the archiepiscopal throne: "The Church of England is the ancient Catholic Church of this

* The Archbishop of Canterbury ranks first. A papal decree of the fourteenth century ruled that Canterbury should have the title "Primate of All England" while the Archbishop of York should be called "Primate of England."

country, the Church alike of Aidan of Lindisfarne and Paulinus of York, and is unbroken in the continuity of its faith, its order and its sacramental life from the earliest times," he declared. ". . . While love and truth demand our practical brotherhood with all who own the name of Christ, and our utter humility towards them, they demand no less our faithfulness to what God has given us in the Catholic Church of this land. As to the comprehensiveness of our Church, this does not mean that several religions are crouching for space under one umbrella. Rather does it mean that the riches of Christ in His Church are apt to elude the grasp of any one of us, or any group of us. . . . If our presentation of the Gospel is to strike home, it must be seen to bear upon the lives of those who work in factory, shipyard, mine and farm. It must correspond to the virility of a sturdy people. It must contain an honest willingness to meet the questions which forthright men and women will ask."

After the sermon the new Archbishop gave his blessing at the high altar and in the nave. The third and final blessing of the enthronement day was given to the throngs who waited under pewter skies outside the Cathedral. Many saw for the first time the man who would sign himself "Michael Ebor:" using the abbreviated Latin word for York and who would be called "Your Grace," the revered form of address shared by archbishops and dukes.

From York Minster the Ramseys were driven to Bishopthorpe. The many changes and additions over a period of more than seven hundred years lend a distinctive but brooding air to this manor house on the edge of the River Ouse. After the old Archbishop's death on New Year's Eve, 1955, it had stood bleak and empty with little prospect that it ever again would shelter an archiepiscopal household. Only the cry of gulls broke the quiet.

"Archbishop Garbett thought he could rule from his grave," explains a diocesan official. "He had taken over Bishopthorpe during the war when the house was in disrepair and the garden in weeds. He was a bachelor who rarely entertained. He found the estate lonely and hard to staff. In his last years he drew up plans to convert Bishopthorpe to a retreat house and conference center. He even selected a smaller house in which his successor could live."

The Ramseys disagreed with these plans, hoping to use Bishopthorpe as they had Auckland Castle. They settled down, temporarily, in one wing of the house while the Church Commissioners, the central board of finance, decided Bishopthorpe's fate. Within a few months the Commissioners ruled in their favor.

With this decision the Ramseys began the same renovation they had given Auckland Castle. Joan Ramsey splashed the old walls with color—regal maroon and white wallpaper for the private dining room, a quaint Victorian pattern for her parlor, big blue roses for a work room, rich gold-and-white-flocked paper for the Archbishop's study, and quantities of glistening white paint for the formal rooms.

Bishopthorpe provided plenty of room for the diverse household the Ramseys assembled. It included Miss Renée Tanqueray, a motherly-looking woman who had resigned her job at Durham High School to become Mrs. Ramsey's companion. Miss Tanqueray's huge boxer, Timothy, roamed the gardens of Bishopthorpe at the Archbishop's side.

Another new member of the household was the secretary, Miss Dorothy Kitchingman—or "Kitch," a fond nickname bestowed by Mrs. Ramsey. Tall with close-cut graying hair, "Kitch" had formerly been secretary to the Bishop of St. Albans. She ran the Archbishop's office with brisk orderliness, typing long theological manuscripts and co-ordinating diocesan business with the offices at York Minster.

There was a third newcomer to Bishopthorpe, the Rev. Martin Kaye, who had been tutor and chaplain at Cuddesdon since 1951. Soon he was called "the Rev" by both the Ramseys. He was given to long periods of quietness but, like "Kitch," was a model of pleasant efficiency.

A cottage near the house was occupied by the butler, Walter Brindle, and his wife and two daughters. Brindle had been brought to Bishopthorpe from Lancashire years before by the William Temples.

A routine of worship and work soon developed. In the beautiful old chapel Ramsey and his new chaplain celebrated Holy Communion each morning and read Evensong at twilight. Now and then diocesan clergy and their wives came for tea and a tour of the house. Sometimes the grounds were thrown open to parish societies. Ramsey especially enjoyed the shipyard workers and miners he had known during his years at Durham. When a group of German students came to see the house, the Archbishop addressed them in their native tongue.

The York Quarterly, founded by William Temple, was revived by Ramsey with an introductory note: "This publication ceased, like other good things, in the first year of the war. The books chosen for review—whether they be for blessing or for cursing —will in every case be books deemed worthy of attention." Again Ramsey wrote the crisp and thoughtful book reviews which had distinguished the Durham diocesan magazine.

The first bishops whom Ramsey consecrated were a new suffragan, George Frederick Townely, who became Bishop of Hull, and Ramsey's old friend, Hugh Edward Ashdown, who became Bishop of Newcastle. Ramsey gave them the counsel he since has tendered every bishop he has consecrated: "Keep this one-in-four rule. Out of every four Sundays, reserve one free of engagements. Devote that day to your own study, meditation and writing."

A new Archbishop is a traditional choice for an honorary degree. Four universities—Hull, Edinburgh, Leeds, and Cambridge —singled out Ramsey for this honor in 1957. His alma mater bestowed an honorary doctorate of divinity with a Latin citation hailing Ramsey as an eloquent orator, in the tradition of Asquith, and praising him for attaining such eminence when barely fifty —*Pro partibus Asquithianis orator eloquentissimus. . . . Vix quinquaginta annos natus ad hoc fastigium emerserit.*

Ramsey's rising prominence brought to the fore a story that had been making the rounds. It concerned his days at Repton when Geoffrey Fisher was headmaster. In a speech at Repton's four-hundredth anniversary celebration the Archbishop of Canterbury declared, "I am thankful to say that Eric Maschwitz nipped in the bud a scandalous reminiscence of Sir Basil Bartlett,* who said that he's heard outside the door the present Archbishop of Canterbury beating the present Archbishop of York. What is more, he said it to the drama critic of a newspaper. By the mercy of Providence, Maschwitz was there, and promptly said, 'Sir Basil Bartlett has always lived in the realms of fantasy,

---

* Both Eric Maschwitz and Basil Bartlett are Old Reptonians who have become prominent playwrights. Maschwitz wrote the scenario for *Goodbye Mr. Chips,* filmed at Repton.

and his memory has been remarkably mistaken all his life.' "

Thousands of miles of foreign travel awaited Ramsey as Archbishop of York. Within a few months after his enthronement he would go to Russia. In 1959 he would visit the United States. And in 1960 and again in 1961 he would go to Africa.

The Archbishop of Canterbury appointed Ramsey to head an Anglican delegation to Moscow for what was, in effect, an ecclesiastical summit conference. Ramsey was chairman of a group of nine churchmen who undertook what he describes as "the first conference ever held with the Russian Church with which contact had been impossible since the Revolution." The Church of England hoped to work slowly toward a "reconciling" of doctrinal differences and subsequent intercommunion. One of Ramsey's colleagues in the ten-day meeting recalls that "in similar sessions the main objective had been a technical one, to gain recognition of Anglican orders, whereas in 1956, the aim was to restate unity in faith."

Ramsey saw the invitation to Moscow as part of a more liberal Soviet policy developing in the wake of Stalin's death. "In spite of recurring political difficulties we ought to draw nearer to them and they to us," he told the Convocation of York just before his departure. "Neither open persecution nor the subtle patronage of the Soviet Government can crush Christianity in Russia."

The Anglican delegation—eight Englishmen and one American—reflected a wide variety of opinion and experience. Canon Herbert Waddams of the Council on Foreign Relations was secretary. Other members were Dr. Paul B. Anderson, an American layman appointed at the Archbishop's request by the Rt. Rev. Henry Knox Sherrill, Presiding Bishop of the Protestant Episcopal Church; the Rt. Rev. H. J. Carpenter, Bishop of Oxford; the Rev. Owen Chadwick, Master of Selwyn College, Cambridge; the Rev. John Findlow, Chaplain of the British Embassy in Rome; the Rt. Rev. A. E. J. Rawlinson, Bishop of Derby; the Rev. Francis John Taylor, Principal of Wycliffe Hall, Oxford; and the Rev. Harry A. Williams, Fellow and Lecturer of Trinity College, Cambridge. Two members of the group, Anderson and Findlow, spoke Russian. Anderson was Director of the Russian YMCA Press in Paris and had traveled in Russia. Findlow, whose wife was Russian-born, had been Assistant General Secretary of the Church of England Council on Foreign Relations before taking charge of the Anglican chapel in Rome. At London Airport the men assembled, dressed in the cassocks they had agreed to wear throughout the trip. "I don't know if we're going as pilgrims or very important persons," Ramsey said to one of the wives, Mildred Rawlinson, who saw them off from London.

It soon turned out that the men were VIP's indeed. At Moscow Airport they were welcomed by the Metropolitan of Moscow, Nikolai Krutitsky, who was in charge of the external relations of the Russian Church. His sleek, black limousines whisked the visitors to the Sovietskaya, a "showplace" hotel with television in every room. "There was, in fact, every comfort," Ramsey recalls. "And let the curious be told at once that vodka was very little in evidence and some excellent light wines from Georgia were usually on the table. We were surrounded by warm, generous and considerate hospitality. The Metropolitan had general overseeing of our visit, though he did not take part in the work of the conference. He won our hearts. The Patriarch of All Russia took a personal interest in everything that happened, and to know him is to have a reverent affection for him."

Some of the Russian churchmen also had been assigned to the Sovietskaya. With the help of Anderson and Findlow, conversation flowed with the smiling Bishop Michael of Smolensk, the Russian chairman, who in turn introduced Bishop Sergei of Starorussii and professors from Moscow and Leningrad. Ramsey and the other two Anglican bishops in their purple robes stood out prominently among the veiled and bearded Russian Orthodox clergy. Ramsey was rotund, weighing well over two hundred pounds, the heaviest he has ever been.

"In the formal conference sessions the familiar issues arose," says Ramsey. "On the one hand Anglicans are perplexed by the Orthodox valuation of Tradition as having authority equal to Holy Scriptures; and perplexity is caused by the place given by the Orthodox to the Blessed Virgin and the Saints. On the other hand the Orthodox complain of the Western addition of the word *Filioque** to the clause in the Nicene Creed about the Pro-

---

* Owen Chadwick recalls a spirited exchange between Ramsey and the Rector of the Moscow Academy (described by Ramsey as "the learned and

cession of the Holy Spirit; they find ambiguity in the Anglican attitude to the authority of the seven ecumenical Councils, and they are disturbed by the Article which distinguishes between the two Sacraments generally necessary to Salvation and the five others 'commonly called Sacraments'; for the Orthodox adhere firmly to seven Sacraments. The question of validity of orders assumes a subordinate place. To the Orthodox, what is requisite for unity is dogmatic agreement: if they came to be satisfied about the full dogmatic orthodoxy of the Church of England, then recognition of orders and intercommunion would follow—the Church of England being acknowledged as itself a part of the Holy Orthodox Church of Christ."

The conferences lasted four hours each day. They were formidable. The Russians read long and weighty papers, leaving no time for discussion. Ramsey yearned to debate the issues. He wished, too, for what he calls "that informal, out-of-conference discussion which oils the wheels of a conference."

Cars were lined up daily to take the visitors sightseeing. Ramsey resented the intrusion but soon found these tours invaluable for understanding the world in which the Orthodox Church was pursuing its ancient course.

The Anglican delegation visited eight of the fifty churches still maintained by Moscow congregations. After years of religious suppression, the Muscovites heard an Archbishop of York speaking in their own churches. Their surprise was lessened by the fact that this venerable figure would, with a beard, look not unlike one of their own patriarchs.

The usual order of service would be interrupted by the parish priest for a welcome to the visitors and a reply by Ramsey. He spoke in the dim light of candles flickering under the golden icons, choosing the simplest terms for the translators to relay. "Whenever possible I made allusion to the dedication of the par-

---

humorous Protopriest Konstantine Ruzhitsky") on the *Filioque*. This is a term inserted into the Constantine Creed at the third Council of Toledo (A.D. 589) after the words *Qui Ex Patre* (who from the Father). Since the eleventh century it has been accepted in the Latin Church to express the doctrine that the Holy Spirit proceeds from the Father and the Son. This doctrine was denounced especially by Photius (867) as heresy and blasphemy. It is commonly considered the chief doctrinal difference between the Eastern and Western churches.

ticular church* for some words of encouragement to the congregation," he says, "and in reference to the unity of our Churches I told them although we had in our Church many customs different to theirs, we worshiped the same Blessed and All-glorious Trinity, and were baptized into His Name, we were fed with the Body and Blood of Jesus, very God and very Man, we honored the saints, we sang the Song of Mary in our evening service every day. In speaking of peace between the nations I said that it would be secure when men everywhere gave glory to God in the highest, and I usually concluded with some words on the glory of heaven which I prayed might be in store for all of us if there is first faithfulness amid our difficulties here and now."

In Red Square and inside the Kremlin walls Ramsey strode where another Archbishop of York, William Maclagan,** had walked at Easter of 1879, and recalled the accounts of that festival day so long ago—thousands of tapers in the hands of thousands of people in the Kremlin courtyards, bells answering bells, incense sweet on the wind, and processions of clergy in cloth-of-gold. "All this is no more," Ramsey noted. "The godless state has come."

Some miles from Moscow, in a village church dedicated to the Transfiguration, the delegation received a welcome of almost heartbreaking warmth. The congregation was huge, evidently drawn from numerous villages where the churches had been closed.

On another foray into the countryside, the delegation spent a day at the monastery of Sergui Sergiuskaya at Zagorsk, a great center of Russian devotion about forty miles from Moscow. "Here, after the liturgy, the Patriarch Alexei entertained many guests at a banquet, and the party included some ecclesiastics from countries beyond the 'Curtain,'" Ramsey wrote in his conference report. "And on the Patriarch's right was the one un-

* "The churches in Moscow which we visited," says Ramsey, "are dedicated to the Resurrection, All Saints, the Seamless Robe of Christ, St. Pimen, St. John the Soldier, Our Lady the Help of the Sorrowful, besides the Cathedral of Our Lady and a church containing the tomb of the Patriarch Tikhon."

** Archbishop Maclagan was translated from Lichfield to York in 1891. He retired in 1908 at the age of eighty-two.

believer present, apart from two interpreters, Mr. G. G. Karpov, an amiable man, the chairman of the Soviet Committee for the affairs of the Orthodox Church." Ironically, it was this unbelieving official who entertained the foreign visitors at a banquet on the last night of their stay in Moscow.

Flying home to England, while the rest of the delegation went on to Leningrad for a longer tour, Ramsey reviewed his observations of the Soviet Union. There might be progress in science and technology but Ramsey had found nothing new or inspired in the art, the sculpture, or the architecture of the new Russia. As for the people he saw in the streets—peasants, artisans, and those who looked like officials—there was a "sameness" and a feeling that they were controlled by forces out of sight.

The religion? Ah, the religion. He had found, happily, that worship, spirituality, and charity are alive in the Church of Russia. With a thwarted existence it yet maintained bishops and clergy and some monasteries and seminaries from the offerings of its own faithful. And it kept alive the faith in a portion of the people, worshiping God with zeal and beauty, living its own interior life.

In the *York Diocesan Leaflet* Ramsey wrote a telling description of the world around the Russian Church: "It knows what the Soviet press and radio tells it. Hence there need be no surprise when it speaks of 'peace.' This fits the notion in the country that the Soviet Union seeks peace and that other nations try to disturb it; and when it desires (as it sincerely does) friendship with those foreign Churches which are doctrinally less remote from it than others, this fits the general Government line of 'selling' things Russian to the outside world. Equally the looking to the Moscow Patriarchate by other Orthodox Churches fits what the Soviet Government likes to see from the satellite countries. But not for a moment do I doubt the charity and sincerity of the Russian Churchmen towards us. Their theological interest is serious, their concern for Christian brotherhood is real. They rejoice in the newly created possibilities of friendship with another Church."

After ten days at Bishopthorpe, Ramsey began a long holiday on August 4. "I shall be grateful if during that time I am spared letters which are not imperatively necessary," he wrote with the frankness of a man who felt to his bones the fatigue of events set in motion eight months before by the Prime Minister's Christmas Eve letter.

The initials "L. C." appear repeatedly in Michael Ramsey's datebook for 1957 and first half of 1958, signifying his increasing attention to details of the Lambeth Conference. There was a prodigious amount of work to be done between January and July when the sessions would begin. But first there was to be a wedding in the village of Bishopthorpe—the marriage of the butler's pretty daughter, Kathryn Frances Brindle. The Archbishop himself presided at the ceremony. The parish church was decorated with white flowers on the Feburary morning when Brindle and his daughter came down the aisle for her marriage to David Alan Haxby. The reception later at Bishopthorpe Palace was attended by the Ramseys, not as host and hostess but as guests of the Brindles.

York Minster became a place of pilgrimage for many of the visitors who assembled from five continents for the Lambeth Conference. On St. John Baptist's Day, June 24, there was a colorful service to honor the Presiding Bishop of Nippon Sei Ko Kai, the Most Rev. Michael Hinsuke Yarhiro of Kobe, Japan; the Bishop in Madagascar,* the Rt. Rev. Thomas Richards Parfitt; and the Bishop of Wangaratta, the Rt. Rev. Thomas Makinson Armour.

Ten days later the Lambeth Conference opened with the traditional ceremony of welcome in Canterbury Cathedral. "It was a gloriously sunny day," Ramsey recalls, "and the stone of Canterbury had an enchanting 'softness' all its own."

Inside the Cathedral a long procession of three hundred and ten bishops and archbishops from forty-six countries moved slowly down the aisle to be received by Archbishop Fisher at the Chair of St. Augustine. The largest group was the body of eighty-eight American prelates headed by their Presiding Bishop, the Rt. Rev. Henry Knox Sherrill.

On the first Sunday of the Lambeth Conference the great

* The term "Bishop in . . ." instead of the customary "Bishop of . . ." denotes the overseas bishoprics of the Canterbury jurisdiction.

family of bishops and archbishops gathered in St. Paul's Cathedral to receive Holy Communion. Ramsey recalls reading the Gospel for the day: "It was the story of the call of St. Peter— 'We have toiled all night and caught nothing: nevertheless at Thy word. . . .': a message of moving appropriateness."

Some of the congregation were from behind the Iron Curtain, present as guests and observers. Of them Ramsey wrote, "Within the company were men who had suffered greatly for the sake of Christ. Christendom is still the scene of heroic faith and love; and God and mankind are served by some 'of whom the world is not worthy.' The authentic marks of the Christian calling are still to be seen in our midst."

The grounds of Lambeth Palace stood in the midsummer of 1958 like a green oasis in a heavily industrialized section of London. Delegates to the ninth Lambeth Conference streamed through the wide Tudor gate into a courtyard that had all the nostalgic spirit of a college reunion. Ramsey himself fell into the bewhiskered embraces of the Russian Orthodox observers who remembered him affectionately from the Moscow conferences of 1956. Their delegation included Bishop Michael of Smolensk and Archpriest Konstantine Ruzhitsky with whom Ramsey had argued the *Filioque*.

General sessions were held in the Lambeth Library with Archbishop Fisher presiding and the Bishop of Peterborough, Robert Stopford, acting as episcopal secretary. In the library, and in the leafy shadows of Lambeth's spacious gardens, the conferees soon came to regard Ramsey—or "York" or "Ebor" as they called him—with considerable interest. His arrivals in the palace courtyard, in a limousine bearing his archiepiscopal flag, were almost theatrical in effect. Some of the bishops and their wives frequently snapped his picture. (The Americans, known as the "camera bugs" of the conference, reportedly had hidden cameras under their robes to take pictures at St. Paul's.)

During the weekend breaks the Ramseys drove to York to entertain a few of the Lambeth bishops and their wives. Over three successive weekends the guests represented many areas of the Anglican Communion—Calcutta, Quebec, Kurunagala, Nyasaland, Ondo-Benin, Washington, D.C., and Perth, Australia.

At Lambeth the delegates worked feverishly to mold many opinions into unified reports on the Bible, the Prayer Book, world peace, foreign missions, family life, and unity, a subject which has been discussed by every Lambeth Conference since 1867.

Ramsey was chairman of the Committee on the Holy Bible: Its Authority and Message. This was the foremost topic on the conference agenda, a position that signifies the Lambeth Conference's progress from the early days when it avoided any discussions of doctrinal issues. The vice chairman was Philip Carrington, Archbishop of Quebec. The secretariat was shared by Richard S. Emrich, Bishop of Michigan, and W. G. H. Simon, Bishop of Llandaff, Wales.

Of the committee's forty-three members, eight were from the United States,* seven from Canada, three each from Wales, Australia, and West Africa, two from India, Pakistan, Burma, and Ceylon, and one each from Scotland, Ireland, New Zealand, South Africa, Japan, and the West Indies, in addition to four extra-provincial bishops. The seven Englishmen on the committee included three who had figured in Ramsey's career—Hugh Edward Ashdown, Bishop of Newcastle, a member of Ramsey's wedding party; A. T. P. Williams, Bishop of Winchester, whom Ramsey had succeeded at Durham; and M. H. Harland, the present Bishop of Durham.

A London newspaper reported, "Dr. Ramsey, Archbishop of York, is giving many hours to the Lambeth Conference report on the Bible. Proofs are now coming from the printers. He is a swift worker, able to read a page of type almost at a glance. In the bishops' discussions on the Bible, Dr. Ramsey presides. Sometimes the bishops think he is asleep in the chair. For he sits with his hands tightly clasped over his purple robe. But he does not sleep. He is on his feet in seconds if he disagrees."

At the close of the Lambeth Conference the bishops issued the traditional Encyclical Letter to the Faithful in Jesus Christ. The beautifully phrased message was followed by the Ramsey committee report forthrightly reaffirming "the relation of the Bible

---

* The American bishops were A. B. Kinsolving, Arizona; W. R. Moody, Lexington, Ky.; Richard Emrich, Michigan; R. S. Hubbard, Spokane; E. H. West, Florida; A. J. Miller, Easton, Md.; C. R. Haden, Sacramento; and J. P. Craine, Coadjutor of Indianapolis.

and the Church which Anglican teaching has always emphasized and the modern study of Christian origins has made more clear."

The Archbishop of East Africa, the Most Rev. Leonard Beecher, says the completed report revealed Ramsey "as a man who not only has deep insights into the Bible but also exercises a warmhearted understanding of its relationship to modern society. One sees Ramsey not with a Bible in his hand but in his heart."

As the 1958 Lambeth Conference ended with a service in Westminster Abbey, Ramsey's chief impression was that of "the fellowship which unites the different parts of the Anglican Communion with one another." In the *York Quarterly* he wrote that "the nature of our fellowship in the Anglican Communion is as hard to describe and to explain as it is inescapable to see and to feel. Embracing as it does people of other races than the English, and of other political systems than the British Commonwealth, its unity must rest upon something other than which is merely English in religion or ethos. It is indeed a unity which includes sacramental communion, creed, the bond everywhere of the bishop exercising the same pastoral office, a worship whose character has been moulded by the Prayer Book, a devotion to the Bible, and a sense of ancient tradition blending with a spirit of experiment. It is possible only to say that here is a portion of the One, Holy, Catholic and Apostolic Church of Christ, not claiming any unique excellence, but living by the principles of a non-papal and scriptural catholicity. But new trends—such as the movement towards greater liturgical diversity in different parts of the Anglican Communion, and the movements of parts of it into reunion schemes in increasingly indigenous Churches—call for fresh thought about . . . the principles on which our unity rests."

After the conference Ramsey returned with pleasure to the comfortable pastime of sitting for a portrait authorized by the Corporation of Church House. The big dining room at Bishopthorpe was turned into an artist's studio.

"It isn't every day one paints an archbishop or a face with that much character," says the young artist, George Bruce, as he thumbs through the preliminary sketches he made of Ramsey as Archbishop of York. "The other portraits at Bishopthorpe differed only in the fullness of the white lawn sleeves of the archbishops.

I decided to break with tradition by doing a full-length portrait of the Archbishop in his cope."

When the sacristy wardrobes were thrown open for Bruce he selected the vestment Ramsey had worn at his enthronement, a rich gold-and-cream-colored cope with orange medallions on its edges.

"Darling, he's picked the shrimps," Mrs. Ramsey called to her husband. ("Shrimps" was the fond nickname for the handsome orphreys or border of the cope.)

At the initial session Ramsey asked who had done Archbishop Fisher's portrait in Lambeth Palace, and Bruce replied, "The artist was A. R. Middleton-Todd, R.A."

The name interested Ramsey. He was fascinated by the initials reversed at the end to show the artist's membership in the Royal Academy. He repeated it over and over, "A. R. Middleton-Todd, R.A. Yes, yes! Well, Mr. Bruce, you shall be *my* A. R. Middleton-Todd, R.A.!"

Sometimes Ramsey fell asleep as he sat for the portrait. Awakening suddenly he would ask, "Am I all right? Have I moved too much?" Occasionally the Archbishop sang aloud. "There now, I couldn't have done *that* with Mr. A. R. Middleton-Todd, R.A."

During the Lambeth Conference weekends Bruce sometimes found at breakfast as many as five foreign bishops choosing between shredded wheat and cornflakes. After the conference Ramsey fell into brooding periods of thought as he sat for his portrait, and this became known to the artist as "the Lambeth Conference look."

Bruce sometimes accompanied Ramsey on visits to churches in Yorkshire. "Paine, the chauffeur, kept the Archbishop's car as clean as a watch, outside and inside," Bruce recalls. "The Archbishop would pull his purple lap-robe up over his knees and slide down in the seat, occasionally looking over the front seat to check the chauffeur's speed. When I told him one day how much I enjoyed his description of Solomon's Temple, he said that he had been imagining how he might have painted the Temple in watercolors. That was the beginning of his interest in painting. I gave him a set of watercolors to take to Dartmoor on holiday. Later he showed me the landscapes he had done. 'I loved dropping the paint in splattering blobs on the paper,' he told me."

Since the Archbishop could give only a few hours a week to the portrait, Bruce hunted for a stand-in. One of the gardeners obliged, but seemed swallowed up in the cope and the thronelike chair. Finally, a sixty-seven-year-old retired policeman, almost as large as the Archbishop, was persuaded to sit. He came regularly to fill the Archbishop's chair while Bruce painted the folds of the heavy cope and other details. The butler, Brindle, never lost the opportunity to ask, "Tea, Your Grace?"

Looking at the picture today, Bruce says, "The left foot protruding from the cope, *that* is the policeman's."

When the painting was finished Bruce had it carefully crated for shipment to London. It was included in an autumn exhibition of portraits of such notables as Sir Winston Churchill, Queen Elizabeth, and Pius XII. The art critic of the London *Times* observed sharply that there were on display "an unpleasantly smooth and characterless study of the Queen, and a scarcely more distinguished bronze of the Pope while Sir Jacob Epstein's 'Maria Donska' carries intensity of expression to extremes. . . . but a portrait of the Archbishop of York mingles formality and informality with conspicuous success."

On the day Ramsey was scheduled to view the portrait the gallery was held open after 5 P.M. Finally the Archbishop arrived, puffing and full of apologies. The lights were turned on and he saw the portrait in its handsome old Georgian frame. "Yes, yes, there I am!" he exclaimed. "And is there a portrait here by Mr. A. R. Middleton-Todd, R.A.?"

After the passing of Pius XII in November, 1958, Ramsey wrote in the *York Diocesan Leaflet* a penetrating and thoughtful tribute. "A few days ago the death of the Pope held the attention of millions throughout the world and stirred feelings beyond the members of the Roman Catholic Church," he said. "It is a sign of a greater Christian charity which is abroad in our times (despite our many failures to practice it) that the emotion of this event was allowed to reach across the ecclesiastical barriers, and that there were no inhibitions in the paying of tributes to a man undoubtedly good and great. The late Pope will have a big place in the history of the Roman church. It was in his time that a new dogma concerning the Blessed Virgin Mary was promulgated, which undoubtedly has sharpened the division between Roman and non-Roman Christianity. . . . But the impression made by the Pope, as he passed to his account and as the significance of his life was summed up, was one of saintliness and humility. It was for this good gift of God that thanks and praise were given. It is saintly lives which are the supreme witness of the Christian faith before the world."

Two occasions in the early summer of 1959 dramatically demonstrated Ramsey's versatility as a modern shepherd of the flock. When he took part in a clerical conference at one of the sprawling Butlin Holiday Camps, Yorkshiremen felt that here was an Archbishop with the common touch. Later they saw an entirely different Ramsey—serious and reverent as he led a pilgrimage to the Holy Island of Lindisfarne.

The Yorkshire Post headline read: ARCHBISHOP BOOKS IN AT BUTLIN'S. A few days later the readers smiled to see pictures of His Grace against the background of streaming banners and swimming pools of the resort. The cottages of the Butlin's Camp at Filey in Yorkshire accommodated the two hundred and seventy-five priests who came to discuss theological issues as well as the problems of working with the very people who had responded to the Butlin advertisement, "Fun for Everyone." In their spare time the clergy strolled about the camp with the teeming crowds of shopkeepers and factory workers and their families on holiday. Ramsey was photographed riding on the miniature railroad with a group of children.

Billy Butlin, who has always provided a resident Church of England "padre" for every camp, came personally to meet the Archbishop. Since then the camp brochure has featured color pictures of Butlin shaking hands with the Archbishop. It implies Church approval of budget vacations en masse.

The second occasion, the pilgrimage to the Holy Island of Lindisfarne, was an unforgettable spectacle. The island is separated from the coast of Northumberland by a stretch of sand covered by the sea at high tide. Ramsey had led his first pilgrimage in 1955 when he was Bishop of Durham. This second pilgrimage drew more than two thousand persons, the largest group since the war. They crossed at low tide following the "Pilgrim's Way," which is believed to have been the route of St. Aidan when he landed on the island in 635 as a missionary from Iona.

Most modern prelates had chosen to ride in motorcars during their pilgrimages, but Archbishop Ramsey walked barefoot at the head of a procession so long that it stretched out of sight on the mainland. His chaplain, Martin Kaye, walked ahead of him, bearing the Primatial Cross of York. Ramsey wore a cassock and the four-cornered velvet "Canterbury cap," or English biretta, and carried his pastoral staff. While many stopped to replace their footwear upon reaching the island, the Archbishop strode on barefoot along the stony road to the village.

In the ruins of the old Priory twelve nuns had kept an all-night watch. They were members of the Order of the Holy Paraclete, a large and thriving Anglican sisterhood founded in 1914 as a successor to the ancient monastic community ruled by the Abbess of Whitby, St. Hilda. The voices of a choir of five hundred voices rang out during Solemn Evensong in the ruins of the Priory where St. Aidan and St. Cuthbert had lived and prayed. *"Praise the Lord, O my soul; and all that is within me, praise his holy Name. . . ."*

After the dramatic pilgrimage to Holy Island, Ramsey turned again to Dartmoor for a quiet holiday. During this vacation he completed his masterful study of Anglican theology of the last half century. It spanned the eventful years from Charles Gore, a dominant figure, to the beginning of World War II when Archbishop William Temple was at the height of his influence. *From Gore to Temple* became the title of this comprehensive survey. Ramsey concluded that "there has been in recent years much striving after order and tidiness. But the theological coherence which a Gore or a Temple exhibited came, not from a quest of tidiness, but from a vigorous wrestling with truth for truth's own sake. Without such theological coherence, the Church's moral witness may appear as piecemeal bits of moralizing, and the majestic unity of the Church's faith may be too faintly made visible."

Ramsey's analysis of Anglican thought formed the basis of the Hale Memorial Lectures he was invited to deliver at Seabury-

Western Theological Seminary in Evanston, Illinois. Preliminary arrangements had been made during the Lambeth Conference when Ramsey met several times with Seabury-Western's Dean, the Very Rev. Charles U. Harris.

While in London Dean Harris and his wife had given a dinner party for the Ramseys at the Mayfair Hotel. It was the beginning of a close friendship between the American couple and the Ramseys. "The dinner was lovely, but I had forgotten that London hotels are not air conditioned, even in July," says Janet Harris.

The Ramseys sailed for the United States in October, 1959. It was Mrs. Ramsey's first visit to America and her husband's third. Once again he saw Lake Michigan and the pleasant suburb of Evanston which he had known first during the Cambridge debate tour of 1925 and again in 1954 when the city had been host to the World Council of Churches.

Ramsey's four lectures in Evanston drew several hundred people every evening. They were given at Garrett Biblical Institute, the Methodist seminary, which has a larger chapel than Seabury-Western.

The Archbishop spent his mornings browsing in the seminary library and chatting informally with the students. Although he did not eat with them in the refectory, he endeared himself to the men by granting them an exclusive tutorial. Neither the graduate students nor the faculty were allowed to intrude. He discussed practical and theological questions with them for two hours. And he expressed again his dismay that the American Church leaves the support of its seminaries to voluntary contributions.

In private conversations with Dean Harris, the Archbishop thought it was unlikely he would be asked to succeed Geoffrey Fisher. There were many factors, he said, including the lack of understanding about his devotion to Anglo-Catholic traditions.

The Chicago press played up Ramsey's presence in Evanston, sometimes called "the Athens of the Midwest." The title Archbishop of York was ancient and impressive to American ears. The man who bore the title was, indeed, a splendid ecclesiastical figure with intelligent and quotable comments on the issues of the day.

At a news conference in the University Club in downtown Chicago, the reporters asked a variety of questions on Roman

Catholicism, Billy Graham, British politics, and Khrushchev, who had just finished his first visit to the United States.

Pope John XXIII's plans for an ecumenical conference, the first in many years, had been disclosed the previous January. When asked if such a council might be an instrument for Christian reunion, Ramsey said, "It is now clear all that is intended is a council of the Roman Catholic Church, because the Roman Catholic Church claims alone to be the Christian church in the world. I don't think it has nearly the significance it seemed to have to some people when the news was first reported—and misreported. On the other hand, the present Pope seems to be one of great Christian good will, filled with the spirit of Christian charity, and of course where Christian charity exists the results are quite incalculable."

Persisting in their questions, the American reporters even imagined that Ramsey might be asked to address the Vatican conference. This was highly unlikely, of course, but Ramsey dealt patiently with the question. "Yes, I would accept on the same principle that I would address any Christian group. I would tell them that I would be willing to accept the Pope as a presiding bishop, but not as infallible. I would be willing to call him *primus inter pares,* first among equals." (This is the same position accorded the Archbishop of Canterbury in the Anglican Communion.)

Only once during the news conference did the reporters consider Ramsey evasive. This was when a reporter asked if he was High Church or Low Church. When the newsmen attempted to cross-examine him, he repeated for a second time, "I am the Archbishop of York and father in God to the whole Church."

The *Chicago American* described Ramsey as "a tall, ruddy, jovial man who never lost his composure as reporters flung questions at him." The weekly Episcopal magazine, *The Living Church,* found him "gray, gay, and forthright." One reporter, Dolores McCahill of the *Chicago Sun-Times,* took up the subject of Ramsey's churchmanship with Dean Harris and reported, "His host . . . afterward said Dr. Ramsey probably could be regarded as High in churchmanship."

The following Sunday, the Feast of Christ the King, the Archbishop was the guest preacher at St. Luke's Church in Evanston.

"On the way to St. Luke's the Archbishop asked me what might be expected of him in the way of ceremonial," Dean Harris recalls. "When I replied that St. Luke's was the leading Anglo-Catholic parish between the East and West coasts, the Archbishop said, 'You don't suppose they'll greet me with *Ecce Sacerdos Magnus,* do you?' On arrival at the church I took my place in the sanctuary and heard, to my surprise, the sound of kettledrums, then trumpets, and finally the organ in a full blast especially written for the occasion. Then, believe it or not, I heard *Ecce Sacerdos Magnus*—'Behold the Mighty Prelate.'"

Under a blue-and-silver canopy the Archbishop walked in procession to the high altar. There a *prie-dieu* draped in cloth-of-gold awaited him alongside a table bearing a tall gold mitre. He knelt in prayer—for so long that the service was thrown off schedule. But the American clergy were undaunted. During solemn high mass they brought forth several mitres for Ramsey to wear and unabashedly took them on and off his head as the ceremony progressed. Even so, everyone agreed afterward that the ceremonial had been most impressive and moving. Later that day the Evensong at St. James' Cathedral on Chicago's north side seemed almost anticlimactic in its adherence to simpler observances.

Ramsey was the preacher at the service which opened the 125th anniversary of the Diocese of Chicago. He was already a favorite subject for television crews, and in the cathedral service they closed in upon him with merciless close-range cameras. All Chicago smiled as the Archbishop, standing before the high altar, was seen unconsciously digging for a handkerchief beneath his vestments.

At its 102nd Convocation Seabury-Western bestowed on Ramsey an honorary Doctorate of Sacred Theology. The ceremony in the seminary chapel was an impressive one with the entire faculty grouped around the Dean's chair to give their assent to the conferring of the degree. Dean Harris acknowledges in his North Carolina drawl that he was more than a little awed at the sight of an Archbishop kneeling before him to receive the degree. There was only one lapse—instead of a doctor's hood there was passed to the Dean a bachelor's hood almost too small to fit over the Archbishop's shoulders.

Evenings at Evanston were spent quietly in the Harris home.

Except for noisy greetings by reporters and cameramen, the Ramseys were spared the speeding police escorts and screaming sirens which had disturbed the last Archbishop of York, Cyril Garbett, on his visit to Chicago in 1944.

Before sailing for England the Ramseys spent a few days in New York as the guests of Dean Lawrence Rose and Mrs. Rose at General Theological Seminary in Chelsea Square on Manhattan's west side. Ramsey had three engagements—to preach on Sunday in the Cathedral of St. John the Divine, to address the Church Club of New York at a dinner meeting at the Hotel Plaza, and to conduct a brief retreat for the clergy of the Diocese of New York.

"I thought I was to talk to the clergy about the Old Testament and the New Testament," recalls Ramsey. "But I discovered on arrival at the meeting that they were having a Quiet Day. I scrapped my lecture and during the morning service I improvised a new meditation and made a 'mental map' of what to say."

Among those present was a bright-eyed young English priest, the Rev. John Andrew, who had been first in line in Ramsey's initial ordination service on becoming Archbishop of York. Andrew was a curate at St. George's-by-the-River in Rumson, New Jersey. "Do you know!" he exclaims. "Do you know that talkative, *chatty* New York clergy sat *absolutely still* throughout the Archbishop's meditation."

Ramsey's address to the Church Club of New York, which includes the leading Episcopal laymen of the area, brought a mixed reaction. Some felt he leaned disconcertingly on his chair as he spoke, indicating he was worn out from his American visit. One clergyman believes Ramsey was in a playful mood that evening. Still another feels that the older members of the club compared him unfavorably with Archbishop William Temple who had addressed them years ago.

The Ramseys sailed the next day aboard the *Queen Elizabeth*. In a shipboard interview reporters asked about the Archbishop's stand on birth control. This seemed a favorite question with newsmen, at home and abroad, a provocative inquiry which pinpointed one of the differences in Anglican and Roman doctrine. Ramsey was asked to comment on historian Arnold Toynbee's recent statement that birth control should be used to avert world famine.

As he had in Chicago, Ramsey again referred to the statement of the Anglican bishops of the 1958 Lambeth Conference. He pointed out their "definite approval of contraceptives in the service of Christian family planning." He added his own belief that "it is utterly wrong for couples to marry with the intention of avoiding or postponing parenthood. I am concerned at the use of contraceptives for promiscuity. As for families, several children make a better family than one child but it is quite impossible to lay down any set rule. The economic situation should be one of the determining factors. I think restriction of population is inevitable and right."

The persistent questioning of newsmen in interviews in Chicago and New York put Ramsey on record about a number of pertinent issues. There emerged a picture of a modern Archbishop who tinged his religious thinking with realism. He matched a variety of questions with a variety of answers on matters spiritual, political, topical, and sometimes trivial.

On faith-healing: "There has been a revival in the Church of England of the ministry of healing. We are anxious that the gifts of healing in the Church should be used with emphasis on the restoration of the whole personality, body, soul, and spirit, to the peace of God, and to avoid isolating bodily healing as a stunt."

On the task of the Church: "First, really worshiping God and helping other people to worship and pray. Second, the effective presentation of the Gospel to the people in every way possible."

On the preference of some Anglicans for Roman Catholic forms of worship: "What I would emphasize is that there is much less party spirit than there used to be. The Church is finding more unity between Catholic and Evangelical factions."

On Billy Graham's meetings in London: "The Graham crusade produced a number of converts to Christianity. I don't know how much it strengthened the fundamentalist cause, [which] I regard as harmful. It did bring some converts, but it repelled many thoughtful people who can't hold such impossible Biblical views."

On Premier Khrushchev's visit to the United States: "We must elicit the love of peace which is in every human heart. We must get past ideology to the individual. His visit to the United States has done something to get foreign affairs into the human wavelength and off the ideological wave-length. No human being is a

100 per cent liar. We can come to know when he tells the truth through greater familiarity with the man. The more coming and going the better."

On the unity of nations: "A sovereign superstate is neither possible nor desirable. However, the sort of international unity which we have among the Atlantic Treaty nations should be intensified, and there must be some willingness to limit sovereignty in the interest of peace. Nations must be willing to abide by international agreements even when, as in such issues as disarmament, it is inconvenient. This is necessary to make peace possible, and this will be the great Christian issue in world affairs."

On Princess Margaret and her renounced love for a divorced man: "She is a devoted Christian woman. I am sure her future will be spent in serving her country, her God, and the Church."

On modern man: "Both in England and America I notice that minds are not happy unless they're on the dance, getting a snippet of this and a snippet of that, a snippet of music, a snippet of literature or a magazine article, a snippet of television. They can't remain long on one subject. Our preoccupation with making money is a terrible thing. It's a form of mental habit."

On rare roast beef: "America can teach us something in this department."

On Yorkshire pudding prepared for a visiting Archbishop of York: "M-m-m-m!"

As he was finishing a celebration of the Holy Communion in the chapel at Bishopthorpe, one morning upon his return from the United States, Ramsey's glasses fell from his cassock pocket and shattered on the marble floor. It was an annoying incident, for considerable reading and paperwork awaited the Archbishop after his absence. He went immediately to be fitted for new glasses. In the routine examination the doctor discovered a hardening of the eyeball.

For the next few weeks Ramsey used a special prescription of eyedrops several times a day. But early in the new year, 1960, it was apparent that an operation was inevitable. On February 15 the newspapers were given an announcement disclosing that "the Archbishop of York will have a minor eye operation at the end of the week, and has cancelled immediate engagements."

The condition had been diagnosed as glaucoma of both eyes. Ramsey underwent surgery in a York nursing home on February 20 and again five days later.

Not until March 3 did the seriousness of the operation become known. On that day a London newspaper headlined, PRIMATE'S SIGHT IS SAVED. In three more weeks Ramsey was able to dispense with bandages and resume much of his work. There was a great deal to do, for he had long ago committed himself to spend six weeks traveling in Africa during the centenary of the Universities' Mission to Central Africa (UMCA).

The churches of Yorkshire were still fragrant with the flowers of Easter when Ramsey left Bishopthorpe on April 19, 1960, to begin his African tour. Accompanied by his chaplain, Martin Kaye, he flew at nine o'clock that evening from London Airport. As the plane headed out over the English Channel, he remembered the missionaries who had a century before endured many hardships in traversing in weeks the distance which now was covered within the span of a single day. Reviewing his itinerary as the plane reached the African coast, Ramsey found that such names as Zanzibar, Muheza, and Songea stood out as exotically as the winding rivers and lakes he spotted in the green jungles far below.

The plane touched down at Salisbury and then flew on to Ndola. Here in the rich copperbelt area the Diocese of Northern Rhodesia was celebrating a "double jubilee"—the fiftieth anniversary of its organization and the centenary of the UMCA.

A day's activities in Africa began very early in the morning. Ramsey customarily celebrated the Eucharist at six or seven o'clock, a gentle breeze stirring the altar cloth and his vestments in the last hour before the start of the oppressive heat. There usually followed a busy schedule of confirmations, blessings and dedication of church buildings, visits to schools and hospitals, tree plantings, civic luncheons, and that English institution which flourishes unimpaired in the heart of Africa—the garden party. The guest lists frequently included the Roman Catholic bishop as well as missionaries of many denominations.

Most days ended with observance of Solemn Evensong. More often than not it was sung at outdoor altars with the African sunset a magnificent backdrop. Congregations ranged from a hundred to three thousand.

One of the most significant services was Ramsey's dedication of a twenty-foot metal cross marking the site of the initial mission station established a hundred years before by the UMCA's first band of priests. Here in Nyasaland, on the edge of the Palombe Plain, in view of the towering mass of Mlanje Mountains where the abrupt curve of a small river gave them shelter on three sides from savages and wild beasts, the first missionaries had established their camp. And it is here that the only known grave of those pioneers, that of Father Henry de Wint Burrup, is found, shaded now by blue-gum trees.

Another memorable service took place at Kota Kota under a huge fig tree that had sheltered David Livingstone's camp a century ago. Appropriately, Ramsey chose as his text, "Now let us praise famous men."

After the Kota Kota service Ramsey was scheduled to visit the Anglican cathedral on Likoma Island in the middle of huge Lake Nyasa. The Nyasaland Railroad had provided a forty-six-foot launch to take the Archbishop on the seven-hour trip to the island. The day dawned stormily, the lake tossing up high waves. The boat captain sent repeated messages of the necessity of delaying the trip—first until nine, then eleven, and again at one and three. At last the launch got underway at eight the next morning but was forced to turn back within two hours. The island trip had to be canceled. There was no telephone or telegraph for communication. Ramsey and his hosts could only hope the islanders would hear on the wireless of the change in plans. (Days later it was learned that the broadcast had reached the island.) The parishioners, having prepared for months for the Archbishop's visit, were enormously disappointed. Their only consolation was in listening to Princess Margaret's wedding which was taking place that day in Westminster Abbey.

At every stop there was evidence of careful planning for the Archbishop's visit. One parish had formed a club called "The Children of the Archbishop" which, five months in advance, had planted flower beds and begun to clear wide paths. The pupils and their teachers had oiled and polished woodwork, washed and ironed curtains, and "distempered" rooms. Manners and conversations were perfected too. On the floor of a church Ramsey visited was found a slip of paper that showed at least one native had spent some time learning a greeting in English. It was a penciled note that read, "Guud aftanuun Yoa Gres."

Much of the trip was by automobile over rough roads. When the car broke down, Ramsey clambered out with the others to give it a push or help change a tire. Frequently, small groups waited at the roadside for the Archbishop's blessing. While driving through a game reserve the car struck a bump and Ramsey's attaché case, containing the sermons for the entire tour, was thrown out of the trunk. A native found it and passed it on to a game warden who eventually returned it to Ramsey's chaplain. The whole chain of events was considered a near miracle.

On long air hops Ramsey saw sun-scorched stretches of the countryside with scattered colonies of grass-roofed houses amid palm groves. Sometimes the pilots swooped low over rivers so that the Archbishop might have a better view of the crocodiles, hippopotamuses, and elephants.

A letter from Denis Foote, a layman of St. Peter's Church at Lilongwe in Nyasaland, gives a picture of Ramsey through a colonial's eyes: "A massive figure in purple cassock and, at a distance, a benign, almost childlike countenance; close, deep-set but incredibly keen and shrewd eyes and a powerful chin."

The letter continues: "The sunlit gardens of the Provincial Commissioner's residence, tea tables under the trees with the communicants of the Anglican Church, Africans and Europeans, and His Grace moving from group to group. . . . The Roman Catholic Bishop of Lilongwe and the head of the Dutch Reformed Church Mission were also there. After an all too brief hour, a move down the hill to St. Peter's Church for Evensong. A minute vestry full of ecclesiastics—the Archbishop and his chaplain, also the Bishop of Nyasaland, the Archdeacon of Kota Kota, our African Catechist; the little church with its normal seating capacity of about eighty increased to just over a hundred chairs from the Boma nearby. The Archbishop's sermon spoken from the steps of the Sanctuary (St. Peter's has no pulpit—only a lectern), clear, simple, stopping every few sentences for one of the African members of the Church Council to translate into Chinyanja. Then the hymn, 'Now Thank We All Our God' and the blessing from the Archbishop, impressive in cope and mitre.

"Later that evening supper for twenty-odd at a Churchwarden's house and the opportunity for real talk with the Archbishop. A happy, friendly afternoon and evening."

The letter concludes: "St. Peter's swept and garnished at 5:30 the next morning. (Our young African verger said he was there at three o'clock lest he might be late.) . . . Dawn still lighting the sky. An early confession being heard of a visitor from sixty miles away, and the first African members of the congregation moving in, then an increasing flow. The Eucharist beautifully enunciated by the Archbishop. Black and white side by side at the altar rails with the Bishop assisting the Archbishop in administering. Again the Blessing—to us all most moving, and then talk on the lawn outside the porch, many kneeling to be blessed. Farewells, and a seven-mile drive to the airport where a Beaver of Central Africa Airways named 'Duiker' was waiting to take the Archbishop, Bishop and Chaplain to Mponda', the headquarters of the UMCA. Sharp at eight o'clock the plane was in the blue sky and away. . . ."

At Malindi Station in Nyasaland, Ramsey's tour ran into trouble. As he put it later in a review of the trip, "The word had been passed round that I was a 'Federation Archbishop,' whatever that may mean." Only twenty people turned out to greet him. But in the afternoon, when he arrived by launch at Fort Johnston, he had an impressive welcome. "A large crowd lined the beach, and as His Grace disembarked everybody sank to the ground for his blessing and then the singing started," a mission priest reported. "He was completely surrounded by people thronging to kiss his ring."

Generous, unusual presents awaited Ramsey at almost every stop. He received a huge ivory tusk and a total of three ebony walking sticks. A native chief gave him a flower-pot stand of carved ebony. And frequently, members of a Mother's Union approached the Archbishop, marching under their banner and carrying a tray of eggs. In one day Ramsey received a hundred eggs and twenty *zawadi* (chickens). But the most touching gift of all was a beautiful ebony crucifix presented by the children of Mkomaindo School in Tanganyika. As it was borne forward the children sang, "Were You There When They Crucified My Lord?"

Ramsey, obviously moved, told the group, "I shall find a special
place for this in my chapel at home. . . . It will tell me again and
again that the Lord Jesus died for the people of Africa, and seeing
that, I will pray again and again for you before this crucifix."

A few days later another parish presented Ramsey with a pair
of carved ebony candlesticks that perfectly matched the crucifix.
Still another memorable ceremony was the presentation of a Bible
in the native language, Swahili, as the congregation sang also in
this native tongue the hymn "Stand Up, Stand Up, for Jesus."

Almost as moving in its simplicity was a song a group of children composed for Ramsey's visit to their school:

> We are very happy today,
> To see the Archbishop of York.
> You have come from a very long way away,
> We welcome you here to our school.
> We thank you for all your work,
> And your help to the UMCA,
> Your Grace, the Archbishop of York,
> We are glad to see you today.

Once the ceremonials were over the local bishops entertained
Ramsey at dinners carefully planned and served by natives.
(A typical menu: chilled papaw and limes, fried fish covered with cheese sauce and decorated with tomatoes, anchovies
and olives, a salad of African fruits, coffee—and sometimes a
cherished bottle of Portuguese white wine.)

The trip had its humorous incidents. Ramsey himself confessed
to a short-cut in language. "When I wanted to say 'thank you'—
which is *Mara Haba*—I just muttered 'Mother Hubbard.' "

More than once the mitre loaned Ramsey was too small and he
wore it perched precariously over his perspiring brow.

One priest wrote to UMCA headquarters in London, "I wish
there was some outstanding incident I could tell you about. All
that occurs to me is that the Archbishop confirmed someone
Tomato instead of Tomaso, and he had a mild struggle in the
sanctuary with one of our priests who insisted on his wearing the
amice round his neck, and the Archbishop insisted on putting it
over his head."

The six weeks in Africa passed as a colorful pageant of one
impressive service after another. Vast congregations of Africans,

Asians, and Europeans heard the Archbishop's sermons in English and in translations to Swahili and Chinyanja. He greeted thousands who never before had seen an Archbishop, and he called on officials ranging in rank from tribal chiefs to the Sultan of Zanzibar.

Ramsey stepped from a plane at London Airport on June 1 carrying one of the beautifully carved ebony walking sticks as a memento of his trip. He returned from Africa at a time when the continent was moving into a new and powerful position of independence and influence. Great changes were afoot politically: in another year the Union of South Africa would withdraw from the Commonwealth, and Tanganyika and other states would establish their own governments. Religious autonomy also was being realized. Within a few weeks the Archbishop of Canterbury, Geoffrey Fisher, would officiate at ceremonies creating the new Province of East Africa.

"For all the vastness of the distances, and the isolation of any African tribe or village from the world, there is the intuitive awareness in the people that Africa is one, and the fate of one part of it quickly affects the other parts," Ramsey said. "Hence Africa is literally crucial for the Christian Church in the world. There is still time, if the service of Christian resources and of Christian lives can be given, for great victories of Christian faith to be won."

In an address to the York Convocation, Ramsey told of his visit to the six African dioceses. "In hours in a little four-seater aircraft flying low, I saw the country in its fascinating variety of mountain and plain," he said. "In hours on roads, so called, I saw many mission stations and villages. What scenes they were, never to be forgotten. And they all add up to this, that in the midst of the surge of nationalistic emotion, tinged as it can be with an anti-European feeling, African Christianity is tough, loyal, zealous, enthusiastic, the fruit of the heroic saintliness of a century."

Ramsey's vivid memory ranged over the whole six weeks of his trip. "I see places by the roadside where African Christians have come many miles to meet me, just because I have come to join them in thanking God for their Christian faith. . . . I see crowds waiting in their little churches of mud and wood to sing a *Te Deum* in their own tongue and to ask for a word of exhortation and a blessing. I see hospitals, sometimes badly needing better equipment—but that is our reproach—unlike other hospitals because the love of God for God's children has been their conscious motive through the years. I see African catechists teaching their little flocks in remote villages in the bush until, all too rarely, a priest comes with the Sacraments. . . . Most moving of all, I see, at very early hours in the morning, churches crowded with worshipers and communicants, knowing and loving every movement, every syllable, of the liturgy in their own tongue, and loving the Lord who feeds them with the heavenly food. All this we saw, again and again, from Lusaka in Rhodesia right on to Dar es Salaam, the island of Zanzibar, and the borders of Kenya where our safari ended."

After fulfilling several engagements—entertaining the Queen Mother for tea at Bishopthorpe, receiving an honorary degree from Oxford, attending an ecumenical conference at St. Andrew's University—the Archbishop began a holiday in southwest England. There appeared on August 25, 1960, in the widely circulated *Daily Mail,* a simple headline, THE HOLIDAY-MAKER, and an uncaptioned picture of a heavy-set man striding with a cane in hand. The article read:

"He arrived with his wife by car and immediately blended with the Dartmoor scene. Tweed cap, loosely-knotted tie, comfortable sports jacket, baggy grey flannels. Just an ordinary holidaymaker. An engineer perhaps.

"The local gymkhana and fete amused him greatly. He had three-goes-for-sixpence on the hoop-la. No luck. He tried the coconut shies. No luck. He took it all in good part.

"In the evenings, although his simple room had a TV set, he liked to come down to the timbered bar and chat with the farm-workers and holidaymakers over their pints.

"*An agreeable chap, they decided.*

"On Sundays he strolled over to Holne Parish Church to listen to a simple sermon by the vicar.

"*The stranger was a good-living chap, too, they decided.*

"Most of them still don't know he is the Most Rev. and Right Hon. Arthur Michael Ramsey, D.D., fifty-five-year-old Archbishop of York."

The Archbishop in mufti took long walks over the Dartmoor hills he knew so well from his two previous summers there. In the quiet afternoons he relaxed with his watercolors, painting in bold strokes the rolling landscapes. And in the evenings as he talked with villagers and others on holiday, he heard more and more about television as a favorite pastime. He was reminded of the questions he had posed in the York Convocation, "Are we as a Christian Church doing a fraction of what we should in meeting men of knowledge on their own ground? If we are, is it made apparent everywhere, on television, on radio, in every place where people exchange knowledge and thought?"

In September when Associated Rediffusion (Britain's second television network) asked him to appear on a telecast from Bishopthorpe, he readily agreed. Entitled "The Pursuit of Happiness," the program was notable for Ramsey's thoughtful answers to an almost hostile line of questioning which bordered on the highly personal. The Archbishop was seated in an armchair in the formal drawing room lined with portraits of his predecessors. He faced the network's interviewer, Dan Farson, an ebullient freckle-faced man in his middle thirties.

Farson [speaking first]: Your Grace, I know this is difficult, but would you define happiness?

Ramsey [at once acknowledging the superficial aspects of dealing with so large a subject in a half-hour]: I couldn't define it. [Then he proceeded to do exactly that.] What I know it as is a sort of serenity that's always there notwithstanding a person's environment. There are plenty of people who are happy if they've got this and that . . . to bolster them up and give them satisfaction. The people to be envied are those who have the sort of serenity which they carry with them to any sort of environment.

Farson: But in the state of the world today, there's a great deal to be unhappy about, isn't there?

Ramsey: Certainly, but I'm a Christian and that means that one feels the state of the world, not less than other people, but sometimes rather more. I'm not for any ostriching about the state of the world; but a Christian, while feeling it intensely, and having a kind of quickened, sensitive sympathy, also has a kind of inner-serenity that he brings to bear upon it. . . . I don't think religion is a sort of cult of happiness. Religion is loving and serving God. And loving and serving your neighbors and forgetting yourself in the process. And, of course, a person who is really self-forgetful has a chance of being immensely happy, but happiness is a by-product. . . . I think that Christianity has got a conception of happiness more consistent in its general applicability to the human race. . . . A sort of happiness that can make sense of life and make sense of life's tragedies, a happiness that is properly balanced between the here and the hereafter.

[The discussion turned to the Church of England with Farson asking about its supposed lack of "appeal and attraction for the public."]

Ramsey: I don't know that the Church of itself has ever had appeal and attraction. The Church is there to be bringing the people to something far greater than itself, namely God.

Farson: Wouldn't you say, also, that the image of the Church today is an extremely unattractive one, particularly to young people, that it's one of discipline and criticism and coldness?

Ramsey: It depends where they get the image from. If they get the image from impressions through press and radio, I've no doubt it's depressing. If they get their image, say, from some of the really live parish churches which I've seen, where simply marvellous work is being done and the people are a real Christian fellowship, it would be very different. And it seems to me to be our task to prevent the dissemination of bad images and to see that those good images, which doubtlessly do exist, are brought into sight.

Farson: How can you do that?

Ramsey: Well, in all sorts of ways, all along the line. The more effective use of this game of TV, which I try to do now, is one of them."

Farson: As a matter of fact, sir, you use the word depressing.

Ramsey: In some aspects it is, to some people. They do not have a total image.

Farson: But when you say to some people, don't you think most people?

Ramsey: Most people I would say weren't interested, knew

nothing and probably hadn't much image at all.

Farson: Isn't this a failure then on the part of the Church that worries you greatly? The fact that most people don't care?

Ramsey: Yes. If all the members of the Church were superb Christians, the impact of the Church would be infinitely greater.

Farson: But the impact of the Roman Catholic Church, at the moment, is greater isn't it?

Ramsey: Greater than that of the Church of England—er—not as far as I know.

Farson: Surely as regards the amount of converts it is.

Ramsey: Have you got the figures?

Farson: No, I haven't . . .

Ramsey: Well, if you looked at the figures both ways you wouldn't be so assured about that I'm sure.

Farson: But don't you think though, at the moment, the Roman Catholic Church has been able to catch the imagination of the people far more than the Church of England?

Ramsey: I think that a minority Church that isn't the established "show" is very often at an advantage in capturing the imagination. . . .

Farson: Are you conscious of any failures in your life?

Ramsey: Oh, perpetually conscious of failures. For instance, when I'm dealing with somebody who needs sympathy, I wish I had more sympathy. When I'm having a discussion with you I wish I was cleverer and quicker. In every situation I regret that one doesn't do better.

Farson: What is the most difficult question that you've ever had to answer?

Ramsey: I can't remember. None of yours.

[In the last minutes of the program, the discussion returned to the subject of happiness.]

Ramsey: I think the secret of happiness is faith in God. I honestly attribute my own happiness to that, because it . . . enables me to be happy not only in quite cheerful or harmless circumstances like the present but in circumstances which aren't naturally cheerful. . . . Beneath moments of unhappiness there is a sort of deep well that one can draw upon.

Farson: If you were able to sum up the meaning of life in one word, which word would you choose?

Ramsey: Loving and serving God and other people for His sake, to the best of one's feeble powers.

[Here the program ended. It had run its allotted time. But the transcribed copy of the whole interview, taken from the files of Associated Rediffusion at Television House in London, reveals that the conversation concluded with an additional question.]

Farson: Would you like to become Archbishop of Canterbury?

Ramsey [promptly, but with a hint of weariness]: No, not a bit, not a bit.

Farson: But you wouldn't refuse?

Ramsey: Well, that's a hypothesis. We're discussing facts, not hypotheses.

Proud, nationalistic Scotland often has been perilous ground for prelates of the Church of England. Ramsey's sermon in Edinburgh on October 9, 1960, was no exception.

Preaching in St. Mary's Cathedral, on the four hundredth anniversary of the Reformation, Ramsey acknowledged that "the Presbyterian tradition can teach us things about the integration of ministries in the Church and the laity." He added, however, that there are "precedents in seventeenth-century Scotland for an episcopate working in a presbyterial setting, for a presbyterianism by no means ruthlessly hostile to the role of the bishop." And he decried the "loss of much sacramental life, the loss of historic succession of the Church's ministry, and the loss of the Christian year with the festivals beloved by Christians of all ages."

Aware that such statements are unusually controversial in Scotland, Ramsey was careful to say that "in appealing to Scripture as the supreme authority in doctrine, we appeal also to creed, episcopate, sacraments, to the whole treasure of antiquity. . . . It is an appeal not national or sectional or denominational at all."

Despite this preface, the sermon immediately aroused the Scottish Presbyterians when reported outside the cathedral. Four days later it came under direct attack in a meeting of the General Assembly of the Church of Scotland.

"We are bound to remember that this Kirk of Scotland is a Church of the Reformation," Sir Thomas Taylor, principal of Aberdeen University, told the Assembly. ". . . Whatever may be said elsewhere by His Grace, the Archbishop of York, or others . . . . we in this hall are not the least inclined to disown our heritage because our fathers, for good reason, set little store by the observance of the Christian year."

Sir Thomas' speech was greeted with loud applause.

"Just because we are a Church of the Reformation, there are certain things that we affirm and others that we deny," he continued. "In particular we repudiate the Mass and we reject Mariolatry in their Roman Catholic, or Anglo-Catholic, or Scoto-Catholic form."

As for Ramsey's suggestion that bishops might function in Presbyterianism, Sir Thomas declared that "in place of a hierarchical system we have in our Kirk a democratic, an egalitarian policy which means that there is parity among all ministers—no more bishops, no deans, and no coat-of-arms. . . ."

The educator's speech was regarded as a fighting answer to the Archbishop, but it was tempered with Scottish humor and a belief the Presbyterians should draw near "in Christian charity" to Anglicans and Roman Catholics. That, in itself, was a long stride. As for the Archbishop, he had eloquently stated his evaluation of a Christian heritage and what might be learned in re-examining the Reformation across four hundred years. It was all a part of the candid statements and opinions necessary to clarify and cleanse the rarefied air of ecumenical progress.

When Geoffrey Fisher disclosed in November, 1960, that he would visit the Vatican en route home from a journey to the Holy Land, the BBC immediately extended an invitation for Fisher to come directly to their studios, on reaching London, to discuss the significance of this first meeting between an Archbishop of Canterbury and a Pope in nearly six hundred years.

"Fisher declined our invitation," says Oliver Hunkin, the producer, one of several Church of England clergymen on the BBC staff. "Apparently he did not think he would show good taste in appearing on television to discuss his private meeting with John XXIII. We had hoped to have Archbishop Fisher and

Britain's highest ranking Roman Catholic prelate, the Cardinal Archbishop of Westminster. When that became impossible, we invited Ramsey to appear with Dr. J. C. Heenan, the Roman Catholic Archbishop of Liverpool. It wasn't easy to arrange, but we did it."

Whether suggested by Lambeth Palace or originated by the BBC, the idea of pairing Ramsey and Heenan was an excellent one, for the two were old friends. In an international meeting at Oxford in September, 1957, they had solved the question of precedence by approaching their seats together, bowing to each other, and sitting down together amid a storm of applause from an audience of six hundred persons.

On Sunday evening, December 4, two days after the historic meeting in Rome, Britons saw on their television screens the program title, *Meeting Point—Rome and Canterbury,* accompanied by the coat-of-arms of the Vatican and of Canterbury. The moderator, Kenneth Harris of *The Observer,* introduced first Ramsey, then Heenan. Turning to Ramsey, Harris said, "May I begin by asking you what are your impressions at the moment of the meeting of the Archbishop with the Pope?"

Ramsey leaned forward, speaking eagerly: "Well, I think that great meeting has given tremendous public expression to something that has already long been warming up in the hearts of Christian people everywhere."

Heenan spoke up immediately: "Your Grace, I very much doubt whether most people realize that. You know, they think that this is more or less a put-up job. You know, it's in the news at the moment, all this meeting together . . ."

Ramsey's enthusiasm for the meeting and Heenan's friendly observance of episcopal etiquette—addressing his old friend as "Your Grace"—created a cordial and sincere mood that underscored their remarks. The two men faced each other, Ramsey in his purple cassock, and Heenan wearing the full cassock, cape, and zucchetto [skullcap] of a Roman Catholic bishop, his glasses occasionally reflecting the lights of the television studio. They spoke of their agreement on common baptism and other issues, and of their tolerance for each other's viewpoint.

In the first direct reference to the historic call at the Vatican, Ramsey pointed out "the field is wider than just the Church of

Rome, Church of England. . . . The Archbishop of Canterbury went [on the same trip] to Jerusalem, and to Constantinople, and to the Eastern Orthodox Church."

Fingering a cross he was wearing with his customary pectoral cross, Ramsey said, "We Anglicans have very warm feelings toward the Eastern Orthodox Church, believing it also to be a true part of the one Catholic Church with us. This cross was given to me by the Patriarch of Moscow . . ."

Smiling, Heenan interrupted: "Well, I can't, Your Grace, possibly allow you to parade your jewelry without just a little of my own." Heenan held up his hand. ". . . This ring belonged to the last [Roman] Catholic Archbishop of Canterbury, Cardinal Pole, and therefore it's a treasure as that [cross] is, I'm sure, a treasure to you . . ."

After this interlude, Ramsey again took up the significance of Fisher's visit. "It shows charity," he said. "The public interest in it shows concern about what really matters—which is God. I mean, the Pope and the Archbishop of Canterbury and Rome, and everything, it only matters because it's God that matters supremely—the claim of God on every man."

The moderator intervened to express his feeling "that a great many people, particularly in this country, do feel that the Roman religion calls on a citizen to offer prime loyalty to the Pope and that this does stand in the way of the kind of unity that both of you are asking for."

Ramsey hastened to reply: "Oh, I feel that the doctrine of the infallibility of the Pope is a bar to unity, and I feel that the recent Mariological doctrines are a bar to unity. These are things we must thrash out [but] there's all the difference in the world between thrashing them out in controversy that's bitter . . . and discussing them with people who are friends in charity—it's that big difference that our Archbishop of Canterbury's visit to the Pope signalizes."

Harris then suggested that "there are certain aspects of Roman teaching which the man-in-the-street finds it awfully difficult to swallow, or even to tolerate, and one is the idea that his first loyalty should be to somebody outside his own country."

This time it was Heenan who had the immediate reply: ". . . You seem to be under the illusion that we have some sort of political loyalty to the Pope. Well, this is back to the sixteenth century, isn't it, when they thought that religious allegiance meant political loyalty?"

The Roman prelate stated succinctly that the Pope is concerned only with spiritual matters, and that the allegiances of Church and State are separate. To this Ramsey added, "I don't look out of England to the Pope for authority. I believe that the Catholic Christian Church, which I belong to, is essentially more than national. We look to something beyond England, beyond any nation —the brotherhood in Christ. I think that a Christian has primarily an allegiance to God and to the Christian brotherhood in the world that is more than national . . ."

Summarizing his viewpoint on the Vatican meeting, Ramsey said, "The moral of this great event is that in the future let us speak about religious differences [while] accepting a spirit of love and charity, and with the utmost effort to combine your own firm convictions with real understanding of the other man, however different that may be . . ."

The program was viewed by many high-ranking clergymen, except Geoffrey Fisher, who says he had no television set at Lambeth Palace. Canon Roy McKay, director of religious broadcasting for BBC, believes Heenan made his points skillfully but that Ramsey came across as a man of encompassing vision.

One reviewer wrote, "The Archbishop of York's craggy features dominated the screen like a benevolent hawk. There is about him a look of medieval times; he would appear at home on an ancient tapestry with a falcon at his wrist."

Ramsey's appearance again linked his name with speculation that he would be the next Archbishop of Canterbury. A London newspaper reported that "a significant statement was made by Dr. Geoffrey Fisher at a private dinner party given for him in Rome by the British Ambassador. Dr. Fisher said, 'I wanted particularly to visit Jerusalem *while I am still Archbishop.*' Clearly Dr. Fisher, seventy-three, now visualizes a time of retirement. His successor? There is one so ready-made that it is impossible to look elsewhere—Dr. Arthur Michael Ramsey, Archbishop of York. . . ."

The rumor persisted through Christmas and into the New Year. His sister, Bridget, asked about it when the Ramseys came to dinner at her home in London. "Mik," she said, "are you going to Canterbury?" and he replied, "Certainly not!"

At Nottingham University, where Ramsey was giving the Firth Memorial Lectures, a university official broached the matter at luncheon one day. Ramsey completely ignored the question.

In Church House, Westminster, a large building encrusted with coats-of-arms, the Convocation of Canterbury assembled in the legislative chamber beneath an inscription in great golden letters marching around its domed ceiling: "Holy is the true light and passing wonderful, lending radiance to them that endureth the heat of the conflict: from Christ they inherit a home of unfailing splendor, where in they rejoice with gladness evermore."

On this drab morning Tuesday, January 17, the bishops, priests, and laymen hardly glanced at the eloquent promise but stared instead at an agenda of familiar topics: the revised catechism, the compatibility of science and religion, the moral aspects of suicide. A dull day, so it seemed, but Geoffrey Fisher would in the next few minutes sweep away the air of moody listlessness. His resignation had been submitted to the Queen a month earlier. The hour had come for him to disclose his plans publicly. He took his place in the president's chair and, after the opening prayer, stood to announce his decision to retire.

"Now the press will have no hesitancy about its speculation," said a London vicar, wearily. "The newspapers will nominate almost anyone for Canterbury. Their speculation is as wide as the list of diocesan bishops is long."

True to the prediction, the British newspapers began that afternoon to suggest the names of the prelates most likely to be advanced to the primacy. The *Daily Express* championed three names—the Bishop of Peterborough, Robert Stopford; the Bishop of Bradford, Frederick Donald Coggan; and a "far out" choice, the Archbishop of Cape Town, Joost de Blank.

Another London newspaper, The *Daily Mail*, outlined the prospects of nine bishops—and surprisingly, a man who was not a bishop. It mentioned Ramsey first, Stopford as a second possibility, and placed Coggan fifth in the running. Others were William Greer of Manchester, Cuthbert Bardsley of Coventry, Robert Mortimer of Exeter, Falkner Allison of Chelmsford, Bertram Simpson of Southwark, Gerald Ellison of Chester, and

Canon Max Alexander Warren, General Secretary of the Church Missionary Society.

"This is a field day for bishop-watchers," said the newspaper. "The picking of a new 'Arch'. . . . is almost as undemocratic as a horse race and provides a great deal of dignified excitement for followers of form in what *The Church Times* once called 'the ecclesiastical rat race'. . . . The field is wide open. There is no certainty."

The *Daily Mail* commented candidly and humorously on each of the candidates.

On Ramsey: "When that great impressive slab of ecclesiastical dignity. . . . envelops some ancient episcopal seat, you feel that all the power and authority of Christendom is concentrated in his stooping presence. The wisdom of ages seems entombed in his craggy head, decorated with its twin tufts of venerable snow-white clerical hair. . . . But what Churchmen keep asking is: When is Ramsey going to do something or say something worthy of the great expectations which were placed in him? When, in other words, is he going to live up to his brand image? . . . He is to be found talking to farm laborers over a pint in the public bar on holiday, or cosily disputing with adolescent humanists in the draughty library of St. Mary's Church, Oxford, or journeying to picturesque Northern churches to preach what people call 'beautiful sermons.' But a great Church leader? Churchmen are shaking their heads on that point. Besides, some of them say, he is inclined to be a bit High."

On Bishop Stopford: "He is just coming up to his sixtieth birthday, and could be mistaken for a milder version of J. B. Priestley. He smokes a pipe fairly continuously, and talks through it in a refreshingly North Country accent. He went to Hertford College, Oxford, which is a little bit unfashionable, but made up for it to a certain degree by becoming a housemaster and senior history master at Oundle. . . ."

On Bishop Greer: ". . . One of those long-headed, big-eared bishops with an unswerving gaze."

On Bishop Bardsley: ". . . An artistic Old Etonian. . . . An able man, with a gift for well-bred self-projection. He knows how to walk and talk like a bishop. He knows how to hold a crowd. But he is a little short of one essential ingredient for the top job—learned theological authority."

On Bishop Coggan: "A learned theological background. . . . He has a strong Low Church leaning, and regards Mr. Macmillan's Premium Bonds as 'a sop to those who have been pressing for a State lottery.' "

On Canon Warren: "He is . . . not a bishop at all, though that need not stop Mr. Macmillan from nominating him. (He is reputed to have turned down two bishoprics already.) . . . It might be worth remembering the name, at a time when the Church is so full of revolutionary ideas."

In Whitehall the machinery of government moved rapidly in order to settle the appointment before the Queen's departure at the end of the week on a trip abroad. The names the newspapers mentioned were well known, of course, to David Stephens, an athletic fifty-one-year-old Oxford man who had been since 1955 the Prime Minister's Secretary for Appointments. The discerning journalist, Anthony Sampson, in his recent book, *Anatomy of Britain*, sums up the situation in this way: "When Dr. Fisher was due to retire, there was great uncertainty about his successor: Fisher himself was thought to favor the Bishop of Peterborough, or Dr. Coggan. . . . Some people regarded Ramsey as too much a pure theologian, and too High Church, and too ineffectual for the big job, with its heavy administrative burden. But others insisted that he alone had the necessary theological toughness and preoccupation with religion, and after a long period of consultation with the clergy, the Prime Minister decided in favor of Ramsey."

Preparing for all eventualities, the wire services sent to their member newspapers advance biographies of likely candidates for use when the selection was made.

Conjecture on new primates is not an innovation of the twentieth century. It has persisted for hundreds of years as many archbishops have come and gone. A fading manuscript written in 1747 (the year the eighty-fourth Archbishop, Thomas Herring, was appointed), found in the British Museum, is entitled "Race for Canterbury: or Lambeth Ho!" The poem, subtitled "The Contention for the Metropolitan See," begins:

> Behold four Bishops, Tooth and Nail,
> Struggling who first shall Lambeth hail.
> The first is old, yet very willing;

> The second's grave at Rebel-killing;
> The third is pious, good and just,
> And worthy of so great a Trust;
> The fourth strove hard to gain the Point,
> And stretched every Nerve and Joint,
> But finding that his Labour's lost,
> He says, he'll not accept the Post.
> . . . But instantly on *Thames* appear'd
> Four Wherries rowing very hard.
> Each Rower clad in Sleeves of Lawn,
> A Trencher-Cap his Head upon.
> Each sweats and toils with Might and Main,
> The noted *Lambeth* Point to gain;
> For that's the Mark, and there's the Prize
> On which they all have fixt their Eyes.

In his presidential address on January 17 to the York Convocation assembled in York Minster, Ramsey said, "A few hours ago the Convocation of Canterbury heard the news that the Archbishop of Canterbury has, with the Queen's consent, resigned the primatial See, from May 31. . . ." He paid tribute to Fisher for "the achievements and the endeavors of his primacy," especially Fisher's contributions to the "cohesion" of the Anglican Communion and his devotion to "keeping the cause of Christian unity in the front of the Church's consciousness." Ramsey concluded on what some felt was a prophetic note: "We are moved today with emotions of thankfulness for what our Archbishop has been to us, and for his example of humble and selfless service to the Church of God both near and far. And we are moved no less to new resolve in serving our Church and its Lord in a new chapter of its history."

The convocation closed and on Thursday, the nineteenth, Ramsey kept a long-standing commitment to make a recording for the BBC's early morning religious program, *Lift Up Your Hearts*. He had a luncheon engagement, also of long standing, at Ampleforth Abbey, a Roman Catholic school for boys.

It was while Ramsey was driving home from Ampleforth Abbey that the Prime Minister's office at Admiralty House, London, released the announcement:

"The Queen has been pleased to nominate the Most Reverend and Right Honorable Arthur Michael Ramsey, D.D., Lord Archbishop of York, Primate of England and Metropolitan, for election by the Dean and Chapter of Canterbury, in place of the Most Reverend and Right Honorable Geoffrey Francis Fisher, G.C.V.O., D.D., Lord Archbishop of Canterbury, Primate of All England and Metropolitan. The Queen has also been pleased to nominate the Right Reverend Frederick Donald Coggan, D.D., Lord Bishop of Bradford, for election by the Dean and Chapter of York in place of the Most Reverend and Right Honorable Arthur Michael Ramsey. . . ."*

A group of reporters and photographers waited at Bishopthorpe as Ramsey's automobile came through the gates of the estate. Inside the house, his wife, chaplain, secretary, and butler were coping with a flood of telephone calls and messages. Ramsey was pleased that the first note of congratulations, pushed under the door, was from the vicar of Bishopthorpe Parish Church.

Joan Ramsey, her eyes glowing with excitement, joined her husband in receiving the reporters. Heavy curtains were drawn against the early winter darkness. Logs blazed cheerfully in the fireplace.

The only questions that distinguished the friendly conference from any that a newly-designated archbishop might hold were those concerning Ramsey's feeling toward the Roman Catholic Church. He was asked whether he would call at the Vatican as Fisher had done a few weeks before. Ramsey replied with enthusiasm, "I should love to meet the Pope. But the union of all churches is a slow process. It is no use hurrying or being impatient."

Later that evening, when a BBC reporter asked for a statement on the relationship of Church and State, he departed again from the familiar statements usually expected of a new nominee. "The Church must live its own life and have some authority for the ordering of its own affairs, particularly over its worship," Ramsey

* Within the year two of the men mentioned by the newspapers as "candidates" for nomination to Canterbury were named to the high-ranking dioceses of London and Winchester. Robert Stopford was translated from Peterborough to London, succeeding Henry Montgomery Campbell, who was retiring. Falkner Allison was translated from Chelmsford to Winchester to replace Alwyn Williams, also retiring, whose translation from Durham to Winchester in 1952 had created the vacant see for which Ramsey was consecrated.

said thoughtfully in a manner that indicated he had long ago sorted out for himself the intricacies of the matter. "We shall presently be asking the State for a greater degree of autonomy to manage our own affairs. I have no doubt we shall get that, and use it wisely."

Word of Ramsey's nomination to Canterbury spread over Britain in the late afternoon newspapers and broadcasts.

In the suburban Highgate section of London, a tweedy, pipe-smoking professor of medicine purchased a late edition as he emerged from the Underground. This was Ramsey's brother-in-law, Dr. Henry Barcroft, the husband of Bridget. As a boy he had attended the King's College Choir School with Michael Ramsey. He had always been fond of him; in fact he named one of his sons Michael. In the two-story house at No. 44 Wood Lane he left the newspaper prominently displayed on the hall table, smiling to himself as he thought of his wife's surprise in finding there the announcement that her brother was to become the hundredth Archbishop of Canterbury.

"My husband managed to contain himself," says Bridget. "I came upon the announcement as I was casually reading the evening newspaper—and it was an immense thrill. My neighbors gave me kudos. A woman two doors away sent me a telegram!"

Ramsey's other sister, Mrs. Margaret Paul, the wife of a philosophy professor at Oxford, was at dinner with her husband and four daughters at their home in Merton Street, Oxford, when the local newspaper telephoned. And in Cambridge, Miss Lucy Ramsey was kept busy answering the door to townspeople who called with congratulations on her nephew's appointment. John Lewis, the vicar of St. Giles, her parish church, stood at her side. "Oh, you mustn't ask Miss Ramsey *that*," he said in reply to almost every question posed by a reporter from the *Cambridge Daily News*.

Mrs. Leslie Owen, the woman who had introduced Ramsey to his wife, heard the announcement just as she was finishing her afternoon tea in the Kensington flat she shares with her daughter, Faith. "I thought back to the 1930's when we had known Michael at Lincoln and to the 1940's when we had known him at Durham," she says. "It has been wonderful to see him fulfill the promise which I felt he had from the first moment I met him."

Another friend of Ramsey's days at Lincoln, Brother Edwin of the Society of the Sacred Mission, was reclining in a battered old upholstered chair in his cell at Kelham when he heard a broadcast by the American Forces Network in Germany. "The chair and the radio are concessions to old age; they are hardly monastic," Brother Edwin explains apologetically. "But I was glad for the radio when I heard of Michael's nomination to Canterbury. I'm afraid I shattered the silence of the corridors. I went through the house telling everybody I met."

The same broadcast was heard in nearby Nottingham where two priests of the Community of the Resurrection were dining with a family. "Both of us broke into cheers," says one of the monks. "Our host looked up, startled, and said, 'I understand Ramsey is High Church,' and I replied, 'Oh, yes, that's why we cheered.' Funny thing, the rest of that meal was eaten in ominous silence."

At Repton School in Derbyshire, the first-day-of-term tea for new boys was interrupted by reporters seeking information on Ramsey's record as a student.

A diocesan bishop who is believed to have been one of the strongest contenders for nomination to Canterbury, Robert Stopford, had gone with his wife late in the afternoon to an exhibition of historical treasures at Burlington House in London. When they emerged into the cold January night they saw the freshly-lettered signboards of a newsstand:

RAMSEY TO CANTERBURY

"I knew the appointment was to be made that day, but I didn't know who was to be chosen," says Stopford, seated in front of the fire in his new study in Fulham Palace, London. "As soon as we reached home I sat down and wrote him a note of congratulations."

In Canterbury, the "Red Dean," Hewlett Johnson, was sought out by reporters who knew that his dissenting opinions, on most matters of Church and State, could always enliven a news story. But on this cold winter's evening the white-haired old man was brief and amiable. "I am not surprised," he said, "and I welcome the decision." But then he added a barbed comment, in obvious reference to Geoffrey Fisher, "It will be a good thing to have a change to less administrative work and more theological work. We should know a little more about God and a little less about organization."

Britain's leading Roman Catholic prelate, William Godfrey, Cardinal Archbishop of Westminster, offered his "warm congratulations" and added, "We pray that he may enjoy health and strength for many years of service in his high office."

The following morning, January 20, 1961, newspapers throughout the world gave front-page notice to the nomination. It was a day of significant events. Forty-three-year-old John Kennedy was inaugurated President of the United States. Queen Elizabeth departed for India, the first reigning British monarch to visit that country in fifty years. Premier Khrushchev had attended the Old Vic's opening performance in Moscow, applauding enthusiastically. Young Thomas Dooley, the American doctor who had pioneered in medical care for Laos, was reported dead of cancer in New York.

Picturesque phrases were used by the British press in its reports on Ramsey.

"So brilliant, so jovial, so friendly, this Friar Tuck of the Church," said the *Daily Herald.*

"The gentle man of York," the *Daily Mail* proclaimed. "The jolly primate," echoed the *Daily Sketch.*

The newspapers noted that the advancement meant an annual salary increase from £5,000 at York to £7,500 at Canterbury. The *Times* of London said editorially: ". . . the Prime Minister has shown a nice sense of balance. . . . Dr. Ramsey would be popularly described as a High Churchman. Dr. Coggan would generally be considered a Low Churchman."

The *Daily Express* agreed: "Well, Mr. Macmillan has balanced things nicely. . . . He himself leans to the High. . . . His elder brother, Mr. Arthur Tarleton Macmillan, is one of the leading Anglo-Catholic members of the Church Assembly, and a great man at All Saints, Margaret Street, famous in the Church of England for its ceremonial."

The *Cambridge Daily News* commented: "In recent times Archbishops of Canterbury have come from Oxford and the break with tradition will be readily appreciated here. The appointment trans-lates to Canterbury one who is not only a native of Cambridge but a son of the University."

The Communist *Daily Worker,* which bills itself as "the only daily paper owned by its readers," headlined in error that Ramsey was the youngest primate ever nominated. Describing him as "a controversial figure inside his own Church," the newspaper re-vived the 1956 charge that Ramsey's friends had campaigned for his rapid advancement.

A direct attack on both Ramsey and Coggan came from Lord Altrincham, a journalist who in 1957 had publically criticized the monarchy and Queen Elizabeth. Speaking at the Strand Unitarian Church in London on the theme "Theology is Bunk," Lord Altrin-cham said it had been a mistake to nominate men distinguished for academic accomplishments rather than for pastoral virtues. Altrincham identified himself as a member of the Church of England, but said he was "a reformer, not a rebel."

While Englishmen read at breakfast of the new nominees to Canterbury and York, Ramsey was on his way to a confirmation service in a Yorkshire village. He had risen before dawn for the fifty-seven-mile drive to Guisborough where a class of fifty-three boys and girls awaited him in the fifteenth-century Church of St. Nicholas. He had celebrated his first mass in a church honoring this saint, and now he came to a church of the same dedication on his first morning after being nominated for the Church's highest office. But in his sermon he did not mention the events of the last twenty-four hours. "I have enjoyed myself very much," he said afterward. "Now I am looking forward to a good breakfast." And off he went for ham and eggs at St. Nicholas' vicarage with the Rev. Cecil Morrison, who had invited him eighteen months earlier for the confirmation.

Late that afternoon Mrs. Ramsey joined the Archbishop for a drive to the village outside the gates of Auckland Castle, their former home near Durham. They were scheduled to attend a civic dinner in a hall above the local cinema. But they first stopped at the local hospital to call on Alexander, the veteran butler of Auckland Castle, who was recovering from surgery. "They had been so wonderful to me," says Alexander. "They sent a telegram before the operation and another one later in the day. Then when they came to see me, the Archbishop went around the ward and spoke to every man and gave his blessing. The hospital administrator was elated to think that a Primate of England had visited the hospital; that night the men in my ward talked for hours, they were so excited to have seen the future Archbishop of Canterbury."

Among the letters that mounted with every post at Bishopthorpe was a request from one of London's most durable and popular tourist attractions, Madame Tussaud's, stating proudly that every Archbishop of Canterbury since the 1820's had been included in the famous gallery of wax models. A likeness of Charles Manners-Sutton, the eighty-ninth primate, had been the first, and his successor, William Howley, had been modeled from life by Madame Tussaud herself. Ramsey agreed to follow his predecessors, greatly amused at this indication of his prominence.

The founder's great-great-grandson, Bernard Augustine Tussaud, came to Bishopthorpe with his public relations man to take measurements of Ramsey's face with calipers and to make photographs for the creation of the wax model. Over tea poured by Mrs. Ramsey, they joked about Ramsey's model taking its place with his Cambridge contemporaries, Selwyn Lloyd and R. A. Butler. With characteristic attention to detail and authenticity, the gallery obtained a purple cassock from the Archbishop's tailor, J. Wippell & Company, and requested from Mrs. Ramsey a paper tracing of the pectoral cross worn by the Archbishop.

A creditable figure of Ramsey was completed in a few months and was placed with the ecclesiastical group in the main hall, one of the first additions after the arrival of an extremely youthful John F. Kennedy. Ramsey's model shares a platform with a seated Pope John, hurriedly created after his election in 1958, and one step below them are the figures of Cardinal Godfrey and Lord Fisher—a presence that disproves the rumor relished backstairs at Lambeth Palace that Fisher's figure at Tussaud's was melted down to create Ramsey's.

A week after his nomination, Ramsey took the 7:23 A.M. York-to-London train for one of the periodic meetings held by the

English bishops at Lambeth Palace. He reached London in time for luncheon at the Athenaeum Club, the favored meeting place of the Establishment. (Its waiters, having seen most of the top-ranking Churchmen at luncheons and dinners, had staked a running bet on who would be the next Archbishop.) At Lambeth that afternoon Ramsey greeted Fisher and Coggan, their first meeting since the announcement of the previous week. The three men were photographed together "in their gaitered glory, looking like distinguished black crows," as one priest put it.

During a subsequent visit to London for the Church Assembly in early February, a date was chosen for the enthronement at Canterbury—June 27. According to custom, the first evening of the Church Assembly saw a dinner meeting of the Nobody's Friends Club, a group described by Fisher as "the somebodies that the nobodies like." Ramsey's introduction to this group is often recalled because instead of making the traditional talk about himself, he chose to read aloud a letter sent to his parents when Fisher was headmaster at Repton. There were guffaws of laughter at the report which some felt went a long way toward proving the adage that "the boy is the father of the man."

The next evening the Ramseys were guests of the Fishers for dinner and for a visit to *Oliver*, the popular West End musical. "We didn't realize they were in the place until somebody happened to spot them at the end of the program," said the theater manager. A newspaper's inquiry at Lambeth drew the cool reply, "It was a purely private affair."

Ramsey's nomination to Canterbury forced some revising of schedule, but he held determinedly to his commitment to give a mission in Trinity College in Dublin. Before leaving for Ireland he wrote in his monthly letter from Bishopthorpe of his reflections on the last five years:

"Many Archbishops have served the Diocese of York better: none, I am sure, can have loved it more. Though the last five years have included the excitement for me of visits to Russia, to America and to Africa, no part of them has been happier than the time spent in the parishes in the Diocese. I join with you in thankfulness for much which has happened; an increase in the ordination candidates, the building of some beautiful new churches, the arousing of a new spirit of giving in the service of the Church, some steps forward in the helping of Church Schools in their work, the increasing use of our Retreat House throughout the year, some new enterprises in evangelism, the inception of the University of York. . . ."

The years of which he wrote had not permitted as much time as he might have liked for talks to student groups, although he had gone as often as possible to the university hostel at Leeds. His missions of earlier years, to Oxford in 1953 and to Cambridge in 1954, were famous, and he planned to develop at Dublin a series of similar discussions on the general subject of the Christian faith.

In the quadrangles of Trinity College, in the heart of the Irish capital, Ramsey's approaching visit had evoked a spirited controversy, the "Mission Mutiny," in which the "Hist" and the "Phil" —the History Society, founded in 1770, and the Philosophical Society, established in 1853—debated the Student Council's request that clubs and societies suspend meetings during the mission. A group of Roman Catholic students prevailed with the reasoning that "it would be discourteous to hold other meetings while the Archbishop is conducting a mission."

Four days before the opening of the mission there appeared on the campus a mimeographed newspaper designed to stimulate interest in the mission. It was called *Joculator,* a name inspired by St. Francis' admonition that his followers should be *Joculatores Dei*—God's jesters. "There will be articles on practically anything from sex to sputniks and profiles solemn and flamboyant," it declared. "We do not aim just to plug the mission line, but rather to display differing and even clashing viewpoints."

The first issue included an article, "A Roman Catholic Looks at the Mission," which declared that "any form of Protestantism . . . is a desirable alternative to agnosticism." There followed in the next issue "A Communist's View of the Mission," presenting the Marxist philosophy as "more Christian than Christian."

The Ramseys made the short trip by plane and were greeted by the Anglican Archbishop of Dublin, George Simms, and Dr. R. R. Hartford, Trinity's Regius Professor of Divinity.

Eight hundred students assembled in the Examination Hall to hear Ramsey's initial address on the subject "God Our Creator." He began with surprising forthrightness: "Let me say two things first about myself: I claim to be a Christian—a very bad one—and I claim also a concern about the dignity of man and the freedom of man."

Then he launched into the issue on which this memorable week would revolve: "I have come here to talk to you about the conviction that the Christian faith makes sense of the puzzling world and shows us how to grapple with it."

Enthusiasm for the first address carried over to the next day's press luncheon. Ramsey spoke carefully to the reporters, mindful that Roman Catholic Ireland did not share as fully as England and the Continent in the "thaw" between Anglicans and Rome. Yet he spoke candidly, pointing out that deep differences "need not prevent the removal of bitterness and the establishment of a more personal friendship and readiness to act together in the practical problems of Christian duty."

The other members of the mission band began their tasks. The Rev. R. P. McDermott, a Belfast-born Anglican priest whom Ramsey had brought to the theological faculty at Durham, conducted the noonday devotional services. As Irish as the character actor, Barry Fitzgerald, he established an immediate rapport with the students. The third missioner was Miss Christian Howard, since 1947 the secretary for women's work in the Diocese of York. Practical, plain-spoken, a keen student of Ramsey's theology, she counseled with students individually and did much to explain the finer points of the theories expounded by the Archbishop.

"His Grace's way of conducting this mission has been a curious one," wrote David Butler, president of the student governing board. "One would expect to find one or more elements in the missioner's talks: a closely reasoned intellectual argument for Christianity [or] a strongly emotional appeal for the support of the audience. . . . Instead, Dr. Ramsey gives us an exposition of his beliefs, stated with remarkable clarity and simplicity, which we are left to accept or reject as we will."

The popular "coffee hours," when Ramsey and the missioners talked informally with the students, aroused the articulate criticism of one undergraduate: "People all over the college have been receiving invitations which, in spite of a small cross in the corner of the card, seemed to whisper of the delights of a judiciously prepared cocktail. But the fact remains that to the agnostic who may be reconsidering his attitude to Christianity, there is nothing more distasteful than being *got at*. The mental conflict involved in an acceptance or rejection of something as huge as the Christian conception of God is an intensely personal thing, and the palsy-walsy get-togetherness of a 'holy coffee hour' will do no good and could conceivably do great harm."

The agnostics and the skeptics came to listen to Ramsey and to question him. When their questions were openly contemptuous or confused in their phrasing Ramsey would say, "Now here is what you *mean* . . ." When one hostile young man asked, "How would you differentiate between reason, knowledge, and faith?" Ramsey shot back, "Reason is an action of the mind; knowledge is a possession of the mind; but faith is an attitude of the person. It means you are prepared to stake yourself on something being so."

One of the women students, Edna Broderick, the daughter of a Roman Catholic mathematics professor, was impressed with the Archbishop's ability to relate the past and the present in realistic terms. "Dr. Ramsey splendidly removed from the cross any aura of glamorous or safe remoteness in time, space, or relevance," she said. "Christ is our contemporary. The New Testament is no history book. The Bread and Wine of Christ's last day are real, then and now."

By Thursday the success of the mission was assured. The weekly college newspaper, *Trinity News,* ran a banner headline across its front page:

HIS GRACE ABOUNDING
Personality of Dr. Ramsey
Impresses Itself Indelibly

". . . A powerful, direct thinker with a marvellous gift for public expression of his thought," said the newspaper of its initial impression of the Archbishop. "Then we met the private man—a kindly, benign, human person without the hint of ineffectuality which these qualities sometimes imply. . . . He will surely fulfill all that anyone could demand from an Archbishop of Canterbury."

A student columnist, writing under the byline of Martin Marprelate, assessed the mission in more colloquial language: "It is unreasonable to cavil at anything which has given us the opportunity of seeing a pair of such magnificent eyebrows as Dr. Ramsey's. . . . This column wishes the new big wheel of the Anglican Communion well, and hopes that under him the Church of England won't be quite so afraid to get its hands dirty."

So the mission ended, not counting its success by the number of converts as Billy Graham might have done, but by the stimulation it had given to undergraduate thought and action.

The week in Ireland was for Ramsey a relaxing break from the tempo and pressure of work that had mounted at Bishopthorpe since his nomination to Canterbury.

The mornings at Dublin were given over to his correspondence and his reading. He valued the opportunities to browse in Trinity's library where the ancient Book of Kells and other early Irish manuscripts are enshrined. In a spacious old mansion in Phoenix Park he lunched with the aging President of Ireland, Eamon de Valera. Another day he was the guest of the Roman Catholic Archbishop, John Charles McQuaid. Tuesday afternoon he drove through Ireland's flat green countryside to Limerick to dedicate a stained-glass window, in St. Mary's Cathedral, in memory of the Stafford-O'Brien family to which Mrs. Ramsey is related. On Sunday he preached in Dublin's Christ Church Cathedral.

When the Ramseys flew home at the end of the mission, little more than three months remained for them at Bishopthorpe and two weeks of that precious time had to be given to a visit to Sierra Leone in Africa.

As Ramsey prepared for his second African trip, the strife in the Congo was constantly in his thoughts. He spoke of it in his Easter sermon in York Minster: "Every man, woman, and child in the world is an heir to eternity, infinitely precious in the light of God. Let races white and black, see one another in the light of Easter, and their separation is at once at an end."

In his diocesan letter he commented on the news that South Africa was leaving the Commonwealth rather than remain under censure for its apartheid policy. "This painful episode brings thoughts both of relief and warning," he said. "We can be relieved that the new African states are *in*; we can be thankful that an immense weight of Commonwealth opinion deploring apartheid has been felt. But we must warn ourselves that, when a

Commonwealth has taken a collective stand against apartheid, it puts itself under obligation to work against every manifestation of it within its own territories. . . . When as a Commonwealth we take a particular moral principle as the basis of our association with one another, we expose ourselves to the warning of Christ, 'Judge not that ye be not judged.' "

Ramsey went to Sierra Leone to attend its independence celebration as a guest of the government and to visit Fourah Bay College at Freetown. Established in 1827 to provide theological training, Fourah had become affiliated with Durham University in 1876, and until World War I was British West Africa's only institution of higher learning. In 1959, Ramsey had accepted the title of President of the college.

The locale was new, but the lush tropical greenness and the welcoming faces reminded him of his African tour the previous year. The heat was so intense that he wore only shorts and high evening stockings beneath his cassock.

Once again Ramsey visited hospitals and schools, blessed natives who lined the roadside, and dedicated new churches. He celebrated the Holy Communion at outdoor altars and preached to vast congregations. A bush woman proudly named her newborn child Arthur Michael in the Archbishop's honor.

At formal garden parties he sometimes chatted with Edward, Duke of Kent. He had a special bond with this gangling cousin of the Queen for, in less than two months, he was to solemnize the Duke's marriage in York Minster to Katharine Worsley, daughter of a distinguished Yorkshire family. When the London press asked Ramsey about the young Duke's demeanor in Sierra Leone, he loyally replied, "I saw him at a great many functions. We were all very impressed by the way he played his part."

Back in England, the Archbishop traveled up to York—his last homecoming to Bishopthorpe—where a round of farewell fetes awaited him. There were teas, sherry parties, dinners, formal banquets, an honorary degree (his seventh) from Manchester University—and a warmly surprising invitation from his old friend, Dr. Heenan, proposing a luncheon at Woolton, his residence, in Ramsey's honor. So it was arranged for him to return to Liverpool, the city of his ordination thirty-three years earlier, as a guest of the Roman Catholic Archbishop. Present were the Ramseys and the Coggans, the Anglican Bishop of Liverpool, Dr. Clifford Martin, and Mrs. Martin, and the Roman Catholic Bishop of Shrewsbury, Dr. John Murphy. The guests spent four hours at Woolton, walking in the gardens, admiring Archbishop Heenan's prize rhododendron bushes, and enjoying a luncheon served by Franciscan nuns. "We took some beautiful color pictures and the Archbishop sent them to Rome," says Heenan's chaplain. "That day was really something to write home about."

Whatever its ecclesiastical overtone, the drive to Liverpool was for Joan Ramsey and Jean Coggan a respite from the chores of packing and moving. Mrs. Ramsey's task was especially complicated; she had to divide her furniture and possessions between two new residences—Lambeth Palace and the Old Palace, Canterbury. She began the laborious job of tagging her furniture to show the movers where it was to go and to distinguish it from pieces that would remain at Bishopthorpe—such as the twenty-foot dining table which has been in the house for more than four hundred years. (Archbishop Lang had discovered it "below stairs" and gave his servants "a fiver" to restore it to the dining room.)

Letters went out from the chaplain at Bishopthorpe to more than three hundred diocesan bishops of the Anglican Communion, requesting them to pray for Arthur Michael Ramsey at the altars of their cathedrals on Trinity Sunday, June 4.

That same Sunday, BBC Television presented Ramsey in a talk with Kenneth Harris, the suave and capable commentator who had moderated the now famous discussion between Ramsey and Archbishop Heenan.

The interview with Ramsey was the second in a series called "The Three Archbishops." Fisher was witty; Coggan was carefully tactful. The conversation with Ramsey was notable for several direct questions, among them Harris' remark, "Another thing that's said about you, Archbishop Ramsey, is that you're a ceremonialist—now what does that mean exactly to you?"

Ramsey smiled broadly. "That amuses me quite enormously," he replied. "Let me say that I value greatly the fact that we are a reformed church. Make no mistake about that. I also value greatly our Catholic continuity and sacramental life—the things that the High Church movement has revived. But I'm not really very interested in ceremonialism. If I go to a church where there's an elaborate ceremonial, I know what to do, and I don't flounder. But I am completely at home in churches where there's the simplest ceremonial. I'm at home and happy, and I am not conscious about ceremonial."

The subject of disestablishment, on which Ramsey had become known as a forceful speaker, was mentioned early in the interview. Harris asked, "Under the conditions of Establishment, Archbishop, how embarrassing are the burdens of the interference and influence of the State?"

Ramsey's reply was pointed. "The State doesn't order me to do anything contrary to my conscience," he said. "If it did, my conscience, and not the State, would come first, be sure of that."

Harris asked respectfully at the end of the program, "Here you are, about to become the hundredth Archbishop of Canterbury. How do you feel about it?"

Replying, Ramsey could have regarded himself as a figure on the stage of history. Instead, he took the occasion to point out the spiritual significance of his position. "People ask, sometimes, am I in good heart about being Archbishop of Canterbury," Ramsey said. ". . . The phrase 'in good heart' sometimes gives me pause, because, after all, we are here as a Church to represent Christ crucified and the compassion of Christ crucified before the world. And because that is so it may be the will of God that our Church should have its heart broken, and perhaps the heart of the Archbishop broken with it, just because we are here to represent Christ and Christ's compassion. But if that were to happen it wouldn't mean that we were heading for the world's misery but quite likely pointing the way to the deepest joy."

In his final diocesan letter in June, Ramsey wrote of the approaching ceremonies "whereby I shall pass from one See to another. . . ." He concluded, "May God forgive all I have done wrongly, and all I have left undone, and help us all, by faith alone in His mercy, to be ready for the final account."

13. PRIMATE OF ALL ENGLAND

The formal election of the hundredth Archbishop of Canterbury took place at noon on Monday, June 5, 1961, in the deep, cool crypt of Canterbury Cathedral.

Notice of the solemn session had been given by the Dean, Hewlett Johnson, a month earlier. In the quaintly-worded form used for centuries ("You are hereby cited and monished . . ."), he had summoned the Cathedral's Greater Chapter—its four regular members and twenty-four honorary Canons—to the four-teenth-century chapel of Our Lady Undercroft where Cardinal Morton lies buried beneath a great slab of blue marble before the altar. They appeared as directed, in their robes of office, to hear read aloud the Queen's Writ of *Conge 'd Elire,* Letters of Patent, and Letter Recommendatory, which concluded with the monarch's wish to advance for election as Primate of All England "a person [of] virtue, learning, wisdom, gravity, and other good gifts . . . the Most Reverend Father in God, Our Right Trusty and Right Entirely beloved Counsellor Arthur Michael Ramsey."

One by one the Chapter recorded its votes in writing. As the ballots were being collected, a group of tourists unexpectedly entered the crypt and were shown to seats, unaware that they were witnessing a historic moment. The Dean did not make the formal announcement of Michael Ramsey's election until after

the First Lesson of Evensong, read before the high altar later
in the day. It was the third time in his twenty-nine years as
Dean that Hewlett Johnson, proclaiming the election of a new
archbishop, had called out for "hearty prayer for His Grace's
long life and happy administration."

The election at Canterbury changed Ramsey's status from
Archbishop-designate to Archbishop-elect, a title he would re-
tain until the confirmation of the election, at St. Paul's Cathedral
on June 21, made him, legally and officially, the hundredth
Archbishop of Canterbury. His enthronement six days later in
the Chair of St. Augustine would be a formal public proclama-
tion—"for all to see," as Ramsey put it—of his claim to the
spiritualities of his ancient see.

The first engagement of the Archbishop-elect was a clergy
meeting at one of the Butlin holiday camps. In olden times a
prelate chosen as Primate of All England might have made
grander matters his concern. But a man who finds himself called
to this office in the middle of the twentieth century wisely wel-
comes his involvement in the routine conferences of clergy.
Ramsey spent three days at the Butlin camp at Clacton-on-Sea.
Here a photographer for *Life* magazine caught him on all-fours
in the grass, attempting to make friends with a baby girl in a
pink bonnet and overalls embroidered with poodles. "The Primate-
to-be of All England rose to his knees in starchy disappointment,"
wrote *Life*. ". . . nine-month-old Denise Carman was having
none of him. As Dr. Ramsey ruefully gave up, his playmate
returned to her blanket, clearly a free-thinker. Anyway Dr.
Ramsey had a more solemn duty to perform next day: the
marriage of the Duke of Kent."

Returning from Clacton-on-Sea, Ramsey found the winding
streets of York decorated with flowers and streaming pennants
for the city's first royal wedding since the marriage of Edward III
in 1328. In the early afternoon a special train brought Queen
Elizabeth and her family and representatives of the royal houses
of ten countries. The passengers included Princess Sophia of
Greece and Juan Carlos of Spain, who in less than a year would
be the principals in Europe's next royal wedding.

The Ramseys reached the Minster an hour before the ceremony, just as the great bells began to peal. The crowds waiting outside gave their warmest cheers to the Archbishop and to the Admiral of the Fleet, Lord Mountbatten of Burma. Another familiar personage, Noel Coward, gave a debonair wave as he entered. One of the last arrivals of the two thousand guests was Douglas Fairbanks, Jr. A loud cheer went up for the bridegroom and his brother, Prince Michael, the best man.

At 2:25 P.M. the Archbishop greeted at the west door Elizabeth II, the Duke of Edinburgh, and Prince Charles, who was shy and self-conscious in a lounge suit with long trousers. The Queen and her husband and son took their places with the willowy beautiful Princess Marina, the groom's mother. In the same row were Princess Alexandra, the sister of the groom; Queen Mother Elizabeth; Queen Victoria Eugenie of Spain; Princess Margaret, and Anthony Armstrong-Jones, not yet created Lord Snowden.

Pages and bridesmaids, in yellow and white, were led by the ten-year-old Princess Anne. The bride, escorted by her father, Sir William Worsley, was met at the nave altar by the Duke of Kent dressed in the dazzling blue-and-scarlet regimental uniform, sword at side, tall bearskin hat under his arm.

When the wedding ceremony was finished, the Archbishop led the couple beyond the choir screen for an additional blessing at the high altar and a brief address heard by Edward and Katharine alone. Then they passed down the nave, making their formal bows to the Queen, and walked outside the Minster under an archway of swords held by the men of the Royal Scots Greys, the Duke's regiment.

Ramsey's last days at Bishopthorpe were as busy as any he had ever spent there. An air of change and transition hung poignantly over the familiar room in which the Archbishop worked steadily amid packing crates and boxes of books. (Even the wing-chair in which he sat was tagged for the move: "Canterbury, Archbps' Study.") The brief, terse letters for which Ramsey was famous now came in a steady stream from his desk whenever he had half an hour between callers. At the end of the week he found it necessary to cancel his plans for a private viewing of color films of the Duke of Kent's wedding. ("I worked on details of diocesan business until my last moment at Bishopthorpe," Ramsey recalls.) When finally he put down his pen, he was driven to the old walled town of Beverley for the annual missionary festival service. As his farewell appearance in the diocese this occasion at ancient Beverley Minster was one of deep emotion for both the Archbishop and his people. With a full heart he took his leave and was driven alone to Mirfield, in an industrial and mining area known as the West Riding, to begin a private retreat in the motherhouse of the Community of the Resurrection.

"C.R.," as the brotherhood's name is abbreviated, occupies a millowner's stark mansion acquired in 1898, shortly after the Order was founded by Charles Gore, later Bishop of Oxford. The monks have added a retreat house, a theological college, and a fortresslike monastery church which Archbishop Temple dedicated in 1938. The grounds, gardens, walks, and paths—even the community cemetery guarded by a huge crucifix—were familiar to Ramsey. In 1957 he had participated in the solemn high mass of Commemoration Day and walked in procession to an outdoor altar to address a crowd of more than four thousand visitors. Once he had officiated at a Good Friday service. And as episcopal Visitor to the Order, he had held personal conferences with each of the monks during the General Chapter of 1959.

The previous winter the Superior had been deeply touched by a letter from Ramsey in which he agreed to continue as Visitor. It had been placed on the mantelpiece of the Community Room for all to read.

In a meditation at Mirfield, Ramsey once had said, "Silence isn't selfish for it brings the fruits of contemplation which you may share with others." Now, on this early summer day, his car swept up the curving driveway, stopping at the blue-painted doors. He crossed the threshold ready to seek in the silence and tranquillity of this place the "fruits of contemplation" he might share with the whole Church in the challenging years ahead.

The heavy wooden gates of Lambeth Palace swung open at three o'clock on the afternoon of June 20, 1961, as the Ramseys arrived to take up residence. Their car passed through the Tudor archway and into the central courtyard where reporters and photographers waited.

"It was just like any new tenant moving in," says a member of the palace staff. "A sniff at the roses, a wander round the gardens with your wife, meeting the people who work in the house, putting in your own books and ornaments. The new folks found the painters still at work in their own flat."

At eleven the next morning the Ramseys drove to St. Paul's for the ceremony which would confirm the election of June 5 at Canterbury. They were accompanied by Ramsey's domestic chaplain, the Rev. John Andrew, who had been recalled from the United States the previous year to succeed the Rev. Martin Kaye, and by the Rev. Simon Ridley, who had been on Archbishop Fisher's staff.

Awaiting them in a chamber near the tomb of Lord Nelson were bewigged election officials and nine bishops appointed to act as "spiritual commissioners" of the Crown. During the ceremony that followed in the magnificently appointed Chapel of the British Empire, Ramsey sat like a penitent in the third row of chairs. In the cautious language of the Appointments of Bishops Law, enacted during the Reformation, the legal requirements were dealt with one at a time: the Archbishop-elect was "a man born prudent and discreet" (of legitimate birth), canonically ordained, of due age—and was, in fact, Dr. Ramsey and none other. J. G. Pembroke, proctor of the Dean and Chapter of Canterbury, declared, "I do here judicially produce His Grace."

First kneeling and then standing, Ramsey took the oath of allegiance to the Queen, made his declaration against simony (buying or selling ecclesiastical office), and subscribed assent to the Thirty-nine Articles.

The Bishop of London, Henry Montgomery Campbell, stirred restlessly, his Scottish patience disturbed by these finer points of the English law. At last the moment arrived for his statement of affirmation: "We have amply found and do find that the said election was rightfully and lawfully made and celebrated by the Dean and Chapter of Canterbury."

Ramsey, his passive role slipping away, walked confidently to the altar to give his first blessing as the fully empowered Archbishop of Canterbury. Then, as he left the chapel, he shook hands with the Lord Mayor of London, Sir Bernard Waley-Cohen, who was to be his host for a luncheon at the Mansion House, official residence of the Lord Mayors.

After the ceremonies of confirmation and homage the Ramseys found themselves caught up again in the elaborate preparations for the enthronement at Canterbury. One event to which they had been looking forward was the arrival of the golden cope and mitre on which Mrs. Mary Ozanne, who had made Ramsey's copes for Durham and York, had asked to work, contributing her labor as a gift.

"We were busy from January to June," says Mrs. Ozanne in the big sewing room of her home at Sawbridgeworth, near London. "Letters went out all over England for the heraldry of the places with which the Archbishop had been associated. Down one side of the cope marched the coats-of-arms of York, Lincoln, Liverpool, Cuddesdon, and Magdalene. On the other side were Durham, Cambridge University, Durham University, St. Benet's, and Boston. The flat hood on the back was reserved for the primatial coat-of-arms. Four women worked with me, and painstaking it was too, almost all by hand."

Rummaging in the chests and cabinets of her workroom, she brings out a brilliant swatch: "*Real* cloth-of-gold costs the world, if you can get it. This is French Lurex. We wanted to use English material, but the French was better. The mitre, incidentally, is ten and a half inches high with featherbone stiffners in back and front. When the cope was finished the neighbors came in to see our handiwork. That was when 'I acquired merit,' as Kipling would say. The next week we drove to Canterbury for the enthronement. It was such a beautiful ceremony that I completely forgot about the Archbishop wearing our cope."

For the second time in four days the Ramseys took up residence in another great house—the Old Palace at Canterbury, the home traditionally occupied by the primate in his role as head of the Diocese of Canterbury. A remodeling at the end of the nineteenth century carefully preserved the ancient stonework and the passageway—or "door to martyrdom"—through which Thomas Becket walked to his death in the Cathedral.

The civic council, which had honored the primate by naming a street Ramsey Close, gave a reception of welcome on Saturday afternoon. In his response to the mayor's address of welcome, Ramsey said, "Eternity is indeed the territory of which an archbishop is concerned. But this Archbishop is like his predecessor, very much concerned also with 1961, with what is happening here and now among his neighbors. There is a saying of a great old Christian writer that the man of faith has two eyes—that with his right eye he sees things of Heaven and with his left eye he sees the things of earth. I conceive it to be the role of an archbishop to keep both eyes open and alert and to help and encourage people to have both eyes open and alert. This is my ideal as a citizen of Canterbury."

Meanwhile, inside "the precincts" as the Cathedral close is known at Canterbury, there continued separate rehearsals of the groups who would participate in the enthronement ceremony.

Invitations from the Dean and Chapter had gone out weeks before with the notation, "This . . . is dispatched at an early date for the convenience of all concerned, without prejudice to the due Election and Confirmation of the Archbishop Designate." Upon receipt of acceptances, additional instructions were sent for reaching Canterbury by automobile or by the special train from London. Motorists received windshield stickers and a map showing the road approaches and the location of parking lots.

Cards of admittance to the Cathedral were in four colors—red for seats in the choir near the high altar, tan for the north choir aisle gallery, pink for the southeast transept and aisle, and blue for the south choir aisle gallery. Eight hundred of the letters carried an additional white card for admittance to the reception in the Great Hall of the King's School in the close.

"In post-medieval times at Canterbury there has been no continuous tradition in connection with enthronements," reads a memorandum drawn up by a Canterbury historian in the spring of 1961. "The business was carried out by proxy and with maimed rites. . . . The ceremony of inthronisation had been so little regarded by post-Reformation primates that Archbishop Tenison [1695] had been the first to be enthroned in person and not by proxy. William Wake [the next primate] followed his example."

The historian's notes continue: "The tradition of the Archbishop knocking on the door *has no place at all* in Canterbury tradition since the Reformation and there is no positive evidence of the practice during the Middle Ages, here, or indeed anywhere else. It is remarkable that the practice is not even shown in post-

Tridentine Roman pontificals, and makes one doubt very much the antiquity of the practice anywhere, either in our own Church or outside it. It is probably some local usage which has been adopted in modern times in other places. Since the post-medieval use of the crosier is of little antiquity anyhow, knocking on the door must likewise be of little antiquity."

The historian could not resist adding, "There was certainly no knocking on the door at the enthronement of Archbishop Lang, in 1928, as I myself was a Boy Scout on duty in a Guard of Honor by the door and had a good view of what went on." And so Ramsey did not knock as he had done at Durham and York.

The men most concerned with the planning in 1961 were Alexander Sargent, Archdeacon of Canterbury; Gordon Strutt, Archdeacon of Maidstone; and Lawrence Lawson, then precentor of the Cathedral.

Canon Lawson, a short, friendly priest with shell-rimmed glasses, remembers: "The precision of the enthronement ceremony's procession—more than eight hundred persons—was planned by locking ourselves in the Cathedral and pacing out exactly how long it would take to walk the required route. We allotted a time of twenty-seven minutes—only one minute short of the time required on the day of enthronement. But the most complex task was issuing tickets for the public. A large block was given out in order of application and, in the last fortnight before the ceremony, not a single ticket remained. Many of the diocesan clergy didn't like their seats, so they crowded in behind the high altar—a rather strange-looking group of spectators, although a few people were kind enough to say that this bit of informality gave the ceremony a homey touch. The night before the ceremony thirty bank managers and estate agents, and their wives, came in and gave the Cathedral what we laughingly called 'a special volunteer spring clean.' Then for a short while the Cathedral stood in absolute readiness for the enthronement."

The newspapers which had commented profusely on Ramsey's nomination to Canterbury surpassed themselves the week before his enthronement.

The *Daily Sketch* ran a four-part series entitled "Primate Extraordinary," anonymously written "by one of the very few people who know him well enough to observe his off-duty life in the peace and privacy of his home." (At the Archbishop's request Chaplain Andrew had supplied notes for the article, saving Ramsey from time-consuming interviews.)

The *Sunday Express* happened upon a young vicar's "open letter" in a church pamphlet and made the comments far more "open" than the cleric may ever have imagined: "The Rev. Nicolas Stacey, 33-year-old vicar of Woolwich, advises the new Archbishop of Canterbury to follow the lead of President Kennedy," the newspaper reported. "Mr. Stacey, a former Olympic sprinter, says, 'Your predecessor tried to run the Church with a staff that a village postmistress would have considered inadequate. But, please God, you will not be too proud to learn from the young Roman Catholic on the other side of the Atlantic. President Kennedy was faced with a similar situation to yours. He started by gathering round him a brilliant team of unlikely men from unlikely jobs. You must do the same, being particularly careful to choose men with the qualities you may lack. You are well known as a man of love, prayer and high intellect, but your greatest fans would not describe you as a fire-eater. . . . If you do give the lead which the Church desperately needs, you will have to turn a blow-torch on the human fossils so securely riveted to every part of the creaking ecclesiastical machine. . . .'"

At Canterbury the day before the enthronement eleven of the twelve honorary chaplains appointed by Ramsey lined up with him for a ceremonial rehearsal. This group was representative of the cherished association of his career as well as of the widespread life and work of the Anglican Communion: his master at Repton, Canon Balmforth, now chancellor of Exeter Cathedral; his chaplain at Durham, the Rev. A. F. Lazonby; the chamberlain of York Minster, the Rev. David Rees, and the synodical secretary of the Province of York, the Rev. H. R. Wilson; the vicar of Bishopthorpe, the Rev. R. L. H. Lloyd; and the Regius Professors at Oxford, Cambridge, and Dublin—Canon Henry Chadwick, Canon E. C. Ratcliff, and Canon R. R. Hartford; also the Rev. Yohana Lukindo, of the Universities' Mission to Central Africa; Archdeacon K. P. Sakyiama, of Ghana; and the Very Rev. Charles

Harris, dean of Seabury-Western Theological Seminary at Evanston, Illinois. Ramsey's classmate at Repton and Cambridge, Canon Charles Smyth, was not present for the rehearsal.

"The *Queen Elizabeth* was fogged in at Cherbourg," says Dean Harris. "My wife and I reached Canterbury only a short while before the rehearsal. The Archbishop himself was not at all hurried as he greeted me and strolled up an aisle of the Cathedral. When I noticed that he was wearing an old cassock that hung in loose folds (he had lost so much weight), I said, 'Your Grace, tomorrow is a great occasion and you *can't* wear that old cassock.' He turned to me and shook his finger in that characteristic gesture we all know so well. 'You run your seminary and I'll mind my cassocks,' he said. And then he told me he was coming to the United States in 1962 and would like to visit Seabury-Western again. As we talked, sightseers streamed through the Cathedral, and one English couple approached the Archbishop and asked to introduce their five-year-old son. The Archbishop shook hands with him. 'Where do you go to church?' The boy replied with the name of his parish and town—it was Saint So-and-So—and the Archbishop said, 'Now be sure and tell your vicar about *this* meeting.' Then he gave a blessing to the boy and his parents."

As the rehearsal ended and the diagrams of the ceremonial were tucked away in cassock pockets, there came from the Cathedral close the sound of a helicopter landing on the grassy lawn. It brought Ludovic Kennedy, one of the best-known commentators of BBC Television, for an interview scheduled to take place on the eve of the enthronement as a segment in the BBC's popular *Panorama*.

At 8:40 P.M., the BBC announced from London: "The new Archbishop of Canterbury, Prime Minister Fidel Castro, and Mr. Julius Nyerere, the African leader—these are three very different men that you'll be meeting in *Panorama* tonight. . . . Let us begin by going to Canterbury. . . . First into the nave of the Cathedral—a lovely building, as you see it half in shadow, half in light. At the far end of the top of the steps all bathed in light, the Chair of St. Augustine, in lonely splendor this evening. . . . Behind it, through the high doorway in the great carved screen of the Cathedral, lies the Choir. . . . And there in the distance the high altar, and walking near the high altar, two men tonight—the new Archbishop and with him Ludovic Kennedy."

Their discussion in the twilight shadows of the Cathedral ranged over the familiar issues of unity, the relationship of Church and State, and the need for stronger Christian influences in everyday life. Ramsey restated his position as he had done frequently since that January evening six months earlier when he was nominated to Canterbury. Kennedy asked if Ramsey would be as "outspoken on controversial political issues" as Fisher had been.

"On political issues the Church has to be stating always the broad Christian principles about public affairs," he replied. "You would say at once that's insufficient and I agree with you. The thing must be more pinpointed in reference to practical issues. Where there is a political issue on which the Christian view is absolutely clear then it's my business to state it, and to call upon Christian people to back me up."

Kennedy's final question was, "What remains for you to do between now and your enthronement tomorrow?"

The Archbishop thought for a moment, then spoke of his new position as he saw it. "I am very, very overwhelmed, indeed," he said. "I mean, here am I, just an ordinary man, and I'm going to shoulder the job of being the leader of a really big portion of the Christian Church, caring for it in the name of God. And that's a task that any man might shrink for and I shrink for."

Next he spoke of the ensuing eighteen hours before he returned to the Cathedral for the ceremony of enthronement. "Well, I'm going home," he said. "We're going to have our usual evening service in the chapel. I'm going to be quiet for the rest of the evening. It isn't surprising that I shall want to be alone with God, is it? Looking to God for some of His strength. In the morning we shall have Holy Communion, and I shall be quiet till the time of the service, and Christian people who are listening to me are going to be helping me with their prayers."

The long-awaited enthronement day was clear and fair, the sky changing from streaks of apricot and mauve to a fine, cloudless backdrop for the Cathedral's spires and the old town's hud-

dled buildings, rooftops, and gables. Fluttering in a slight breeze
above the Old Palace was a bright new flag displaying the coat-
of-arms of the primatial see.

The little hotels and lodging houses were filled to capacity.
Soon the narrow streets were crowded with the visitors and
vehicles, including a police escort for an automobile bringing
from Corpus Christi College, Cambridge, the priceless Canterbury Gospels on which the new Archbishop would take his oath
of office.

The Union Jack flew high; bunting decorated the lampposts. A
shop displayed magnificent vestments worn by Archbishop Lang.
In the Olive Branch, a pub across from Christ Church Gate, the
story was told of another enthronement day, in October, 1294,
when Robert Winchelsey, the fiftieth Archbishop, once a poor
boy in Canterbury Grammar School, had entered the town in
glittering array, astride a white horse.

Ramsey's relatives gathered at the County Hotel—his aunt, his
sisters, with their husbands and children; and the widow and
daughter of his brother, Frank. (Frank's elder daughter had died
in her teens.) The women had new outfits, and the men wore
morning coats, striped trousers, and gray top hats. The Pauls'
four daughters had hats for the first time. One of the Barcroft
sons, fourteen-year-old Roger, related his trials in being excused
from school: "Finally I had to go right to the headmaster to explain the matter. I said, 'Please, sir, may I be excused? You see,
sir, my uncle's being upped in the Church tomorrow.'"

For Frank Ramsey's widow, Lettice, and her daughter, Jane,
the party was a family farewell before their departure the next
day for a year in the United States. Jane's husband was to do
atomic research at Oak Ridge, Tennessee.

At luncheon in the hotel, with their Aunt Lucy at the head of
the table, the family fondly recalled how the Archbishop always
burst in on such gatherings, looking around and asking, "Well,
who's here?" Today he had sent them a letter that his elder sister
began to read aloud.

"Dear Everybody," he had written. "Who's here? And who's
Archbishop of Canterbury *now*? . . ."

There converged on Victoria Station in London, two hundred

and fifty-four guests who had been assigned places in the eleven carriages of the British Railways Enthronement Special. The atmosphere was as jolly as a seaside excursion. One of the newspaper photographers persuaded two Greek Orthodox prelates, the bearded Metropolitans of Mytilene and Rhodes, to pose rather unconventionally—leaning out the window of the train.

"Oh, do let us meet Archbishop Nikodim," cried Mrs. Hugh Gaitskell, wife of the Labor Party leader. She entered a compartment to be formally presented to the Russian Archbishop and to Moscow's leading Baptist minister.

One carriage was entirely taken over by Greek, Turkish, Rumanian, and Bulgarian archbishops, laughing and talking as the train pulled out of the station. The remainder of the carriages were occupied by the British priests and gaitered bishops—quiet, solemn, and rather gloomy. "This train is the Church of England on wheels, and if it crashes the junior clergy would be grieved," said a Church Commissioner. "They would be *very* grieved—and *very* quickly promoted."

The train sped through the London suburbs and the villages and bountiful orchards of Kent. Its passengers were served a light luncheon (tomato soup, turkey and ham salad, peach Melba). In an hour and twenty-five minutes they caught the unforgettable sight of Canterbury Cathedral across a broad expanse of meadow.

Eight coaches of the East Kent Bus Company took the distinguished visitors from the station to the Cathedral, where they robed and assembled for the procession.

In the Old Palace, Ramsey left his second-floor bedroom and walked briskly downstairs to greet his honorary chaplains in the dining room. "Your Grace, may we have a prayer?" asked John Andrew. Ramsey, apparently called from the depths of concentration, flashed him a glance of surprise, then began. As he prayed, briefly and movingly, a spontaneous petition, there streamed through the nave of the Cathedral a long procession of robed officials and foreign and domestic clergy. In the choir stalls were the Archbishop's family, his secretaries and staffs from Bishopthorpe and Lambeth, a few retired priests, wives of many in the ceremony, and fourteen monks and nuns representing seven monastic communities of the Anglican Communion.

The best-known faces among the dignitaries were those of gov-

ernment officials—the Lord Chancellor, Viscount Kilmuir; Hugh
Gaitskell; and two who had been Ramsey's colleagues years earlier in the Cambridge Union, R. A. Butler, Home Secretary, and
Selwyn Lloyd, Chancellor of the Exchequer. (A new crisis in
Berlin had detained Prime Minister Harold Macmillan in London. As for royal guests, the long-range planning of the Queen's
schedule had called for her to take up residence in late June at
Holyrood Palace in Edinburgh. On the afternoon of June 27 she
was accompanied by the Duke of Edinburgh to open a gasworks
in Fife. The Queen Mother was launching a ship at Newcastle
upon Tyne. Princess Margaret, awaiting the birth of her first
child, had canceled most of her public appearances.)

The last person in the preliminary processions was the Bishop
of London, Henry Montgomery Campbell. As he turned into his
stall a tiny red light glowed on a stone column near the high
altar, signifying to the organist and musicians the Archbishop's
presence at the great west doors. Trumpeters sounded their melo-
dious fanfare as he entered the Cathedral.*

The sight and sound of the exquisite music and enthralling
pageantry was carried to almost every corner of Britain and to
some areas of the Continent, the first Canterbury enthronement
ever televised. Two cameras were placed atop Christ Church
Gateway to pick up the crowds and processions. Inside the Cathedral, camera positions were improvised above the main door,
at the south end of the choir screen, on an especially constructed
bridge in the nave, and on a platform that spanned the entire
length of the north and south aisles of the choir. (A giant lens
crashed at the feet of one of the Archbishop's cousins.) The vast
congregation in the nave followed the ceremonies at the high
altar, obscured by the stone choir screen, by watching small
monitor sets lashed to the pillars of the nave.

A temporary shed and the crypt of the Cathedral housed trans-
mission facilities, the heavy cables and control boards contrasting
curiously with the ancient stonework and low, vaulted ceiling.
From here the cameras were directed in sweeping, breath-taking
panoramic views and intimate close-up portraitures: the Archbishop using both hands to secure the mitre on his head, nuns

* Excerpts from the Enthronement sermon appear in Part I, pp. 2-7.

bowing deeply in acknowledgment of episcopal authority, his wife genuflecting as he passed to the nave, his papers rustling in the wind as he gave a final blessing from a small wooden platform outside the Cathedral.

The ancient words and music resounded in a darkened room at the London headquarters of American Express where tourists who were unable to secure seats in the Cathedral followed the ceremony on television. They were given official programs especially sent from Canterbury.

The principal figure of the last enthronement, Geoffrey Fisher, now Lord Fisher of Lambeth, and Lady Fisher, sat before a television set in the home of neighbors of their son, H. A. P. Fisher, at Hazelmere, in Surrey. (Fisher's enthronement in April, 1945, had included British and American military personnel and a prayer "for the Allied Nations. . . . and our enemies.")

Mrs. William Temple, widow of the ninety-eighth Archbishop and daughter-in-law of the ninety-fifth, saw the service in the quarters of the chaplain of Winchester prison where she had spent the morning visiting and counseling with prisoners.

An ordinand from Lincoln, Lawrence Frost, recalls he was working in a mental hospital at Chester: "It was amazing. The whole ward went quiet. There was hardly a sound for an hour and a half."

At Kelham, two hundred ordinands, novices, and monks of the Society of the Sacred Mission watched on two television sets in the Common Room of the motherhouse. At Mirfield the monks scattered to the houses of the village to see the ceremony.

The staff of Durham's County Hotel, where Ramsey had attended innumerable luncheons and dinners, gathered in the new television lounge. And in his house near the gate of Auckland Castle the Ramseys' former butler, Ernest Alexander, still convalescing from the operation of the previous January, followed the program closely, hunting for his daughter in the crowd.

The ninety-minute service ended with the emergence of the clergy and choristers, blinking in the bright sunlight, and winding out of sight around a corner of the Cathedral. Richard Dimbleby, the BBC's commentator, completed his masterful narration: "Michael Ramsey, one hundredth Archbishop of Canterbury, successor among a multitude of others to Augustine, to Cranmer, to Laud, to Temple, and to Fisher, now proceeds to the cloister and then to the chapter house and finally to his new home in the Palace in all its sweet and calm in the shadow of this great Cathedral."

Twenty-four hours after his enthronement Ramsey was re-admitted to the House of Lords with the same formalities that had marked his coming to Durham in 1952 and to York in 1956. "The Lord Chancellor took his seat on the Woolsack at half past two o'clock," says the official record. "The Archbishop of Canterbury took the oath and subscribed the roll. Dr. Ramsey's sponsors were the Bishop of Norwich and the Bishop of Chelmsford."

Unbowed by the burden of recent ceremonial, the Archbishop welcomed at Lambeth Palace many of the dignitaries who had attended the enthronement. First there was an evening reception for members of the Orthodox and Old Catholic Churches. The next afternoon seven hundred guests attended a garden party in Lambeth's spacious grounds, queuing up in a long line to greet the Ramseys. A tireless young man sang out strange, evocative names announcing without stumbling "The Archbishop of Thyateira . . . the Metropolitan of Carthage . . . the Archbishop of Uppsala . . . the Metropolitan of Sardis . . ."

Ramsey was in great good spirits; he clasped his large hands over those of an old schoolmate, enjoyed a joke with two monks, patiently explained to some Americans the symbolism of the pectoral crosses he wore, and responded repeatedly to the traditional embrace and kiss of the Orthodox clergy. Occasionally he put an arm around his wife's shoulders, drawing her close to chat with a guest.

After greeting their host the visitors moved on to the refreshments—cups of tea or glasses of grapefruit juice, tiny cakes and bowls of strawberries and cream. Among the hollyhocks, delphiniums, and snapdragons of this most English of gardens wandered exotic Armenian monks with pointed hoods, tall-hatted Greek Orthodox priests, and the familiar gaitered bishops.

Reporters sought out Archbishop Nikodim of the Patriarchate of Moscow, a man whose dignified bearing and full beard gave the impression that he was at least fifty. He anticipated their questions on his age, his background, and the status of religion in Russia: "I am only thirty-two. I have been a priest since I was seventeen. My grandfather was a priest, but this did not influence me. Religion is a deeply-rooted need in all Russian people. It is simply not true, as many think in England, that our people are not religious. True, many members of my own family are not. But we are all on the best of terms I assure you."

At the back of the garden roamed aimlessly a tall harassed priest from Istanbul. "I have lost my Metropolitan," he chanted. "Has anyone seen my Metropolitan?"

Nearby, a woman in a large broad-brimmed hat peered down at a plump hen scratching in the grass. "My word!" she exclaimed. The presence of domestic fowl behind the sedate walls of Lambeth Palace was for many guests the most fascinating discovery of the day. "Doubtlessly a gift from the Diocese of Rhode Island," a bishop laughingly suggested. Actually, the twenty-eight hens had been brought to Lambeth by Archbishop Fisher's sister-in-law, Miss Foreman, for many years the warden (or chief housekeeper) of the Lambeth Palace hostel for visiting dignitaries. Ramsey said with tolerant amusement and pride, "Those hens supply all our eggs"—a remark that conjured up visions of a churchman who appreciated a penny saved and would likely do wonders with skimpy ecclesiastical budgets.

That evening Ramsey appeared, shaved and refreshed, for a formal dinner in the Guard Room, the great hall built in the fourteenth century for soldiers and arms. (Troops had been billeted there as late as 1780 to protect Lambeth from a group of marchers called the Protestant Association.) One hundred and sixteen guests, including Ramsey's friend, the Roman Catholic Archbishop of Liverpool, gathered under the finely-carved, vaulted ceiling, surrounded by portraits of primates from the fifteenth to the eighteenth centuries. Looking down in their lawn-sleeved magnificence, they might have mused that "the new man" was cutting quite a swath.

Despite the entertaining that dominated his first ten days in office, Ramsey devoted considerable time to Church business. At Lambeth, in the interval before going to Canterbury, he had met with the Church Commissioners and held private conferences with the Anglican Bishop of Amritsar, India, and the Rev. J. G. Baker, joint secretary of the Anglican Communion's Advisory Council on Missionary Strategy.

After the enthronement the first person Ramsey received in his study at Lambeth was the general secretary of the World Council of Churches, W. A. Visser 't Hooft. (Their meeting on June 29, 1961, was a few weeks short of the twenty-fifth anniversary of the day William Temple had introduced them at Bishopthorpe.) The following morning he saw the executive officer of the Anglican Communion, Bishop Bayne. Other priority appointments on his schedule were given to the Rev. John Satterthwaite, general secretary of the Church of England Council on Inter-Church Relations, and to Canon McKay of the BBC.

On July 4 Ramsey met with the Archbishop-designate of York, Dr. Coggan, presided the next day in the Lambeth chapel at the confirmation of Coggan's election, and attended a reception for him in the drawing room. The Bishop of New York came to luncheon on the 20th and the Bishop of Jamaica and his two sisters on the 26th. Outside engagements included a tour of the *Church Illustrated*'s new building, a meeting at the British Museum, a garden party at Westminster Abbey, a tea in the House of Commons, and a civic reception at Croydon. One evening the Ramseys attended the Lord Mayor's dinner for bishops; another night they dined with the Bishop of Southwark.

"My new job won't stop us from going to Devon. Why should it?" Ramsey asked, looking forward to his August holiday. They went loyally to their usual retreat in Devonshire, an antique inn, which provided room and board for slightly more than £10 a week. Ramsey abandoned his customary gaiters and cassock to tramp the moors in a vacation ensemble of cloth cap, tweed sports jacket, and flannel bags. He returned near sundown, ready for a simple, hearty meal at the inn. "It's good plain stuff," he purred. "And I like a drop of cider with it. The cider rounds off the meal."

One more opportunity for rest and peaceful work awaited the Archbishop before the busy schedule of the autumn months: a quiet weekend at Cuddesdon, conveniently near the International Congress of the New Testament which was to meet at Oxford. He was driven there alone. Mrs. Ramsey was on a visit to relatives in Ireland, and his chaplain on holiday in South Africa.

A Cuddesdon history published in 1930 refers to the college as "a nursery not only of priests but of bishops . . . [and] at last there came from its seventy-five years of life one who as Primate of All England has never forgotten the happiness and privilege of being a Cuddesdon man." This was Cosmo Lang who was greatly devoted to his old seminary. Ramsey, the second alumnus to become Archbishop of Canterbury, was to receive a proud welcome from the seminarians. They were waiting in the Common Room to greet him when they heard a knock at the back door.

"The 'Princeps' was so nervous he nearly jumped out of his chair," recalls one student. "I went to answer, thinking it was the garbage collector calling at a most inappropriate time. I opened the door—and there stood the Archbishop. His car had already pulled away. He had alighted at what had been the main entrance when he was here."

Cuddesdon's suite for special guests was in shining order for Ramsey's occupancy. Here he completed his addresses for Oxford and for a conference of Old Catholic and Anglican theologians at Amersfoort, Holland, later in the month. In the mornings he chatted with bricklayers working on a modernistic structure to replace the Bishop's Palace that had recently burned. And he took a few swings at croquet on the green lawns of the college, saying to those who were timid in trying to defeat him, "Well, I see we are playing *seminary* croquet!"

Preparations for the Third Assembly of the World Council of Churches in New Delhi demanded much of Ramsey's time upon his return to Lambeth. Fisher had asked Lord Denning to raise £50,000 as Britain's contribution toward a new headquarters building at Geneva. Ramsey joined in this drive and up to a week before his departure was sending carefully worded personal letters to banks and leading businessmen for the cause he described as "international, while being in the fullest sense Christian, humanitarian and world-wide."

Departure for India was scheduled for November 15. From Palim Airport, New Delhi, the Ramseys were driven to No. 2 King George Avenue, the handsomely landscaped residence of the British High Commissioner, Sir Paul Gore-Booth and Lady Gore-Booth. They would be the Gore-Booths' guests for the next three weeks along with Satterthwaite of Lambeth's "foreign office" (a delegate and also Ramsey's chaplain) and Colonel Robert

Hornby, Chief Information Officer of the Church Assembly, who would handle the Archbishop's press relations.

Life moved at a gracious pace in the High Commissioner's residence, an island of comparative peace in the increasingly crowded city. Nearly six hundred delegates were arriving with scores of alternates, official guests, advisers, observers, assistants, newsmen, and tourists. Hotels and housing accommodations were woefully inadequate; head colds and "Delhi-belly" were prevalent.

One of the visitors Ramsey received, prior to the opening of the Assembly, was Billy Graham, who had come to the conference as an observer. (Graham's church, the Southern Baptist Convention, is not a member of the World Council.) "Ah, Billy!" the Archbishop cried out to the surprise of Satterthwaite and others who had rarely heard him call an acquaintance by his first name. The evangelist addressed Ramsey as "Your Grace" as they reminisced of their earlier meetings, including the time the Ramseys and the Grahams were house guests of the Duke of Hamilton, in Scotland. Graham had said then, "Let me walk behind you and I'll know what to do because an Anglican bishop can't go wrong." Later they appeared together on a program at the Delhi YMCA and were publicly photographed. It was at least one moment of prominence for Graham who otherwise remained on the sidelines at the meeting, wearing a sportcoat that contrasted with the ecclesiastical robes. He departed at the end of the week with the comment, "This meeting needs to get its vision focused on a risen triumphant Christ."

A white banner sagged in a slight breeze over Moulana Azad Road proclaiming the World Council's central meeting hall, the strikingly modern Vigyan Bhavan, or House of Learning. At 10:30 A.M. on Sunday, November 19, a small sedan sped along this dusty thoroughfare and careened to a stop in front of the hall. Several smiling Englishmen peeled away—Satterthwaite, Hornby, and others—and out stepped Joan Ramsey and the Archbishop in his familar purple cassock.

"It's the Archbishop of Canterbury," the whisper went round the crowd of spectators. Hands on hips, Ramsey stood looking up at the boxish architecture of the Vigyan. He peered at the photographers and the crowds, smiling and shooting his eyebrows up and down in a characteristic gesture. "Yes, yes," he said to nobody in particular and strode into the building.

A half hour later, Ramsey emerged midway in a line of several hundred clergy and laity. They came alphabetically, representing one hundred and ninety-eight churches in sixty countries: Coptic priests with black onion hats and heavy rosary beads, the shaggy-faced Orthodox, Congregationalists and Presbyterians in Geneva gowns, and Anglicans walking with the measured pace perfected in long years of processing up the aisle every Sunday morning.

The uneven ranks moved toward a multi-colored *shamiana* or tent erected for the opening service of worship. A choir, seated cross-legged on a platform, hummed Indian tunes to the accompaniment of string instruments. Ramsey found his seat, twelve rows from the front, as a small electronic organ took up a familiar hymn. The congregation sang in a babble of tongues that, taken together, was surprisingly melodic: the Third Assembly of the World Council of Churches was beginning.

At the business sessions in the Vigyan's main auditorium, Ramsey occupied an aisle seat with the new Archbishop of York and four other Church of England delegates. They sat directly in front of the American Baptist Convention and behind the delegates from the *Eglise évangélique du Gabon*. The scene resembled the United Nations: tiers of chairs and desks equipped with identifying nameplates and earphones for language translations. There was even a group from the Soviet Union. The reception of the Holy Orthodox Church of Russia, as a member of the Council, was one of the most moving events of the meeting at New Delhi. Ramsey and the entire hall applauded as the bearded Russians paraded to the stage, among them Archbishop Nikodim who had so recently walked in the gardens of Lambeth Palace.

Ramsey's days at New Delhi fell into a pleasant routine, beginning at 7:30 A.M. in a side chapel at the Cathedral of the Redemption. ("Don't be surprised if the Archb. celebrates in his bare feet when he returns, as that is the custom at the altar here," wrote Satterthwaite in a letter to London.) He hurried to breakfast at the High Commissioner's, attended the meeting of the Section on Unity from 9:45 to 12:45, and usually appeared for meetings of a committee on Faith and Order from 4:30 to 6 or the general sessions from 6:30 to 8. "I am very happy to be one of the mob," he said to Canon C. B. Mortlock, ecclesiastical correspondent for the *Daily Telegraph*. "This is the first big conference at which I have not felt tired. I can cut a session now and then."

During the morning recess Ramsey moved swiftly through the corridors to call personally for messages and letters at the first floor mail desk. He stopped now and then to greet visitors or for the embraces of the Orthodox. ("I do *love* the Orthodox," he said.) Often he sat quietly on a sofa outside the main auditorium. Photographers soon discovered that anyone photographed with the Archbishop usually ordered several prints.

One morning the Archbishop slipped away early to pray barefoot at the shrine of Gandhi, an act of reverence he appeared particularly anxious to perform. He added a large wreath to the flower-bedecked cement block that is Gandhi's memorial on the banks of the River Jumna where the leader's body was cremated in January, 1948. Later Ramsey spoke of the need Christianity has to present itself as "applicable to all the world and not just a part of European culture."

As he was driven to and from the Vigyan in the High Commissioner's stately black Rolls Royce, Ramsey became familiar with the panorama of life in New Delhi. He saw the Indians squatting, drowsy or meditative in the hot, midday sun; women in saris moving gracefully with jugs of water balanced on their heads; and the carnival attractions drawn by the international meeting—the snake charmers with their flutes, the mangy black bears made to dance by a rope cruelly inserted through their noses.

In the meetings of the Unity section the Archbishop spoke occasionally, raising his hand to be recognized by the speaker and then waiting for the signal that the translators were ready. He identified himself simply: "Ramsey, Church of England." To interviewers he described the work of this section as "that part of the World Council that deals specifically with Christian unity in a theological way, thrashing out some of the points of doctrine that divide us and seeing how far we can reconcile them."

Ramsey made his major address to the Assemby on the evening of its sixth day. "Just as our mission is unity, holiness, truth, all three, so our scandal is the distortion of unity, holiness, truth, all three," he declared. ". . . The world does not hear the call to holiness, and does not care for the truth in Christ. But the world has its own care for unity, albeit conceived in a secular way: longing for peace, it desires that men and nations shall be joined to each other and the forces which separate them removed. And the world, caring thus for unity, is shocked when the Church fails to manifest it."

He warned that "a movement which concentrates on unity as an isolated concept can mislead the world and mislead us, as indeed would a movement which had the exclusive label of truth." He recommended slow and thoughtful deliberation: "If we will be patient, true theology, good theology, is something which unites. But it will not be true unless it keeps itself and us near to the Cross whence the call to holiness comes."

Two days later Ramsey again was a central figure in the events of the Assembly—the occasion of the first "open" Eucharist ever conducted by Anglicans at a meeting of the World Council. It had required weeks of careful planning and involved many doctrinal issues (for example, Methodists objected to the use of fermented wine: they insisted on using plain grape juice), as well as arrangements for an estimated fifteen hundred people to receive the Sacrament from thirty priests ministering at several improvised altars.

Ramsey's absence from the procession (he had left it to enter at the side of the *shamiana*) gave rise to the rumor that he did not wholly approve of the open service, a belief that seemed to be corroborated by his presence in the sanctuary without officiating. Later a spokesman explained that Ramsey had left the procession to follow the Metropolitan of India, Pakistan, Burma, and Ceylon, Aurobindo Nath Mukerjee, who could not walk the length of the cavernous tent. And it was pointed out that he had communicated, receiving the Holy Communion at the hands of the celebrant, the Bishop of Delhi, and the Cathedral's native vicar, Ernest John.

At the same hour the Archbishop was attending the open service, there was broadcast by short wave from New Delhi a tape recording he had made with the Secretary General of the Methodist Church of Australia, W. F. Hambly. "Don't expect the World Council itself to produce a plan of unity after a fortnight or so," Ramsey warned. "But do expect this: that as a result of the converse together here at New Delhi the churches when they go home will be in lots of ways in a closer relation than they were before. That is what will happen."

Asked about "the next step" toward unity, he replied that "wherever possible there should be actual unions of churches as in the case of South India where there has been a remarkable coming together of different traditions in one Church with the historic episcopate as the backbone." Ramsey pointed out that "for centuries the Orthodox has been very isolated but now it is finding unity and strength within itself and is going on to the general task of unity. I think it is about the biggest and most significant thing of the lot."

Much of the Archbishop's time was given to official entertaining—and to being entertained. At the Jesuit College Ramsey and other Anglican prelates dined with the Roman Catholic Bishop of New Delhi and his coadjutor. One evening Ramsey held a reception for the Anglican delegates. Another night he received the Orthodox and Old Catholics, and they responded a few days later with a reception honoring him. In an informal address he thanked them, adding with a smile as he looked around the room, "If I could collect all these beards I would have a holy mattress!"

The most splendid of all the receptions was that given by the Vice President of India, Sarvepalli Radhakrishnan, in the formal gardens of the impressive red sandstone building that was once the palace of the British Viceroys.

Indian guardsmen in full uniform stood at attention at intervals along the paths of the serene acropolis in the heart of the spaciously laid out city. Ramsey went immediately to greet Radhakrishnan, a friendly man in white turban and steel-rimmed glasses who had been for sixteen years Spalding Professor of Eastern Religions and Ethics at Oxford. (A noted author, Radhakrishnan is frequently quoted on his description of Christians as "ordinary people making extraordinary claims.") Whereas the delegates and visitors had reluctantly approached the Archbishop during his first few days at New Delhi, now they crowded around him. He probably met more people on this afternoon than at any other time during the Assembly.

The Archbishops of Canterbury and York both participated in the morning service at the Cathedral on their last Sunday in New Delhi. Ramsey preached the sermon and attended a breakfast on the broad front lawn. A red-coated band, sent by the President of India, played under the trees. Urging his parishioners to gather around him to hear his address of welcome, the vicar, Father

John, said in an aside to Ramsey, "My people are backward about coming forward!"

That afternoon the Ramseys and a group of distinguished churchmen had tea at St. Stephen's Mission Hospital on the outskirts of Delhi. An Anglican nun, Sister Vivian, of the Community of Jesus the Good Shepherd, showed them through the maternity wards. As the Archbishop passed, the young mothers placed their hands together in the reverent greeting of the East. In the stone chapel, built in 1898 in the hospital courtyard, Ramsey stood silently before the altar.

When his limousine pulled away from the hospital, the Canterbury flag waving from the right fender, a visitor remarked to Sister Vivian,

"Quite a day for St. Stephen's, Sister."

"Very!" she replied, her eyes glistening with tears.

After a few minutes the automobile turned from the rutted road into the grounds of the Church of St. James Within the Kashmir Gates where Ramsey was to preach at Evensong. A small Indian girl, her dark eyes wide with awe, silently regarded the Archbishop in his cope and mitre. When he had passed into the church she ran to find her mother in the parish house. "Mommy," she exclaimed, "I've just seen the Archangel Gabriel with wings and a tall hat."

At the Hotel Ashoka, in New Delhi's embassy district, Sir Kenneth Grubb sat at dinner, thinking back over the weeks of the Assembly. Sir Kenneth, a man of many activities and once an explorer in South America, has in recent years held simultaneously three key positions—the chairmanship of the House of Laity of the Church Assembly and of the Commission of the Churches on International Affairs, in addition to the presidency of the Church Missionary Society. "I asked how long they would carry on this morning, and they said an hour," Sir Kenneth remarked. "I asked Mike Ramsey how long he would preach and he said a quarter of an hour. He kept his promise but the rest didn't. These ecclesiastics have no respect for time. As for the Archbishop, he is a good soul, a good theologian. His brilliance saves him from laziness. When he went to Canterbury I told him, 'You are supposed to bear fools with gladness. You've also got to gladden the fools!' "

Not until the Assembly entered its final week did the Archbishop have an opportunity to see the countryside beyond New

Delhi. On Monday he went with his party to Agra to address a convocation at St. John's College and to walk in the gardens and along the white marble terrace of the Taj Mahal.

"What a country of contrasts it is," he wrote after this trip. "The old life of country villages and the new life of the industrial belts, the great modern buildings of the British Raj and the monuments of ancient Indian civilization, the juxtaposition of wealth and extreme poverty and squalor. . . . It is a country which to see is to love quickly; and despite the intensity of nationalism, the friendship with us, the country of India's former rulers, is wonderfully great."

In New Delhi the delegates assembled in one of their final meetings to hear Prime Minister Nehru. He appeared in his familiar white trousers and cap, the inevitable red rose in the buttonhole of his gray coat. He spoke but briefly and hurried away. The time was less than a month before the invasion of Goa.

The Assembly closed with a new presidium at the helm. To almost no one's surprise, Ramsey was among the six presidents, for he was the logical successor to fill one of the vacant places. Ramsey stood at the center of the group for pictures on the steps of the meeting hall and in the garden. The presidium included, besides Ramsey, Archbishop Iakovos of the Greek Archdiocese of North and South America; Dr. Martin Niemoeller, president of the Evangelical Church of Hesse-Nassau; Dr. David Moses, principal of Hislop College, Nagpur, India; and, for the first time, two laymen—Sir Francis Ibiam, governor of the Eastern Province of Nigeria, a physician and distinguished Presbyterian; and Charles Parlin, outstanding Methodist layman and a senior member of a law firm in New York City.

In retrospect Ramsey found that the World Council had come a long way in correcting its "unrepresentative character of a body overwhelmingly Protestant in composition and definite in its dominant tone." Secondly, he felt it had escaped "from the impression that Western Civilization is a kind of norm for Christian life, thought, and culture."

While the meeting was still in progress some leaders praised it as "the second Reformation" and the "greatest gathering of Christians since the sixteenth-century Council of Trent." Ramsey spoke more realistically: "New Delhi is a symbol; a milestone on a journey, but also a signpost telling us to go on."

The official schedule for the Archbishop's last six days in India was as varied as those of his two African trips. It began on December 6, the day the Ramseys flew to Calcutta, and included such notations as:

> Visit to Leper Dispensary, Manicktolla.
> Dinner party at residence of N. Stenhouse, Esq., to meet Old Reptonians.
> Bishop of Barrackpore will fetch Archbishop by car, and they will visit villages south of Calcutta till lunch time.

The busy program continued through the final evening when Ramsey preached in St. Paul's Cathedral and was guest of honor at a dinner given by the Deputy High Commissioner, Major-General W. H. A. Bishop, in whose home the Ramseys had been visiting. They left the house the next day at 5 A.M. for Dum Dum Airport, Calcutta, and the long flight home. A cable confirming their safe departure was dispatched to the Foreign Office in London and was relayed within the hour to Lambeth Palace. A tall, beautifully decorated Christmas tree stood at the top of Lambeth's main stairway to welcome them.

Another royal occasion, the baptism of Princess Margaret's infant son, awaited Ramsey on his return. Official notification of the child's birth, on the morning of November 4, had been made in telephone calls to the Queen, the Prime Minister, the Home Secretary, and the Archbishop. The Ramseys had responded immediately with a large bouquet of white roses and carnations personally delivered to Clarence House by Chaplain Andrew. On the afternoon of December 19, Ramsey stood in the white-and-gold music room of Buckingham Palace to give the child his Christian names—David Albert Charles. The Queen, as the principal Godparent, had held the baby while a choir from the Chapel Royal sang the hymn, "Loving Shepherd." She passed him to the Archbishop, softly repeating the names. Ramsey used water from the River Jordan in a silver-gilt font made more than a century ago for the baptism of the first of Victoria's children. Afterward, in a parish register and again in the royal register, he recorded the baptism.

Preparations for Christmas crowded in upon the Archbishop no less than any other subject of the realm. Fortunately, the Ramseys' own holiday greetings had been ordered and addressed before their departure for India. They had chosen a tan paper for the imprinting of a 1498 wood engraving of a Nativity scene by a French artist, found in a Latin Book of Hours in the Lambeth Palace Library. Inside was the printed message: "Christmas Greetings from the Archbishop of Canterbury and Mrs. Ramsey, Lambeth Palace and the Old Palace, Canterbury." And to this Joan Ramsey often added a personal note in her large, distinctive handwriting.

Lambeth Palace was completely closed a few days before Christmas. The Ramseys drove to Canterbury for their longest stay of the year. Among the calls they paid in the area was a visit to one of the Archbishop's aunts, Miss Phoebe Ramsey, who at ninety-five was a patient in a nursing home in Kent.

Ramsey was asked to write special messages for publications ranging from the mass-circulation *TV Times* to the Canterbury newspaper, *The Kent Messenger*. But the matter to which he gave closest attention was an address from the Cathedral to be televised by the BBC on Christmas night.

The Queen's customary address was heard at 3 P.M., and the Archbishop followed at 6:55. Seated before the high altar of Canterbury Cathedral he came across warmly and simply. "Christmas is nearly over," he began. "What a happy day it has been, hasn't it, for you, listening there in your home." He moved on to the meaning of Christmas: ". . . To this act of God's love reverberating down the ages you can be indifferent or you can be just rather vague and sentimental, or you can respond with gratitude, love, belief. And the moment you respond there begins a real bond between Christ and you, between you and Christ . . ."

He departed, momentarily, from his prepared text: "I am not just making this up, you know. This is how it is . . ." And he continued with the story of Bethlehem.

"So Christmas passes on its way once more," he concluded. "It is nearly over; it has swept on its course through the hours and the minutes and all the joys we have been having. . . . If you know that there is room in you for Christ you will not end your

Christmas Day saying, like the people of Bethlehem, 'If only we had known.' "

At the year's end it was obvious that Ramsey's manifold activities had allayed the anonymously written declaration of *Crockford's Clerical Directory* that the Church would not want just "a quiet, colorless, efficient administrator" in the wake of Fisher's extraordinary primacy.

The new Archbishop was energetic and imaginative in his participation in many aspects of the Church's life at home and abroad, especially the movement toward Christian unity. A meeting at the Old Palace the previous September with Monsignor Jan Willebrand of the Vatican Secretariat for Promoting Christian Unity would lead to a luncheon at Lambeth the following August with Augustin Cardinal Bea,* the German-born Jesuit who heads the Secretariat. In October, Ramsey had welcomed His Beatitude, Patriarch Benedictos of Jerusalem, presenting him with the coveted Lambeth Cross and receiving in return the star-shaped Order of the Holy Sepulchre.

Such experiences, emphasizing Ramsey's position as the spiritual leader of a world-wide communion, reminded him of his old feeling that the term "Anglican Communion" is a limited and unsatisfactory name. "It suggests Englishness, Englishness," he says, with his characteristic musing repetition.

Meanwhile, the public and the press continued their assessment of Ramsey's character and capabilities. "Dr. Ramsey's basic beliefs are as simple as they are firm," observed one newspaper. "He holds that faith is hard, religion is no cult of happiness, some questions have no answers." *The Church Times* commented editorially that "his finest triumph . . . would be to recall the Church of England to her knees [and] the whole English people to their knees—and their salvation." Something of the same sentiment was echoed in Anthony Sampson's comprehensive survey, *Anatomy of Britain,* which observed that under Ramsey the Church "may not obviously become a greater force in the land, but is quite likely to become more religious—with possible consequences which no one can predict."

* His visit on Sunday, August 5, 1962, marked the first time a Roman Catholic Cardinal had visited Lambeth since the primacy of Cardinal Pole 404 years earlier.

IV MICHAEL CANTUAR

London lay under a record snowfall during the first week of January, 1962, when the hundredth Archbishop returned from Canterbury to begin at Lambeth Palace the first full year of his primacy. He rarely paused now as, almost automatically, he signed his name "Michael Cantuar:"—the abbreviation of the ancient Latin for Canterbury. His successive signatures, "Michael Dunelm:," "Michael Ebor:," and "Michael Cantuar:," represented his personal odyssey, his ascent in less than a decade from newly-consecrated diocesan bishop to the highest position in the Anglican Communion. At New Delhi he had signed photographs and speeches "Michael, Archbishop of Canterbury," explaining with a smile that the longer title "seems to give the people more for their money." Back in England, he returned to the ancient form.

The stately buildings in which this hundredth Archbishop lives and works from Monday mornings until Friday nights, occupy land acquired by the forty-second primate, Baldwin, when he was weary of tedious disputes with the monks of Canterbury. Originally a royal manor house believed to have been owned by a sister of Edward the Confessor, the property was willed to the Bishop of Rochester and his monks and came into the possession of the Archbishop of Canterbury in an exchange of lands sometime between 1185 and 1190. Nearly seven hundred years later the convening in 1867 of the first Lambeth Conference signified that a place acquired during a domestic quarrel inside the Church of England had become a symbol of unity, a focal point of the whole Anglican Communion.

More than fifty people live behind the high brick walls that surround the palace grounds. A quadrangle of cottages to the right of the palace provides housing for numerous members of Archbishop Ramsey's domestic and official household. Others come in to work during the day.

One member of Ramsey's staff has described the palace as "a place of offices and long corridors, cream-painted and impersonal." Others are charmed by the restrained elegance achieved in the architecture of many centuries. Almost everyone feels a deep sense of history that speaks of hundreds of years of devotion to God.

Lambeth Palace is the first and only London home Ramsey has known. Although he passed through London as a schoolboy going to Sandroyd and Repton and occasionally came to the city for meetings in the 1930's and 1940's, he had never spent long periods in London until becoming a bishop in 1952. In that year he visited Lambeth Palace for the first time. After that, he returned regularly to London for meetings of bishops, the Church Assembly, and the House of Lords.

The area known as Lambeth (derived from Loamhythe, or marshy area) is mainly industrial, lying between the Thames and Waterloo Station. Its name is associated with a dance fad of thirty years ago, the Lambeth Walk. Devotees of Somerset Maugham know it as the setting of his first novel, *Liza of Lambeth*, written when Maugham was a medical student at St. Thomas Hospital across the road from the palace. In February, 1952, the palace was mentioned in newspaper accounts of the death of George VI and the thousands who formed "a somber line that stretched four miles outside Westminster Hall, past the scaffolding of Victoria Tower, along the north banks of the Thames, over Lambeth Bridge, down the Albert Embankment, and back around Lambeth Palace where the Archbishop lives."

A caller approaching Lambeth Palace sees first of all the square stone tower of the Parish Church of St. Mary, Lambeth. "We always speak of the palace as being next to St. Mary's, not of St. Mary's next to the palace, because St. Mary's was here first," explains the rector, the Rev. H. Hedley. Mentioned in the *Domesday Book* as the house of worship in the manor of Countess Goda, it has been closely associated with the Archbishops who came to live at Lambeth. Five of them (Bancroft, Tenison, Hutton, Cornwallis, and Moore) are buried in front of the high altar. St. Mary's proximity to the center of activity of the Anglican Communion is emphasized by a large stained-glass window which depicts a global map, the four saints who brought the faith to Britain—Augustine, Patrick, Ninian, and David—and Christ's command, "Go ye into all the world." Ten days after his enthronement Ramsey made his first official visit to St. Mary's for the annual service for overseas missionaries.

The entrance to the palace grounds is only a few feet from the churchyard. It was Cardinal Morton who in the 1490's built the Tudor gate of red brick between the two older towers which he restored. His audience chamber, used today as one of the archive rooms of the palace library, arches above the passage. A ground-floor flat is occupied by the gatekeeper, Jack Papworth, a short, muscular man who was for twenty years a policeman on the docks of London. He busies himself in his small woodworking shop when he is not opening the gate for automobiles or the small postern door. If a visitor's name is not on a list sent from the secretary's office, Papworth politely telephones to the palace. The majority of unexpected callers are petitioners, pickets, and religious fanatics. One, identifying himself as an Ethiopian businessman, left behind five pieces of matched blue leather luggage which the London police eventually claimed. On a cold Sunday afternoon early in 1962 a well-dressed man in a bowler marched back and forth with a neatly-worded sign: "I want this place destroyed!" For years the palace gatekeepers and staff have agreed, "Every nut in the Kingdom comes to Lambeth sooner or later."*

Visitors cross a courtyard to the main door opening on a hall that is three stories high, its walls hung with paintings and halberdiers' pikes from the times when Lambeth had to be defended from mobs. In one full sweep the eye follows the broad blue-carpeted

---

*Cosmo Lang had an especially strong regard for the dignity of the palace. His biographer relates that Lang "treated the intrusion of a burglar in the summer of 1933 almost as an affront. The man climbed in through Lang's open bedroom window, later admitting astonishment at finding 'an old man in bed' where he had expected a drawing room."

staircase to the graceful triple arches which frame the main corridors of the first and second floors.

A fresco of Christ's resurrection from the tomb is centered above a long console table. This table holds a large framed mosaic of the madonna and child, and frequently there is a blooming plant or a fresh bouquet of flowers. To the left is the door to the Archbishop's study, and here the senior chaplain, Noel Kennaby (former provost of Newcastle), or the domestic chaplain, John Andrew, stand to welcome the primate's callers. If a visitor is early he is shown into the chaplain's study until the Archbishop is ready to receive him.

Near the staircase is a small table reserved for a guest book. A fresh page is always turned for the Prime Minister and royal visitors.

The central hallway is lined with portraits of primates of the nineteenth and twentieth centuries. Other portraits hang in the formal dining room and in the Guard Room.* On the staircase to the Lambeth hostel, a wing reserved for bishops and other guests, are displayed the large photographs of the Lambeth Conferences in which can be readily traced the changes in tonsorial fashions from the bearded bishops of the 1860's to the smooth-faced prelates of recent years.

The Ramseys' most spectacular refurbishing at Lambeth may be observed in the formal drawing room where the once dark walls are covered with scarlet brocade. Pale blue draperies can be drawn across the broad windows when Mrs. Ramsey works in the evening at her voluminous correspondence. Her demure writing table is outfitted with a crimson-and-purple desk set, the gift of an Orthodox prelate.

Across the hall, the Archbishop's study has a square bay of windows looking out on the spacious grounds where the Westminster choir boys come to play cricket. In the distance are a few of the tall office buildings new to the London skyline. Two walls are filled with handsome glass-fronted bookcases. The fireplace

---

*"I am afraid we have an imposter in the Guard Room," reported the Lambeth librarian, Geoffrey Bill, in a memorandum to Ramsey. "The portrait claiming to be Archbishop Abbot is in fact a portrait of Thomas Bilson, Bishop of Winchester. The portrait is clearly marked anno 1611, and the age of the sitter is given as sixty-four. Archbishop Abbot was only forty-nine in that year, though it fits the age of Bilson."

is flanked by a door to a secretary's office and another to a private lavatory. There is bright grass-green carpeting on the floor, and the walls above the white wainscoting are covered with a wall-paper of gold-and-white design. A familiar framed print of the crucifixion, acquired by Ramsey years ago, hangs above a mantel-piece that displays interesting personal mementoes: a photograph of the interior court of Magdalene College, a color picture of the enthronement at Canterbury, snapshots of recent trips, and small gifts from visitors.

A dominant piece of furniture in the room is a round table with neat stacks of newly published magazines and books. There is also a large desk, but Ramsey almost never uses it, preferring to work in a wing-chair with a lapboard on his knees.

A private dining room is closed off by sliding double doors from the formal dining room. The smaller room has as its principal feature illuminated cabinets displaying the palace's best china and glassware. The china used on the Archbishop's table is white with a wide border of purple edged in gold. Its only decoration is the archiepiscopal mitre in black and white at the center of the plate. In this small dining room the Ramseys first entertained Prime Minister Harold Macmillan and his wife with a private luncheon on January 11, 1962, which also happened to be the fifth anniversary of Macmillan's election to office. Besides luncheons, the Ramseys frequently give sherry parties, especially during the weeks of convocation and the Church Assembly. ("They make you know how genuinely glad they are to see you," says one guest. "One never feels it is an 'official squash' in which people are being ticked off.") A caterer was the first person Mrs. Ramsey received at Lambeth in preparation for the enthronement garden party the following week.

The late Bishop of Derby's widow, Mildred Rawlinson, has known Lambeth during the reigns of five Archbishops: "In Archbishop Davidson's time it was like a country vicarage—cozy, comfortable, and unmodernized. Since there were no bathrooms, the old and faithful servants brought in large cans of water so guests could have a hip-bath in their bedrooms in front of the fire. Lang succeeded Davidson, and the next time I went to Lambeth the whole place had gone tremendously grand. I was reminded of the lines, 'Four and twenty bathrooms and a ghost on every floor;

Seven things for breakfast and often many more.' There were so many silver platters of food we could only wonder who ate all of it. Then William Temple, *poor* William, stayed in two rooms in the rubble of bombed-out Lambeth. The Fishers endured the same thing at the beginning, living 'below-stairs' in a palace of windswept corridors and roofless chambers. Joan Ramsey was dropped by divine helicopter to help restore the Church's castles and palaces."

A walk with the Ramseys through the corridors of Lambeth reveals the fascinating souvenirs of many eras. One finds, for instance, a plaque bearing a coat-of-arms with an alligator rampant and the inscription: "A Silver Jubilee Gift to the Archbishop of Canterbury and the Mother Church from the Diocese of the Nile, 1926-1951." Glass display cases in a corridor leading to the chapel contain, among other items, vestments that belonged to Cardinal Pole and the illuminated parchment manuscript given by the city of Toronto to Archbishop Davidson, "the first Primate of All England who has visited this continent, 3 September 1904." In another gallery, one comes, surprisingly, to the portraits of three women, the wives of Davidson, Temple, and Fisher.

A small elevator near the main staircase offers the Ramseys easy access to their flat tucked away on the second floor. (Having been trapped in "the lift" one evening shortly after she came to Lambeth, Mrs. Ramsey may now regard with caustic amusement a small sign that proclaims, "Doors will open automatically when this car has completed its journey.") A grandfather clock stands in the foyer of the private quarters, and the walls are decorated with landscapes painted by a cousin of Mrs. Ramsey.

French doors open from the foyer onto a tiny roof garden. Here the primate and his wife may while away an hour on a mild summer evening. A short corridor called "Crooked Lane," which is lined with several prints of County Durham, leads to an unpretentious but comfortable sitting room with a piano Mrs. Ramsey sometimes plays. The hallway also leads to a guest room and the Ramseys' airy bedroom overlooking the gardens. A restful blue wallpaper is figured with silver flowers. The bed has a white spread and a half canopy. A dressing room and bath complete the suite.

Another private flat within the palace is occupied by the warden of the Lambeth hostel. When Lord Fisher's sister-in-law resigned this job, the Church Commissioners employed Mrs. George Edward Brigstocke, whom the Ramseys had known well during their years at Durham. With her husband, a retired canon of Durham Cathedral, she came to live at Lambeth at the same time the Ramseys took up residence there.

Molly Brigstocke, a cheerful and efficient woman, supervises the domestic staff of cleaning women, three serving maids, and a cook. Two of the jobs as maids are reserved for German girls, usually Lutheran, who spend a year "in service" at Lambeth while perfecting their study of English. The third maid is an older Englishwoman whose name sometimes startles and amuses guests —Mrs. Pope.

A case of tea is used each month at Lambeth even though the Ramseys themselves frequently prefer coffee. Venison from the royal parks is sometimes supplied the palace kitchen on the token payment of one pound by the Archbishop. Most of the vegetables served are grown at Lambeth by the chief gardener, Charles Skinner, who also tends the formal rose garden and the other flowers. He does extremely well, despite London's polluted air, its flocks of pigeons, and soil depleted from centuries of use.

The twenty-eight Rhode Island hens, the talk of the Ramseys' first garden party, are no longer at Lambeth, but their eggs were pickled and served for some months thereafter by the resourceful cook, Audrey Heaton. This Westmoreland lass is the joy of Lambeth. She serves for breakfast the lightest, fluffiest rolls in all of England. ("These rolls are the best part of staying at Lambeth," confides the Bishop of Coventry.) For the Archbishop's birthday, just before he flew to India, Audrey prepared his favorite dishes— "roast duck, plain and very English, for lunch, and a mixed grille for dinner." Both fulfilled the requirements of the high-protein diet prescribed for Ramsey while he was still at York. A big birthday cake remained hidden in the kitchen because the Archbishop is forbidden breads and pastries. Melons are a fondness in which he may indulge at any meal.

Ramsey begins each day at Lambeth with the celebration of the Holy Eucharist in the palace chapel. A different diocese and diocesan bishop is remembered daily until a whole rotation of the Anglican Communion is gradually completed and then resumed.

The chapel, restored after World War II, is a symbol of that widespread communion: the organ was given by Americans, the sanctuary carpet by New Zealanders, the altar frontals and furnishings by Canadians, the altar linens by Japanese.

At breakfast with his wife and chaplain in the small dining room, Ramsey glances through the morning post, smiling and sometimes laughing aloud, occasionally frowning, discussing an invitation with Mrs. Ramsey, giving instructions to his chaplain. From breakfast he goes directly to his study.

An indefatigable worker, Ramsey sees callers until 7 P.M., the hour of Evensong, and after dinner he almost invariably returns to his study. He is often still at work there when the sound of Big Ben, somberly stroking the hour of midnight, is heard across the Thames. Guests returning late to Lambeth have seen the Archbishop padding in stocking feet about the halls, sometimes going into the secretaries' office to look over the file of the day's correspondence—a purple-clad figure casting an immense shadow in the stark light.

There is a stenographic staff of four. The senior member is Priscilla Lethbridge, whose youthful appearance belies the fact she came to Lambeth as social secretary to Mrs. William Temple. She speaks of Fisher and Ramsey as two men who "are as different as cheese and chalk."

Adjoining Ramsey's study is the office of Robert Beloe, who since 1959 has had the official title "Secretary to the Archbishop of Canterbury." Beloe's record suggests that, far from being a courtier, he is capable of careful judgments that complement those of the Archbishop's other advisers. Educated at Oxford, he was a master at Eton before becoming a professional educator. He was Chief Educational Officer for nearly twenty years and also served as a member of the Royal Commission on Marriage and Divorce, the Electoral Boundary Commission, and the Higher Agricultural Education Committee. During meetings of the Church Assembly, he wanders in and out, listening but appearing to avoid conversation, and wearing at all times an entirely noncommital expression. It would be difficult to enumerate all his duties at Lambeth Palace, even if they were known, but an indication is the fact that his name is signed to numerous letters to both clergy and laity. And he is believed to advise on and draft many others signed by the Archbishop.

The Rt. Rev. Stephen Bayne* describes his working relationship with Archbishop Ramsey as "anything that has to do with Ramsey's role as patriarchal head of the Anglican Communion, nothing that has to do with his role in the Church of England."

Bayne, a lean, crisp-spoken man with steel-gray hair and a nononsense attitude looks more like a corporation executive than a former bishop of the Pacific Northwest. He was for twelve years bishop of the Diocese of Olympia, Washington.

The Lambeth Conference outlined a total of thirty-two distinct functions or official tasks for the new Executive Officer, and many other jobs are inherent in the title. In the first two years he traveled more than 260,000 miles and visited almost all of the eighteen churches in communion with the See of Canterbury. He regards as a principal responsibility, the work of two groups—the Advisory Council on Missionary Strategy, established in 1948, and the Consultative Body of the Lambeth Conference. The Archbishop of Canterbury is chairman of both groups, and Bayne, often called "the Rt. Rev. Marco Polo," is the administrative officer.

Arriving in London in January, 1960, Bayne worked for ten months in an office adjoining Archbishop Fisher's study at Lambeth. In October of that year he moved with his staff to a handsome town house at 21 Chester Street in the area of Belgrave Square. (Lambeth maintains a direct line—extension 54—to Bayne's assistant.) From its façade three flags whip the breeze— the red, white, and blue ensign of the National Council of the Protestant Episcopal Church, flanked by the Union Jack and Old

---

*Said the 1959-1960 edition of *Crockford's Clerical Directory*, "In Bishop Stephen Bayne, whose appointment . . . [as Executive Officer to the Anglican Communion] was announced in April, 1959, the authorities have chosen one who made perhaps the most profound impression of any bishop at the Lambeth Conference. It is to be hoped, however, that he will not attempt to introduce into Anglican affairs those aspects of American organization which have been so much criticized in the affairs of the World Council of Churches, and it is perhaps important that Dr. Fisher's successor at Lambeth should be a man whose sympathies do not lie in that direction."

Glory. In a comfortable, informally furnished study that stretches across the second-floor front of the building, Bayne works among souvenirs of his travels and autographed pictures of such personages as Eisenhower and Kennedy. There is one of Lord Fisher inscribed, "To Stephen Bayne with affection and respect, *Christo Fratres*, Geoffrey Cantuar: May 31, 1961."

A few weeks after Ramsey's enthronement, Bayne wrote to this author, "I agree with your impression of Archbishop Ramsey as a colorful and dynamic man. While he has very big shoes to fill, I do not at all question the fact that he will do so, and more. He will become far better known throughout the Anglican Communion than he is now, as time goes on. He is young, and of course these early years have been lived under the shadow of Geoffrey Fisher, a giant. But there is no question in my mind as to the size of the man, and his very exciting leadership."

In an interview six months later he recalled a day near the end of the 1958 Lambeth Conference when Ramsey had challenged some of the conclusions of the Commission on Family Life, of which Bayne was chairman.

"He might scare some who don't know him," Bayne says. "He seems ponderous and perhaps forbidding, hunching up his shoulders and drawing his eyebrows together. His long silences might be puzzling, but he is only framing a good answer."

Bayne compares the primates in this way: "Fisher liked to see people often and for short periods. Ramsey sees people less often and for longer visits."

He regards Ramsey's greatest task as one that will not be worked out in any short amount of time: helping the Anglican Communion to function internationally, intercontinentally, and interracially in the world community. At the same time, the Archbishop must encourage the younger churches not to be dependent.

In his first months as Archbishop of Canterbury, Ramsey impressed Bayne as "a priest-bishop—a priest's bishop, and a bishop's bishop. He has spent most of his life teaching people to be parsons and he understands and likes them. . . . He is interested in the Church from the inside. He is more of a Temple than a Fisher or a Davidson. Ramsey brings just that kind of leadership he has in his skin to give. Therefore, he is sometimes opaque to the layman. Americans and others abroad will not find a Fisher, if that is what they expect when they meet Ramsey, but they will find other qualities equally good. I believe he was well received at New Delhi. He has a title everyone knows, of course, and he is a kind of third force or factor between the East and the West. There is a tendency to cow-tow to him, and he always discourages it." As for the impression that the Archbishop may be absent-minded, Bayne adds, "People will find he is about as absent-minded as a computer."

A man who watches both Ramsey and Bayne with keen personal interest is Lord Fisher of Lambeth. During the first year of his retirement the ninety-ninth Archbishop of Canterbury frequently corresponded in his own hand on stationery that bore the heading, "The Most Reverend Archbishop Lord Fisher of Lambeth, Hound Street, Tudor Cottage, Sherborne, Dorset."

Until he and Lady Fisher settled in the spring of 1962 in an Elizabethan house in Somerset, they spent much of their time at their sons' homes. Lady Fisher, long active in the Mother's Union and other organizations, was affectionately known as "Mrs. Lambeth." She crisply introduces her husband with a single, brief remark: "Now here is the Archbishop."

As bright-eyed and alert as ever, he rises to greet a caller. His conversation ranges over many subjects from his years at Repton to his historic call at the Vatican. "I still exchange greetings with the Pope," he says. "I sent him a recorded message for his birthday, and the Vatican acknowledged it. My visit to him opened the way for calls by other churchmen—for instance, the moderator of the Church of Scotland. It is a thing that could not have happened with the former Pope. He was a diplomat who would have looked at the matter from many sides, and one cannot tell what he would have answered. And with a question of the Church of England calling on a Pope for the first time in hundreds of years, we would not have taken the chance of being turned down."

Fisher does not believe the Church should supply a retired Archbishop with secretarial help because "most of my work is of my own making. I am beginning to taper off." Even so, he remained much in the news during Ramsey's first year in office. When thirty-two theologians sent an open letter to the Archbishops of Canterbury and York, Fisher wrote an article explaining its meaning. And the day before Ramsey's return from India, it was Fisher who addressed a large group in London on the significance of Anglican participation in the New Delhi meeting. Of his own enthronement address in April, 1945, he said, "I suppose I'd forgotten the next day what I said. It was wartime and newspapers didn't have space to reprint it. When Canon Charles Smyth wanted to put it into a book, the only copy we could find was among the papers I had left to the Lambeth Library. The televising of Ramsey's enthronement was to be expected because it took place in an age which televises all sorts of events. The coronation of Elizabeth II was the first great event on television. I was in on the planning, and the powers-that-be didn't know how it would be taken [by the people]. We decided to omit the Communion Service—when the Queen and Duke received the Communion—because it was an intimate part of the ceremony. Now I would include it because I have heard of the immense devotion with which the coronation was watched. People felt as if they were in church. Businessmen in the City who had laid on a lunch, thinking they would take time out to entertain and that people wouldn't watch all the ceremony, found they were watching. Afterwards, women told me they didn't even think of having tea. And nobody smoked. It was like being in church."

Fisher speaks of his travel throughout the Anglican Communion and of his final Lambeth Conference which had seen the creation of the post Bishop Bayne holds: "It was the outcome of talks we had begun in 1948 in an effort to relieve the Archbishop of Canterbury who had always been the link from one Lambeth Conference to another. Now we have the assurance of more continuity of work between the conferences. In reviewing my years as Archbishop, I must mention that I inherited a report of a commission on canon law. We have had a need for more operative canon law. Our goal was not merely to produce a code, but to pull the Church together. I left my responsibility for it within sight of completion."

The ancient Roman wall surrounding the center of Canterbury has seen a hundred primates come and go. It parallels the road along which the present primate is chauffered from London in the luxurious black Daimler supplied by the Church Commissioners. Darkness has usually fallen by the time the Ramseys reach Canterbury on Fridays. The limousine moves through Christ Church Gateway into the Cathedral grounds and down a short incline to the homey, welcoming porch of the Old Palace.

It is a rambling house of great and mellow charm. On the ground floor are the studies of the Archbishop and his domestic chaplain, the kitchens, and the dining room dominated by a dark ceiling beam carved with the words, "Make not thy boast of to-morrowe for ye knowest not what maye happe to-daye: Proverbs XXVII. A.D. 1539."

A private chapel is located on the second floor. Above its altar has been placed the large ebony crucifix presented to the Archbishop in Africa in 1960. A small alabaster statue of Our Lady, on the wall to the left of the altar, was discovered by Mrs. Ramsey in a shop window in London.

The second floor also contains a wing of bedrooms, a small sitting room, and a drawing room where the eye is caught instantly by a handsome blue chair with the royal cipher "E R II." Identical chairs are found in the homes of almost everyone who had a special seat at the coronation.

The household at Canterbury includes Brindle and his wife, and also Miss Tanqueray, her boxer, Timothy, and Mrs. Ramsey's cat, Pudsey. Timothy has claimed the foyer as his special province, seeking in the summer the coolness of the white marble floor and in the winter the warmth of the welcoming fire. Panting and lamentably unsuspicious, he is usually at Brindle's side when the butler answers the door. As Brindle shows in callers to the Archbishop's study, he places his foot on the dog's ample backside and trundles him amicably along the corridor.

Pudsey scampers about from the kitchen to the third-floor guest rooms until he hears Mrs. Ramsey's "Pudsey! Pudsey!" calling him for a walk in the Archbishop's garden. "Poor Pudsey, he's gone from Durham to York to Canterbury," says Mrs. Ramsey. "Every move is harder for him."

At Canterbury the Archbishop takes up his diocesan duties. He works with two suffragans and an assistant bishop in this diocese of 320 parishes staffed by 340 priests. "As the premier diocese, Canterbury feels it must do everything well and set the lead in most," says a diocesan official, the Ven. J. A. M. Clayson, in his office on Lady Wooton's Green. "When Archbishop Fisher retired, the most frequently heard comment in this building was, 'It will be Ramsey by the end of the week.' When the new Archbishop arrived some of us said, 'Now we won't have a headmaster-type after us any longer,' and Ramsey replied, 'That's right. Now you'll have a university don.'"

Ramsey acknowledges only one respite that Canterbury offers from his heavy schedule. "Saturday mornings," he says, "that's the time for a good sleep-in." Saturday afternoons are ordinarily occupied with confirmations or with the institution of a new rector in a country parish. As he stands waiting in the foyer for the arrival of his limousine, Ramsey is likely to spin on his toes, cassock flying. Sometimes he throws his cap into the air and catches it. He is lighthearted and jovial in these moments, clearly more relaxed in the less hurried surroundings of Canterbury.

The rural visitations are reminiscent of those Ramsey knew in County Durham and Yorkshire. He is greeted by the vicar while his chauffeur and chaplain take from the trunk of the automobile the cases containing his robes and the primatial cross. Later the chaplain reverently lays the cope and mitre on the altar of the church while the Archbishop enters the pulpit to preach. Tea in the parish house or community hall is certain to follow the service, with the country women passing around platters of buttered biscuits and tiny pancakes.

Such afternoons can be exhilarating and exhausting. Back at the Old Palace the Archbishop usually has a brief rest and another cup of tea before reading Evensong in the chapel.

If there are guests in the house, Ramsey may meet them in his study for sherry before dinner. He still wears his purple cassock, but has exchanged his shoes for comfortable evening slippers with large silver buckles. He tosses down the sherry like an oyster but does not care for hard liquors. "I remember people in the United States offering me whiskey while calling it Scotch. 'Have some Scotch,' they say." Ramsey has a don's taste for cider and wines—especially the dry, white German Hocks—but abstains in Lent and also foregoes his penchant for making epigrams. One weekend his hand was badly gashed when a cider bottle shattered as he attempted to open it in a door jamb. (The injury was reported in *The Times,* again reminding Ramsey of the newsworthiness of even minor events concerning the primate.)

At dinner the Archbishop enjoys carving. He sends heaping plates down the table with a special comment for each guest. "Here's a fine helping for an angry young man," he says with a laugh to one of his clergy. Ramsey is at his wittiest at dinner, and his humor can be infectious. Scenting fun, the Archbishop has been known to invite a few guests, especially close friends, upstairs to see his collection of hats. He first brings out a great ecclesiastical beaver.

"How d'you think this one looks?" he asks, a sandy eyebrow seesawing. "Fine, don't you think? Splendid!"

Next he produces a frayed straw hat, then changes to a jazzy check-cloth cap. "My incognito," he calls it. ("He likes to think it makes him look anonymous," says a friend. "Actually it would make him stand out at a race track.")

Story-telling and mimicry, favorite ecclesiastical sports, have a champion in Ramsey. Mimicry is his best defense against people who delight in mimicking him. One of the best imitations is reportedly given by the Archbishop of York.

Ramsey finds humor in history, too. In a Bayeux tapestry he discovered a column of marching soldiers followed by a Norman bishop prodding the last man with the point of his sword. "The fine lettering underneath is 'The Bishop comforteth his soldiers,' " reported Ramsey.

Another time he referred to Marston Moor as "the place where the battle was—held!" And that word "held," where ninety-nine out of a hundred would have said "fought," contains at once a delicate and delightful mockery.

Ramsey's great rollicking laughter can banish the tension of an embarrassing moment and it can transform an amusing situation to the realm of hilarity. Some are reminded of the rumbling laugh of the late actor, Sydney Greenstreet. Others compare it to "the wonderful, musical, good-humored laughter of William Temple that rang throughout the Church of God."

True to his belief that "administration is something to be got on with and not deified," Ramsey usually works through the evening in his study at Canterbury. (As late as eleven o'clock on Saturday night he may step into the chaplain's adjoining office to review name by name a list of priests: "Is this the man I saw at Lenham? And is this the one the Archdeacon mentioned?") He works in his favorite wing-chair near the mantelpiece that bears the date 1900 and the initials "F. C." for "Frederick Cantuar:" (who sold a country estate he found too luxurious). Ramsey's collection of icons, gifts of the Orthodox clergy, are placed about the room. On one wall are pictures of four of his predecessors at Durham—Lightfoot, Westcott, Moule, and Henson.

Sunday mornings the Archbishop stands before the high altar of the Cathedral to begin the celebration of the Eucharist. He faces the altar in silent prayer for almost five minutes. Then, just before the Cathedral chimes strike the hour, he begins to repeat aloud the Lord's Prayer. About eighty people usually attend the early morning service, receiving the Holy Communion at the hands of the Archbishop and the Dean of Canterbury.

Ramsey returns for breakfast in the Old Palace and an hour or so with the newspapers—the *Sunday Times*, the *Sunday Express*, and *The Observer*—which a newsboy has dropped through a window in the foyer. Shortly before eleven he prepares to return to the Cathedral for the service of matins.

After luncheon he goes to his study again for a second look at the newspapers and whatever work awaits him in the bulging briefcase at the side of his wing-chair. He sinks back in the chair and takes up his lapboard, a contrivance that resembles a card table with two legs. Ramsey calls it "my Eric Abbott" after his friend, the Dean of Westminster, who gave it to him as a wedding present.

The lengthening shadows of the afternoon find Ramsey still hunched over his work. This is how he writes his sermons, his addresses, and his letters. And this is how he conducts the business of the Church of England.

In addition to the lapboard he must have a great pot of good black ink into which he can dip a pen. "He wants to get down to some writing when he is staying with me," says his Aunt Lucy at her home in Cambridge. "He says, 'Oh, Aunt Lucy, give me a pen I can *write* with.' Then he somehow balances that inkpot on the arm of a chair."

A member of the Archbishop's staff confirms this procedure:

"He is always writing and he has a ghastly series of pens which he is always losing. And he splashes the ink as he writes in scrawling hieroglyphics across the pages, uneven, unlevel, and undecipherable to all except a patient and tried private secretary. His writing is distinctly better when he is working on a train. He has to write slowly and try harder. But he still loses his beastly pens on trains. When he had 'flu' at York and was ordered to bed he saw a chance to assemble material for a new book. He sent for his pen and inkpot and began scribbling away, surrounded by piles of books and discarded papers. The inkpot was overturned twice. But a new book was created. When he is well he plans his books late at night, sitting in his wing-chair, and the next morning the secretary finds a mound of notes to transcribe."

Ramsey takes almost no physical exercise except for the long walks of his summer holidays. He has been known to play a card game called "Patience" but he usually prefers to read whenever there is a free moment. His favorite subjects are theology and political biography. Vacation reading may include a Sir Walter Scott novel or even a detective "thriller."

An opportunity to browse in the stacks of a good library is almost irresistible. When he cannot be located at Lambeth the staff has learned to look first of all in the library. (In Canterbury, when he borrowed some books from St. Augustine's College, the students rushed in to see the library card signed "Michael Cantuar:"—as grand and historic and official as it looks on charters and great documents.) Browsing was his pastime at St. Deiniol's, too, the church library in Wales where he went so often in the 1930's and 1940's. When he was staying at the General Theological Seminary in New York in 1959, he turned up in the library before it had officially opened for the day. "Our Irish cleaning woman was the only one here," recalls the librarian. "The Archbishop came in and bowed to her as if she were the Queen of the May and asked permission to see the books. It didn't make any difference that he was an *Anglican* Archbishop. She thought it was the most wonderful thing that ever happened."

One of Ramsey's most remarkable traits is his superb memory. Many have found it surprising in a man with a reputation for absent-mindedness. He is known to repeat dates, texts, and subjects of sermons that he and other men have preached in a particular church. Letters written or received years before are sometimes quoted verbatim. When he drives past a church and vicarage he can recount the date of his last visit, what he said, what the vicar was like and how many children he had. One priest who was rash enough to challenge the Archbishop to remember his name received in reply not only his full name but also the date he had begun his pastorate, and the text of the sermon he had preached on that occasion.

"His Grace combines a powerful brain with an equally strong humanity," says one of his associates. "Lying is the one thing he cannot bear. If he catches someone at it, he can thunder in a voice that reduces them to tears. This is almost the only time, outside the pulpit, that he chooses to raise his voice. And the effort can make him ill with distress. When he is upset about a case of misconduct or some other situation, I have seen him, disconcerted and pained, pacing the length of the room time and again, lost in agonized thought, wheeling and turning until the thing has been thought out and he is ready to speak. We who know him well can tell how fast his brain is racing by the speed of his walk. I have seen him streak past the window and set off at a great clip along the riverside path at York, coat forgotten in the rush. When we heard his tread on the stairs we knew that he was coming to put on paper thoughts that had been clamoring for expression. Soon the energetic pacing would be resumed in the garden as the next point was hewn and struck into shape. We never worried about it. It cleared his mind. And it did him good."

At Canterbury, Ramsey and the famous "Red Dean" have scrupulously observed the ancient custom that the Archbishop must inform the Dean of his desire to come into the Cathedral. Faithfully each Saturday the chaplain telephones the Dean's residence to relay the Archbishop's wishes, and just as faithfully the Dean comes to the cloister door to accompany the primate.

Ramsey is the fourth Archbishop whom Dean Hewlett Johnson has known at Canterbury. At eighty-eight the Dean still drove his own car, used glasses only to read the Lesson during services, had a firm handshake and a strong voice. Above the entrance to the Deanery, his fine house in the Cathedral precincts, he erected a neatly worded sign: "Christians, Ban Nuclear Action." He says he was inspired to do so after seeing the motion picture, *On the Beach*, made from Nevile Shute's novel of the world's destruction.

The Dean speaks readily of his relationships with the Archbishops: "Lang I knew well, of course, after I became Dean of Canterbury in 1931. He used to say, 'I've had to smack you down in public but don't let it make any difference in our private arrangements.' Temple would correct me and suggest other courses for me. But Fisher was, from the start, a blank wall, a stone wall. He would never let me talk about my Communism. I was in China three times and in Russia five or six times, but Fisher never allowed me to tell him a word about it. You'd think he would be curious, politics completely aside, but he would always stop me. Ramsey I hadn't known before he came to Canterbury. Fisher and Ramsey bring to mind a tree in the spring: the bark protects it, tends to constrict it, and it has to burst with new life. Ramsey is that resurgent life. I liked what he said first of all when he came here, 'I want to make man aware of God.' That's what Ramsey said, but the other man, Fisher, wanted to tie God up so he wouldn't thrash about too much. Ramsey called on me one morning when he first arrived. Brought his wife with him; she's charming. I believe he will do a great deal toward stirring up the Church for its own good."

Few would have believed that Michael Ramsey or any other Archbishop of Canterbury might be so active and effective in the initial years of a primacy.

He had begun at once by presiding over the Church Assembly with a firmness that some had thought unlikely. Then, mindful of his pledge to reach the nation in the most effective ways possible, he had asked for television time to encourage the prayers for world peace, a fearful anxiety that had dominated his mail during his first months at Lambeth. His statement was one of great simplicity: "We do turn to God when we feel on the edge of the precipice. . . . I want to say to you, precipice or no precipice: pray now, today, and again tomorrow—pray always. *That* is the real answer."

Ramsey's promise to re-evaluate the system of Crown appointments and liturgical reform was implemented in February and in May, 1962, by the appointment of new commissions on both subjects. His interest in a more cordial relationship with the Roman Catholic Church was encouraged by the Vatican's invitation to send Anglican observers to the ecumenical council meeting in Rome.* And his longtime friendship with the Orthodox was strengthened anew by his visits to Turkey and Greece in May and to Russia in July.

In the House of Lords, where he had spoken on five occasions in previous years, the Archbishop voiced his strong opposition in March, 1962, to the Commonwealth Immigration Bill. Its discrimination against colored people was, he said, a reversal of one of Britain's greatest traditions and revealed a failure to solve housing problems and related conditions that had caused the color issue to loom so large.

Ramsey's diverse interests and wide travel must at all times be compatible with his traditional duties which, taken alone, constitute an almost overwhelming schedule. He frequently is asked to commit himself two or three years in advance of an occasion.

England and the whole Anglican Communion has customarily looked to the Archbishop of Canterbury for opinions on temporal and spiritual matters. Ramsey has not been disappointing in that regard, choosing in most instances to re-emphasize or expand on statements he had made at Durham or York. Many of his thoughtful pronouncements are telling indications of what his position and course of action may be in future years. Here, culled from speeches, interviews, diocesan bulletins, and other sources, are his viewpoints on a variety of issues:

On the Virgin Birth: "It is possible to believe that Jesus is divine without believing in the virgin birth, though if you do believe Him divine then the virgin birth becomes congruous. I believe it is quite in order for a person to stand up in church and recite the Creed even if he has scruples about the virgin birth, provided he believes in the pattern of faith as a whole."

On hell: "It is certainly not a physical place. It is the state of those who make hell for themselves by denying God a place in their lives."

*On July 5, 1962, Ramsey announced the Anglican Communion would be represented by an Englishman, an Indian, and an American: the Bishop of Ripon, the Archdeacon of Colombo, and the Rev. Frederick Grant, sometime Dean of Seabury-Western Theological Seminary.

On heaven: "Heaven is not a place to which we humans go in our present bodily state, nor is it a place for Christians only. Those who have led a good life on earth but found themselves unable to believe in God will not be debarred from heaven. I expect to meet some present-day atheists there."

In regard to Adam and Eve: "That must now be regarded as a parable because it contradicts what geology tells us of the origin of the world and what biology tells us of the evolution of the human race. But it is a true parable of the fact that in some early stage of his development man disobeyed God and lost fellowship with Him."

On the continuity of the Church: "When an Anglican is asked, 'Where was your Church before the Reformation?' his best answer is to put the counter-question, 'Where was your face before you washed it?' "

On divine punishment: "I do not believe that God deliberately sends calamity as punishment for wrongdoing. But I do believe that where the course of wrongdoing leads to calamity—as it usually does—God does not prevent this result. I believe that mankind is free to bring judgment upon itself as a result of choosing between good and evil. And I do not believe God is such a softie as to intervene to stop us from getting hurt if we have chosen the road that leads towards us getting hurt."

On the discipline of fasting: "I often think the doctrines of fasting in Lent and having meatless days are old-fashioned. As a discipline and reminder of Christ's sufferings, both are right in principle, but I think we need to find more modern forms of self-discipline. For instance, instead of giving up meat once a week it might be better to give up television. That would be a more meaningful self-denial in this day and age."

On ordination of women: "The work of a priest is that of the father of a family. But I should like to see gifted women used more widely—in specialist posts, for example. And remember this —although Our Lord valued women so much, he chose only men to be His Apostles."

On homosexuality: "Those who are criticial of the relaxation of the criminal law which is proposed [that homosexuality involving the consent of two adults is not a crime] need, I think, to distinguish clear moral thinking from moral sentiment. Christianity abhors the indulgence of lust, whether by fornication, adultery, or homosexuality. It would be possible and logical to bring all three of these within the criminal law, and there have been communities which have tried to do this. But morality is not best promoted by giving criminal status to every kind of grievous sin; and the status of a crime rightly goes with acts which, besides being sinful, inflict direct injury on the rights and persons of other people or imperil the community. A little thought shows that incest stands apart in having properly the character of a crime."

On nuclear weapons: "I believe the existence of nuclear weapons has in the last decade probably had the effect of preventing a general war from breaking out. It has acted as a general deterrent—a force for peace—but it is very dangerous to go on depending on such a deterrent, and the only answer is general disarmament. But it must be a general disarmament—not only with nuclear weapons but with all kinds of weapons."

On sex education: "We need sex education that talks about sex from the start with complete freedom and frankness, and so robs it of any sense of being nasty or not to be spoken about. Sex is not an act we do behind God's back. It is something to be known about and freely talked about, appreciated and reverenced. There should be neither a falsely coy reticence nor an unwholesome obsession with it."

On responsibility for the aged: "If our State was one that emphasized responsibility upon the individual, then the care of the aged would be one for the family. But in our Welfare State, which robs the individual of initiative, it is not fair to say to him, 'It's your job to look after the old folk.' . . . With the sort of communities we are developing with workers' flats and housing estates, it may well be that we are returning somewhat to the tribal system rather than the family unit, where the children play together, and the old folk sit by the fire together. This needn't be a bad thing."

On the clergy: "No jokes about the clergy and no running down of the clergy except over my dead body. By and large the clergy are wonderfully hard-working and self-sacrificing and are devoted to their job and to their people."

On bingo: "The bingo craze is a symptom of our failure to find sensible ways of using our spare time and money. Mind you, as a form of gambling bingo is not particularly evil. It's a jolly form of social amusement and relatively harmless. I can understand its fascination, but I do think it's a great pity it has become a craze."

Most of Ramsey's associates become aware of two traits: he serves best if he is chairman of a committee rather than a member, and, as a chairman, he knows how to appoint the best men for the jobs to be done. These are characteristics he has evidenced at Lambeth, and no one has doubted he will be more than an adequate administrator. There remains his deep desire to be understood as a "non-partisan" Archbishop who, regardless of his own preferences, can listen to the views of others and can give what he calls "equal attention to every persuasion within the Church."

In addition, there is Ramsey's longing for the Church of England "to be its own self as a part of Christ's Catholic Church that is able to be both scriptural and liberal."

In a personal aside, he remarks, "I've never been much of a typical Anglican. I have a lot of the Non-Conformist *and* a lot of the Anglican. But I could be happy only as an Anglican. It is only in Anglicanism that there exists Catholic religion and intellectual liberty."

The imaginative child who played in the garden of Howfield in the early years of this century has come to a lofty eminence. He has walked in splendid processions, taken solemn oaths on ancient gospels, sat enthroned in glorious cathedrals, lived in famous palaces, spoken in the councils of State, and is hailed with respect wherever he goes in the world, all of which has had its influence— a humbling influence—on the man. He has been careful to stand uncompromisingly for the living ministry of the sacrament and the word. Reverence, awe, and wonder are the marks of his regard for the worth of the individual and for Christian doctrine.

There is every possibility that Michael Cantuar will be regarded, within his own lifetime, as a brilliant leader of men and one of the great Archbishops of Canterbury.

THE ARCHBISHOPS OF CANTERBURY
FROM THE CONSECRATION OF ST. AUGUSTINE

		A.D.
1.	Augustine	597-604
2.	Laurentius	604-619
3.	Mellitus	619-624
4.	Justus	624-627
5.	Honorius	627-653
6.	Deusdedit	655-664
7.	Theodorus	668-690
8.	Beorhtweald	693-731
9.	Tatwine	731-734
10.	Nothelm	735-739
11.	Cuthbeorht	740-760
12.	Breguwine	761-764
13.	Jaenbeorht	765-792
14.	Aethelheard	793-805
15.	Wulfred	805-832
16.	Feologild	832
17.	Ceolnoth	833-870
18.	Aethelred	870-889
19.	Plegmund	890-914
20.	Aethelhelm	914-923
21.	Wulfhelm	923-942
22.	Oda	942-958
23.	Aefsige	959
24.	Beorhthelm	959
25.	Dunstan	960-988
26.	Athelgar	988-990
27.	Sigeric Serio	990-994
28.	Aelfric	995-1005
29.	Aelfheah (or Alphege)	1005-1012
30.	Lyfing	1013-1020
31.	Aethelnoth	1020-1038
32.	Eadsige	1038-1050
33.	Robert of Jumièges	1051-1052
34.	Stigand	1052-1070
35.	Lanfranc	1070-1089
36.	Anselm	1093-1109
37.	Ralph d'Escures	1114-1122
38.	William de Corbeil	1123-1136
39.	Theobald	1139-1161
40.	Thomas Becket	1162-1170
41.	Richard (of Dover)	1174-1184
42.	Baldwin	1185-1190
43.	Hubert Walter	1193-1205
44.	Stephen Langton	1207-1228
45.	Richard le Grant	1229-1231
46.	Edmund Rich	1234-1240
47.	Boniface of Savoy	1245-1270
48.	Robert Kilwarby	1273-1278
49.	John Pecham	1279-1292
50.	Robert Winchelsey	1294-1313

		A.D.
51.	Walter Reynolds	1313-1327
52.	Simon Mepeham	1328-1333
53.	John Stratford	1333-1348
54.	Thomas Bradwardine	1349
55.	Simon Islip	1349-1366
56.	Simon Langham	1366-1368
57.	William Whittlesey	1368-1374
58.	Simon Sudbury	1375-1381
59.	William Courtenay	1381-1396
60.	Thomas Arundel	1396-1397 / 1399-1414
61.	Roger Walden	1398-1399
62.	Henry Chichele	1414-1443
63.	John Stafford	1443-1452
64.	John Kemp	1452-1454
65.	Thomas Bourchier	1454-1486
66.	John Morton	1486-1500
67.	Henry Dean	1501-1503
68.	William Warham	1503-1532
69.	Thomas Cranmer	1533-1556
70.	Reginald Pole	1556-1558
71.	Matthew Parker	1559-1575
72.	Edmund Grindall	1576-1583
73.	John Whitgift	1583-1604
74.	Richard Bancroft	1604-1610
75.	George Abbot	1611-1633
76.	William Laud	1633-1645
77.	William Juxon	1660-1663
78.	Gilbert Sheldon	1663-1677
79.	William Sancroft	1678-1690
80.	John Tillotson	1691-1694
81.	Thomas Tenison	1695-1715
82.	William Wake	1716-1737
83.	John Potter	1737-1747
84.	Thomas Herring	1747-1757
85.	Matthew Hutton	1757-1758
86.	Thomas Secker	1758-1768
87.	Frederick Cornwallis	1768-1783
88.	John Moore	1783-1805
89.	Charles Manners-Sutton	1805-1828
90.	William Howley	1828-1848
91.	John Bird Sumner	1848-1862
92.	Charles Thomas Longley	1862-1868
93.	Archibald Campbell Tait	1868-1882
94.	Edward White Benson	1883-1896
95.	Frederick Temple	1897-1902
96.	Randall Thomas Davidson	1903-1928
97.	Cosmo Gordon Lang	1928-1942
98.	William Temple	1942-1944
99.	Geoffrey Francis Fisher	1945-1961
100.	Arthur Michael Ramsey	1961-

(In some instances dates indicated are approximate.)

INDEX

Christ Church Cathedral. *See* Canterbury Cathedral

Christ Church Cathedral, Dublin, 196

Chrysostomos, Abp., 101

Church of England: Church Assembly of, 19, 21, 189, 192, 219, 224, 230, 233, 236, 247; Church Commissioners of, 27, 146, 212, 216, 235; Church Missionary Society of, 183, 224; Council on Foreign Relations, 148-49; Council on Inter-Church Relations, 217

Church of England Newspaper, 138

Church House, Westminster, 182; Corporation of, 156

Church Illustrated, 217

Church-State relations, 5-6, 9, 16, 18, 82, 181, 186-87, 199, 210

Church Times, The, 53, 183, 228

Churchill, Winston, 9, 34, 117, 132, 158

Churchmanship, 28-29, 74, 82, 141, 162, 163, 184, 189; Ramsey's, 141, 142, 162, 183-84, 188-89, 198-99; *see also* Anglo-Catholic observances

Cincinnati, University of, 52

Clayson, J. A. M., 241

Clement VII, 15

Coe College, 53-54

Coggan, Frederick Donald, 24, 182, 184, 186, 189-90, 192, 198, 217

Coggan, Mrs. Frederick D. (Jean), 198

Colombo, Archdeacon of, 248

Columbia Broadcasting System, 84

Columbus, Christopher, 14

Commons, House of, 18, 34, 43, 49, 217; *see also* Parliament

Communists, 132, 190, 193, 247

Congregational Church, Congregationalists, 2, 5, 23, 33, 37, 54, 55, 111, 220

Cook, A. M., 80, 82, 84

Coolidge, Calvin, 50

Cornell College, 53

Cornwallis, Frederick, 17, 231

Coronation. *See* Elizabeth II

Corpus Christi College, Cambridge, x, 103, 211

Cosin, John, 125-27

Coventry: Bishop of, 182, 235; Cathedral, 110

Coward, Noel, 47, 202

Cowper, William, 37

Craine, J. P., 155

Cranmer, Thomas, 10, 14-16, 24, 25, 28, 214

Crockford's Clerical Directory, 118, 228, 237

Cuddesdon College, x, 58, 69, 146, 205, 217-18; Ramsey's student years in, 59-68

Culver Military Academy, 52

Cuthbert, St., x, 143, 160

Cyprus, Orthodox Church of, 3

Daily Express, London, 182, 189

Daily Herald, London, 189

Daily Mail, London, 173, 182, 183, 189

Daily Sketch, London, 189, 208

Daily Telegraph, London, 221

Daily Worker, London, 190

Darwin, Charles, 37, 47

Darwin, Horace, 37

Davey, Noel, 76

David, St., 231

David, Albert Augustus, 69, 71

Davidson, Randall T., 17, 18, 19-20, 22, 23, 24, 25, 28, 29, 70, 233, 238

Davidson, Mrs. Randall T. (Edith Tait), 18, 234

Davie, David, 61, 66

Dawdi, King (of Uganda), 128

de Blank, Joost, 182

Delhi, Bishop of, 222

Dennett, Stephen, 92

Denning, Lord, 218

Derby, Bishop of, 95, 148, 233

Deusdedit, Abp., 22

de Valera, Eamon, 196

Devlin, Patrick, 50-54, 57

Dimbleby, Richard, 214

Disestablishment. *See* Church-State relations

Dominican Order, 137

Donegan, Horace, 3

Dooley, Thomas, 189

Downey, Richard, 70

Dublin: Abp. of, 3, 193; Abp. of (R.C.), 196

Duff, James, 108, 120

Dunstan, Abp., 12, 22, 31

Durham: Bishop of, x, 23, 71, 80, 106, 117, 118, 121, 155; Bishop's residence at (*see* Auckland Castle); Castle, 106, 107; Cathedral, 2, 92, 105, 119, 123, 125, 132, 235; Chapter of, 2; Dean of, 2, 130; Diocese of, x, 119, 186; Light Infantry, 133; Ramsey as Bishop of, 122-43, 159

Durham County Advertiser, 109

Durham Essays (Ramsey), 143

Durham Evening Chronicle, 120

Durham University, x, 105, 116, 194, 197, 205; Ramsey as professor in, 106-15

Duse, Eleonora, 37

Dutch Reformed Church Mission, 169

Earlham College, 52, 54

East Africa: Abp. of, 156; Province of, 20, 172

East Lansing State College, 52

Eastern Orthodox Church. *See* Orthodox Church

Easton (Maryland), Bishop of, 155

Eden, Anthony, 39, 138

Hambly, W. F., 222
Hamilton, Duke of, 219
Hamilton, Eric K. C., 108
Hamilton, F. A. C., 108
Hamilton, Joan. *See* Ramsey, Mrs. A. M.
Hamilton, Ouida Mary, 108
Hardy, Edward R., 78-79, 90
Harland, M. H., 155
Harris, Charles U., 161-63, 209
Harris, Mrs. Charles U. (Janet), 161
Harris, Kenneth, 179-80, 198
Harrison, Rex, 51
Harrow, 39
Hartford, R. R., 193, 208
Harvard, John, 46-47
Harvard University, 78
Haxby, David Alan, 153
Hayward, H. C., 41
Heaton, Audrey, 235
Hedley, H., 231
Heenan, J. C., 179-81, 197-98
Henry I, 13
Henry II, 13-14, 25
Henry VIII, 14-16, 25
Henson, Herbert H., 128, 244
Hereford, Bishop of, 44
Herring, Thomas, 24, 184
Hertford College, Oxford, 183
Hicks, Nugent, 80
High Church. *See* Churchmanship
Highcliffe, Vicar of, 71
Hilda, St., 160
Hillsdale College, 52, 54
Hindson, Colin, 125
Hislop College, 225
Hitler, 20, 79, 104
Holland, 29; Student Christian Movement in, 78
Holne Parish Church, 173
Holy Island of Lindisfarne, 159-60
Holy Paraclete, Order of the, 160
Holy Sepulchre, Church of the, 47
Holy Trinity, Cambridge, 37, 64
Homosexuality, Ramsey's statement on, 249-50
Honorius, Abp., 22
Horbling Parish Church, 34
Hornby, Robert, 99, 219
Hornby, W. M., 39
Hoskyns, Edwyn, 43, 44
Hoskyns, Edwyn Clement, 58, 118
How, J. C. H., 70
Howard, Christian, 194
Howley, William, 17, 27, 28, 191
Hubbard, R. S., 123, 155
Hull: Bishop Suffr. of, 147; University of, 147
Hunkin, Oliver, 178
Hutton, Matthew, 24, 141, 231

Iakovas, Abp., 100, 225
Ibiam, Sir Francis, 100, 225
Illinois, University of, 52
India, 17, 189; Church of South, 139, 223; Ramsey's 1961 visit to, 29, 100, 218-26
India, Pakistan, Burma, & Ceylon: Church of, 155; Metropolitan of, 222
Indiana University, 52
Indianapolis, Coadjutor of, 155
Inge, W. R., 71
International Affairs, Commission of the Churches on, 224
International Conference of the New Testament, 217
Iowa, University of, 53
Iowa State College, 53
Ireland, Church of, 155
Isherwood, Christopher, 44
Islip, Simon, 22

Jamaica, Bishop of, 217
James Milliken University, 52, 54
Japan, 155
Jarrow, Bishop Suffr. of, 107, 109, 123
Jerusalem, Abp. of, 3
Jesus the Good Shepherd, Community of, 224
John de Ufford, 31
John, Ernest, 222, 224
John, King, 25, 26
John XXIII, 26, 162, 178, 191
Johnson, Hewlett, 3, 77, 188, 200-201, 246-247
Johnson, J., H.C., SSJE, 118
Jordan, Bishop in, 3
Juan Carlos, Prince (of Spain), 201
Justus, Abp., 22
Juxon, William, 16, 24

Kalamazoo College, 52, 54
Karpov, G. G., 152
Kaye, Martin, 146, 160, 167, 204
Keble College, Oxford, 62
Kelham. *See* Sacred Mission, Society of
Kemp, John, 14, 23
Kennaby, Noel, 232
Kennedy, John F., vii, 189, 191, 208, 238
Kennedy, Joseph P., 84
Kennedy, Ludovic, 209-10
Kent, Duke of. *See* Edward
Kent Messenger, The, 227
Khrushchev, Nikita, 162, 165, 189
Kilmiur, Lord, 213
King, Edward, 77
King's College, Cambridge: Choir School of, 38, 39, 76, 187; Dean of, 57
King's School, Canterbury, 206
Kinsolving, A. B., 155
Kitchingman, Dorothy, 146

Knell, Eric Henry, 60
Knox, John, 15
Knox, Ronald, 47
Kota Kota, Archd. of, 169
Kranesborough, Bishop Suffr. of, 123
Krutitsky, Nikolai, 149

Lambeth Conference, 10, 29, 232, 237; of 1867, 18, 229; of 1878, 18; of 1888, 18; of 1897, 19; of 1908, 19, 128; of 1920, 19; of 1930, 20, 29; of 1948, 21; of 1958, x, 153-57, 165, 238, 240; Consultative Body of the, 237
Lambeth: Mayor of, 2; Palace, 10, 17, 18, 19, 26-28, 98, 99, 110, 154, 198, 203, 215-17, 229-36
Lancaster, Bishop Suffr. of, 123
Lanfranc, Abp., 13, 22
Lang, Cosmo Gordon: childhood of, 23; as Abp. of York, 24, 43, 61, 77, 198; as Abp. of Canterbury, 9, 19, 22, 27, 28, 29, 30, 104, 207, 211, 218, 231, 233, 247; and abdication of Edward VIII, vii, 25, 82; in retirement, 20, 27, 108
Langton, Stephen, 25
Lateran Treaty, 71
Laud, William, 16, 22, 26, 215
Laurentius, Abp., 22
Lawson, Lawrence, 207
Lazonby, A. F., 208
Leeds University, 147
Lethbridge, Priscilla, 236
Lewis, John, 187
Lewis, Sinclair, 51
Lexington (Ky.), Bishop of, 155
Lichfield, Diocese of, 108, 151
Life, 201
Lightfoot, Joseph B., 126, 244
Lilongwe, Bishop of (R.C.), 169
Lincoln: Bishop of, 28, 34, 77, 80, 123; Cathedral, x, 74, 76-77, 90
Lincoln Theological College, 73, 85, 107, 109, 110, 115, 119; Ramsey as sub-warden in, 74-80
Lindberg, Marguerite, 63-64
Lister, Hugh, 63
Liverpool, x; Abp. of (R.C.), 70, 178, 197, 216; Bishop of, 69, 198; Cathedral, 70, 77; Post & Mercury, 69-70
Living Church, The, 162
Livingstone, David, 168
Llandoff, Bishop of, 155
Lloyd, Geoffrey, 50-54
Lloyd, R. L. H., 208
Lloyd, Selwyn, 48, 191, 213
London: Bishop of, 18, 19, 20, 24, 71, 204, 213; Diocese of, 24, 186; Lord Mayor of, 204, 217; University of, 121
Longley, Charles Thomas, 17-18, 23, 24, 141

Lords, House of, 10, 118, 121, 215, 230, 248; see also Parliament
Low Church. See Churchmanship
Lukindo, Yohana, 208
Luther, Martin, 15, 16, 77
Lutheran Church, Lutherans, 2, 54, 235

McCahill, Dorothy, 162
McDermott, R. P., 194
McKay, Roy, 181, 217
McPherson, Aimee Semple, 54
McQuaid, John Charles, 196
Macaulay, Rose, 118
Maclagan, William, 151
Macmillan, Arthur T., 189
Macmillan, Harold, 9, 184, 189, 213, 233
Madagascar, Bishop in, 153
Madame Tussaud's, 191
Magdalene College, Cambridge, x, 32, 33, 39, 67, 103, 104, 119, 136-37, 205, 233; Ramsey's student years in, 46-58
Magna Carta, 25
Maidstone, Archd. of, 207
Manchester: Bishop of, 43, 47, 55, 123, 182; Cathedral, 69
Manchester Guardian, 139
Manchester University, 197
Manners-Sutton, Charles, 9, 24, 191
Manners-Sutton family, 84
Manning, Bernard, 78, 90
Mansbridge, Albert, 67
Manson, Terence Leslie, 61
Margaret, Princess, 25, 97, 166, 168, 202, 213, 226
Marina, Duchess of Kent, 97, 202
Marquette University, 52, 54
Martin, Clifford, 198
Mary, Queen, 128
Mary Tudor, 15-16
Mascall, Eric, 110
Maschwitz, Eric, 147-48
Matthew, Tobias, 141
Maugham, Somerset, 230
Maurice, F. D., 77
Maurice, F. D., and the Conflicts of Modern Theology (Ramsey), 116
Mellitus, Abp., 22
Mepeham, John, 26
Methodist Church, Methodists, 2, 54, 71, 107, 111, 161, 222, 225
Michael, Bishop (of Smolensk), 149, 154
Michael, Prince, 97, 202
Michelangelo, 14
Michigan, Bishop of, 155
Middleton-Todd, A. R., 157-58
Miller, A. J., 155
Milner-White, Eric, 38, 57-58, 97, 119
Mirfield. See Resurrection, Community of
Mkomaindo School, 170
Monteigne, George, 141

Montgomery Campbell, Henry, 139, 186, 204, 213
Moody, W. R., 155
Moore, John, 17, 24, 231
Morehouse, Clifford P., viii
Morrison, Cecil, 190
Mortimer, Robert, 182
Mortlock, C. B., 221
Morton, John Cardinal, 14, 200, 231
Moses, David, 100, 225
Moscow: Academy, 149; Metropolitan of, 149; Patriarch of, 180, 215; Patriarchate of, 152
Mothers' Union, 170, 239
Moule, H. C. G., 128, 244
Mountain, Tom, 84
Mountbatten, Lord, 202
Mukerjee, Aurobindo N., 222
Murphy, John, 198
Mytilene, Metropolitan of, 2, 12

Nehru, Jawaharlal, 225
Nelson, Lord, 204
Netherlands Reformed Church, 2
New Delhi: Bishop of (R.C.), 223; Cathedral (of the Redemption), 220, 224; Jesuit College of, 223
New York: Bishop of, 3, 17, 217; Cathedral (see St. John the Divine); Church Club of, 164; Diocese of, 164
New York Times, vii, 139
New Zealand, 155
Newcastle (Upon Tyne): Bishop of, 75, 123, 147, 155; Diocese of, 232
Newman, John Cardinal, 49
Nicene Creed, 149
Niebuhr, H. Richard, 129
Niebuhr, Reinhold, 78-79, 90, 129
Niemoller, Martin, 100, 225
Nikodim, Abp., 212, 215, 220
Nile, Diocese of the, 234
Ninian, St., 231
Nippon Sei Ko Kai, Presiding Bishop of, 153
Non-Conformists, 2, 55, 56, 82, 113; see also Free Churchmen, Methodists, Congregationalists, etc.
Northern Rhodesia, Diocese of, 167
Northwestern University, 52, 54
Norwich, Bishop of, 215
Nottingham University, 182
Noyes, Alfred, 47
Nuclear weapons, Ramsey's statement on, 250
Nyasaland, Bishop of, 169
Nyerere, Julius, 209

Observer, The, London, 118-19, 179, 244
Oda, Abp., 22
Ohio University, 51
Old Catholic Church, 2, 215, 218, 223

Old Palace. See Canterbury
Oldham, J. H., 78-79, 90
Olympia (Wash.), Diocese of, 237
Orthodox Church, 112-13, 150, 152, 180, 215, 220-21, 223, 244, 248; see also Greek Orthodox Church, Russian, etc.
Oundle School, 183
Owen, Faith, 74, 92, 109, 187
Owen, John, 74
Owen, Leslie, 74, 107, 108
Owen, Mrs. Leslie, 74, 187
Oxford: Bishop of, x, 53, 59, 67, 148; University, 23, 34, 44, 60, 74, 114, 133, 173, 179, 184, 187, 189, 193, 208, 223, 236; see also Hertford Colllege, Trinity College, etc.
Ozanne, Mary Wilde, 119-20, 130, 205

Pakistan, 155
Papworth, Jack, 231
Parfitt, Thomas Richards, 153
Paris: King of, 11; University of, 23
Parker, Matthew, 10, 16
Parliament, 2, 6, 31, 49, 50, 65, 105; see also Commons, Lords
Parlin, Charles, 100, 225
Patrick, St., 231
Paul, Mrs. See Ramsey, Margaret
Paul, Prince and Princess, 97
Paulinus, 145
Pecham, John, 22
Pembroke, J. G., 204
Pepys, Samuel, 58; Library, 47
Peterborough, Bishop of, 154, 182, 184
Philadelphia, Bishop of, 17
Philip, Prince, 97, 131, 202, 213
Photius, 150
Pilgrim College, 82
Pilgrims, 81, 84
Pittsburgh, University of, 51
Pius XI, 71
Pius XII, 158
Poland, Orthodox Church of, 3
Pole, Reginald Cardinal, 16, 180, 234
Pontefract, Bishop Suffr. of, 123
Port, Sir John, x, 41
Portugal, King and Queen of, 33
Prayer, Ramsey's views on, 73, 247
Presbyterian Church, Presbyterians, 2, 23, 54, 111, 177-78, 220, 225; see also Scotland, Church of
Priestley, J. B., 183
Pudsey, Bishop, 126, 143
Purdue University, 52
Puritans, 16

Quakers, 107; see also Friends, Society of
Quebec, Abp. of, 155
Quick, Oliver Chase, 114

259

St. Michael le Belfry, York, 144
St. Nicholas, Guisborough, 190
St. Nicholas, Liverpool, 110; Ramsey as curate of, 69-73
St. Paul's, London, 154, 201, 204; Dean of, 71
St. Peter's, Lilongwe, 169
St. Peter's, Rome, 14
St. Stephen's Mission Hospital, Delhi, 224
Sakyiama, K. P., 208
Salisbury, Robert Lord, 130
Salter, F. R., 63
Sampson, Anthony, 184, 228
Sandroyd, 41, 230; Ramsey as student in, 39
Sardis, Metropolitan of, 215
Sargent, Alexander, 207
Sasse, Herman, 78-79, 90
Satterthwaite, John, 217, 219-20
Scholae Cancellarii. See Lincoln Theological College
Scotland, 177; Church of, 2, 71, 155, 177-178, 239 (*see also* Presbyterians); Episcopal Church in, 3, 17, 63; Primus of, 3, 70
Scott, Sir Walter, 126, 245
Seabury, Samuel, 17
Seabury-Western Theological Seminary, 160-61, 163, 209, 248
Seaton, James B., 61
Secker, Thomas, 17
Selby, Bishop Suffr. of, 123
Selwyn College, Cambridge, 148
Serbia, Orthodox Church of, 3
Sergei, Bishop (of Starorussii), 149
Sergui Serguiskaja, Monastery of, 151
Sex education, Ramsey's statement on, 250
Sharpley's Kindergarten, Miss, 36, 37
Sheffield, Bishop of, 123
Sherrill, Henry Knox, 148, 153
Shrewsbury, Bishop of (R.C.), 198; Bishop Suffr. of, 108
Shute, Nevile, 247
Simms, George, 193
Simon, W. G. H., 155
Simpson, Bertram, 182
Sitwell, Edith, 47
Skinner, Charles, 235
Smith, Alfred E., 54
Smith, Linton, 44
Smyth, Charles, 43, 131, 209, 240
Snowden, Lord (Anthony Armstrong-Jones), 39, 97, 202
Society for Promoting Christian Knowledge (SPCK), 113
Sophia, Princess (of Greece), 201
South Africa: Church in, 155; Union of, 172, 196
South India, Church of. See India
Southern Baptist Convention, 219

Southwark, Bishop of, 182, 217
Southwell, Bishop of, 43, 123
Soviet Union. See Russia
Spokane, Bishop of, 155
Stacey, Nicolas, 208
Stafford-O'Brien family, 108, 196
Stalin, 148
Stenhouse, N., 226
Stephens, David, 184
Stockdale, Grant, viii
Stopford, Robert, 24, 154, 182-83, 186, 188
Strand Unitarian Church, London, 190
Stratford, John, 22
Strathmore, Lady, 71
Strutt, Gordon, 207
Sudan, Bishop of, 3
Sudbury, Simon, 22
Sumner, John Bird, 17
Sunday, Billy, 54
Sunday Express, London, 208, 244
Sunday Times, London, 244
Swanson, Gloria, 51

Tait, Archibald Campbell, 17, 18, 19, 23, 24
Tait, Edith. See Davidson, Mrs. Randall T.
Tanqueray, Renée, 146, 241
Tatwine, Abp., 22
Taylor, Francis John, 148
Taylor, Sir Thomas, 178
Temple, Frederick, 17, 18, 19, 24, 26, 28, 244
Temple, William: childhood of, 23; early career of, 40, 43; as Bhp. of Manchester, 43, 44, 47, 53, 55; as Abp. of York, 44, 78-79, 83, 90, 108, 146-47, 160, 164, 203, 217; as Abp. of Canterbury, 9, 10, 24, 28, 29, 215, 234, 238, 243, 247; death of, 20, 111, 118
Temple, Mrs. William (Frances), 79, 90, 143, 214, 234, 236
Tenison, Thomas, 17, 206, 231
Theobald, Abp., 13
Theodorus, Abp., 12, 22, 26
Thyateira, Abp. of, 215
Tikhon, Patriarch, 151
Time and Tide, 139
Times, London, 30, 31, 136, 158, 189, 242
Topolski, Felix, 130
Townley, George Frederick, 147
Toynbee, Arnold, 164
Transfiguration, Church of the ("Little Church Around the Corner"), 54
Trinity College, Cambridge, 44, 46, 148
Trinity College, Dublin, Ramsey's mission to, 192-96
Trinity College, Oxford, 60
Trinity News, Dublin, 195
Truro, Diocese of, 24
Tussaud, Bernard Augustine, 191

261